EGYPT EXPLORATION SOCIETY IN COLLABORATION WITH
THE ROYAL ONTARIO MUSEUM

THE CEMETERIES OF
QAṢR IBRÎM

PLATE I
FRONTISPIECE

Air photograph of the concession with the town of Qaṣr Ibrîm in the centre and the cemeteries on each side

FIFTY-FIRST EXCAVATION MEMOIR
EDITED BY T. G. H. JAMES

THE CEMETERIES OF QAṢR IBRÎM

A REPORT OF THE EXCAVATIONS CONDUCTED BY W. B. EMERY IN 1961

BY A. J. MILLS

WITH CHAPTERS BY
N. B. MILLET AND
EDMUND S. MELTZER

and illustrations prepared by
ALAN HOLLETT

EGYPT EXPLORATION SOCIETY
3 DOUGHTY MEWS, LONDON WCIN 2PG
1982

LONDON

SOLD AT

THE OFFICES OF THE EGYPT EXPLORATION SOCIETY

3 Doughty Mews, London WC1N 2PG

British Library Cataloguing in Publication Data
Mills, A. J.
   The cemeteries of Qaṣr Ibrîm: a report of the
   excavations conducted by W. B. Emery in 1961.
   — (Excavation memoir, ISSN 0307-5109; 51)
   1. Tombs — Egypt — Qaṣr Ibrîm
   2. Excavations (Archaeology) — Egypt — Qaṣr Ibrîm
   3. Qaṣr Ibrîm (Egypt) — Antiquities
   I. Title II. Series
   932 DT60
   ISBN 0-85698-078-1

Printed in Great Britain
at the University Press, Oxford
by Eric Buckley
Printer to the University

PREFACE

WHEN Professor W. B. Emery died suddenly and tragically in Cairo on 7 March, 1971, he left unpublished much of the work which he had undertaken for the UNESCO campaign to salvage the monuments of Nubia on behalf of the Egypt Exploration Society. The Society asked me to make arrangements for the publication of this work. Mr Anthony J. Mills had assisted the Society throughout the Nubian campaign, and had worked with Professor Emery throughout the autumn of 1961 recording the cemeteries of Qaṣr Ibrîm. I therefore invited him to publish Emery's results on behalf of the Society. By this time, Mr Mills had become a curator in the Egyptian Department at the Royal Ontario Museum at Toronto, and in addition had large publication commitments of his own, more especially to the archaeological survey which he undertook for the Sudan government in Sudanese Nubia from 1964 onwards. Nevertheless, Mr Mills generously agreed to publish the cemeteries of Qaṣr Ibrîm, and the present volume is the result of his labours: the Society is deeply grateful to him.

In the circumstances, it was decided that this publication should present an objective record of the excavations and of the material finds. It would not include detailed archaeological and historical commentaries; these should await the completion of the excavations of the Fortress of Qaṣr Ibrîm which are still continuing. Mr Mills has, therefore, confined his report to a presentation of the information preserved in the existing records of the excavations of the cemeteries.

H. S. SMITH

TABLE OF CONTENTS

INTRODUCTION

WHEN, in 1959, the Egyptian government asked UNESCO to assist in discovering and rescuing the ancient remains in the area designated to be permanently inundated by the lake above the giant new dam, the Sadd el-ʿAli, being built at Aswân, a world-wide appeal was launched. Part of the response made by Britain to this appeal was that the Egypt Exploration Society assumed the responsibility for the excavation and recording of the site of Qaṣr Ibrîm. The concession was selected on the advice of W. B. Emery, who was well aware of the importance of the site to our understanding of Lower Nubia during the first millennium of our era. Emery had visited the site in the 1930s[1] and had made *sondages* in one of the cemeteries (193), but had not fully explored it at that time due to its location above the 124-m. contour, which had been his working limit. This limit was now superseded by the new 180-m. contour line, and it was decided first to excavate those parts of the concession, the low-lying cemeteries, which were in the most immediate danger of flooding. It is the excavation of those cemeteries, numbered 192 and 193, during the autumn of 1961 that forms the subject of this memoir.

Initially, the staff of the field party consisted of the late Professor Emery, Mrs Emery, Mr Aly el-Khouly, seconded to the expedition by the Egyptian Antiquities Service, and A. J. Mills. The field headquarters was established on the dahabîya *Bedouin*, which was moored against the west bank opposite Qaṣr Ibrîm. Excavation began on 16 October 1961, and two days later we were joined by Dr R. A. Caminos, who had come to undertake the epigraphic recording of the graffiti and New Kingdom shrines in the cliff face at Ibrîm.[2] Three weeks later, on 6 November, the staff of the Society's Sondage Survey of unexplored areas of Egyptian Nubia[3] joined the expedition, adding H. S. Smith, Mrs Smith, D. B. O'Connor and M. A. P. Minns to the strength to assist with the recording. The field-work was completed by 30 November and the dahabîya returned to Buhen.

Two preliminary reports were written by Emery concerning this excavation. The first appeared in the *Illustrated London News* of 20 October 1962, 605–7. The second, 'Egypt Exploration Society Preliminary Report on Excavations at Kasr Ibrim 1961', appeared in *Fouilles en Nubie (1961–1963)* (Cairo, 1967). There was also a brief notice in the editorial of *JEA* 48 (1962), 1.

The main element within the Society's concession is the large walled town, which sits atop a high bluff, in 1961 about 60 m. above the Nile (pl. I). It is situated on the right bank of the river some 233 km. upstream of Aswân (pl. II). It lies opposite Anîba, which was, at the time of the Nubian Campaign, the administrative centre of Egyptian Nubia; and it is within Mudrîyet Aswân and Mahafazet Baḥr el-Aḥmar. The concession extends for roughly 1 km. both north and south of the town site ending in each case in the rocky outcrops that descend into the river, and eastwards from the river bank for 700 or 800 m. back along the wâdis. The town at Ibrîm consists of a cluster of stone and brick buildings inside a large, heavy stone wall, which acted, presumably, as both a retaining wall and a defensive wall. It is roughly triangular in shape, due, no doubt, to the shape of the hilltop itself. Entry into the fort was, in recent times, through a gateway in the north face of the wall, but anciently there was also a second access in the southern wall. This fortress has been the

[1] W. B. Emery and L. P. Kirwan, *The Excavations and Survey between Wadi es-Sebua and Adindan 1929–1931* (Cairo, 1935), 268–77.

[2] R. A. Caminos, *The Shrines and Rock-inscriptions of Ibrîm* (London, 1968), E.E.S. Archaeological Survey Memoir XXXII.

[3] H. S. Smith, *Preliminary Reports of the Egypt Exploration Society's Nubian Survey* (Cairo, 1962).

subject of excavation by Professor J. M. Plumley since 1963,[1] and more recently by Professor W. Y. Adams and R. D. Anderson.

Two wâdis debouch on to each of the plains that lie to the north and south of the fortified town. The rugged relief of the sandstone in the area gives rise to a large number of smaller drainage elements, which come together in the larger wâdis. These in turn descend to the river, in each case a pair uniting just before reaching the Nile. These wâdis and the riverside plains are surfaced with a fossil alluvium soil, of no agricultural use, but of great value to a tomb digger, for although it is as dry as sand it is sufficiently compacted to enable a hole to retain its shape, yet it is considerably less consolidated than stone and is correspondingly less difficult than either to excavate. The thickness of this surface layer varies at Qaṣr Ibrîm up to about 3 m. from a few centimetres and it overlies the local sandstone. Almost all the graves excavated at Ibrîm had been cut into the fossil alluvium only and it was only occasionally that bedrock was penetrated. The major exception to this is area 192B, where all the features are built on to or cut into the sandstone. It seems likely that the extent of the cemeteries was governed to a major degree by the extent of the fossil alluvial ground.

The cemeteries were numbered by Emery and Kirwan,[2] in the system begun by Reisner,[3] as 192 and 193. The former is all that area to the north of Qaṣr Ibrîm town and during the present excavation has been further subdivided into 192, the major X-group area; 192A, a Meroïtic and X-group area well to the north of 192; 192B, a Meroïtic, X-group and Christian area overlooking the river bank, to the west of 192; 192C, a Meroïtic cemetery, largely overtaken by Muslim graves, also to the north of 192; and 192D, a small group of X-group tombs at the east side of 192. Cemetery 193 is that area in the plain and

wâdis which is immediately south of the town. It is composed of X-group and Christian burials.

Historically, the cemeteries do not quite reflect the occupation of the site. The earliest evidence from the site is the Middle Kingdom graffito of Mentuhotpe,[4] which does not indicate more than Egyptian presence in the area. The shrines[5] are most probably to be associated with Mi'am, the Egyptian settlement across the river.[6] The earliest remains in the town site are the large building blocks in the church, which have been interpreted as having been reused from the temple of Horus of Mi'am.[7] These blocks bear cartouches of Tuthmosis III and of Taharqa. No other sign of such early settlement was seen on the site, although recently Professor Plumley has indicated that both New Kingdom and Taharqa temples did exist on the site.[8] There is, however, no indication of either New Kingdom or Napatan occupation to be found in the cemeteries.

The date of the foundation of the Meroïtic settlement at Ibrîm is uncertain. Meroïtic interest in Lower Nubia stems from the third century B.C., with the reign of Ergamenes (= Arqamani, 248–220 B.C.), who entered into joint building projects at Philae and Dakka with Ptolemy IV Philopator. The initial northward Meroïtic thrust probably coincided with the establishment of an overland trade route, for there is no evidence for any Meroïtic settlement in Lower Nubia at this early date or, indeed, for any river traffic. The real colonization of the region was brought about by the introduction of the *saqia*, which enabled sufficient agricultural resources to become available to support a settled population. The first firm date at Ibrîm is about 23 B.C., when Gaius Petronius, a Roman Prefect, led a punitive expedition against either Queen Amanirenas or Queen Amanishakhete which resulted in the sacking of Napata and the occupation of Primis[9] (= Qaṣr Ibrîm), where the

[1] Preliminary reports in *JEA* 50 (1964), 3 ff.; 52 (1966), 9 ff.; 53 (1967), 3 ff.; 56 (1970), 12 ff.; 60 (1974), 212 ff.; 63 (1977), 29 ff.   [2] Loc. cit.
[3] G. A. Reisner, *The Archaeological Survey of Nubia. Report for 1907–1908* (Cairo, 1910).
[4] Caminos, op. cit., 94.

[5] Caminos, op. cit.
[6] G. Steindorff, *Aniba* (Glückstadt and Hamburg, 1935; Glückstadt, 1937).
[7] G. Steindorff, *Aniba*, ii. 20.
[8] *JEA* 60 (1974), 1.
[9] The etymology of this name is usually given as being

Roman frontier was established. The town was occupied for several years, until better relations were established and the Romans withdrew their frontier to Maḥarraqa. The Romans actually stormed a Meroïtic town at Ibrîm and occupied it, so settlement there dates from at least some time in the first century B.C., and it is assumed that the Meroïtes reoccupied the town as soon as the Romans withdrew. That it was an important Meroïtic centre is clear both from the temple and other stone architecture in the town, and from the obvious quality of the tombs, particularly in Cemetery 192C. It is to be regretted that probably most of the Meroïtic cemetery remains at Ibrîm could not be excavated due to the same area having been subsequently used by the Muslim occupants of the town. An indication of the brevity of the Roman occupation here is the total absence of any Roman burial remains in the vicinity.

The detailed exposition of the history of the occupation at Ibrîm and its place within the cultural development in the Nile Valley must be the province of Professors Plumley and Adams when their excavation of the site is completed. It is enough to state here that the cemeteries bear evidence of each successive phase at the site down to its abandonment by the Mamelukes shortly after they drove out the forgotten Bosnian garrison in A.D. 1811. Certainly, a survey of the objects from Cemeteries 192 and 193 will confirm Emery's impression that the culture they resemble so strongly is that represented by the royal tombs at Ballâna and Qusṭul.[1] The pottery, glass, bronzes, and wooden objects all are paralleled many times over between the sites. In the interests of expediency, a detailed comparative analysis of objects has been omitted from this volume.[2] Although none was excavated, the extensive number of Christian tombs adjoining Cemetery 193 and the Christian

reuse of the X-group tombs bear witness to the large Christian occupation at Ibrîm.

The Recording

Emery has generally described the methods by which he excavated and recorded a site,[3] but it is felt that a brief exposition with particular application to the Qaṣr Ibrîm cemeteries would be profitable here. As there was considerable uncertainty about the availability of a local labour force, the entire crew of over one hundred men was brought from Quft. Work was begun in Cemetery 193, initially, after the surface of the site had been inspected and details and general information recorded. The tumulus of grave 193.30 was largely removed in order to ascertain whether it contained objects, like those at Qusṭul, or not, as at Ballâna. When it was determined that the latter was the case, the tumuli were subsequently mined straight to the burial. Evidence for the size of each tumulus was left by the workmen so that it could be recorded at the same time as the grave. The recorded size and composition of each tumulus reflect a combination of the weathering and erosional process at the site, and the removal of part of the feature prior to recording. Certainly, most of the tumuli were probably originally larger.

When the tomb was opened, a portion of the stone blocking slabs, brick vaulting, or other roofing, was left in position for recording purposes. Occasionally, when such a feature appeared to be intact, it was recorded photographically and in drawings prior to the opening. Any artefact or bone which appeared to be in its original position was recorded *in situ* before being moved, but those objects encountered in the fill of a tomb were removed from their context prior to recording. Any objects or bones recorded in the grave plans in this volume were recorded as having been *in situ*. A scale drawing

from the Roman word for it. Strabo (*Geography* xvii. 53–4) in his account of Petronius' campaign gives us the earliest Roman name of Qaṣr Ibrîm as Premnis. The earliest name of the site, however, may be the Meroïtic *Pedeme*, dating slightly earlier, to the reign of Netakamani (Griffith, *JEA* 15 (1929), 71), and it must be supposed that the Romans took over the existing local name for this site. See also Caminos,

op. cit., 4 f.

[1] W. B. Emery, *The Royal Tombs of Ballana and Qustul* (Cairo, 1938).
[2] Such a study of all Ballâna-related material is now in the hands of Roger Allen.
[3] W. B. Emery, *Egypt in Nubia* (London, 1965), 51 ff.

was made of the plan and section of every grave excavated and the orientation, fill, and constructional details noted at the graveside. Photographs were generally not taken of graves unless exceptional circumstances occurred. At the time of recording, each tomb was assigned a number, which was painted on a rock which was placed at the same corner of each grave.

The contents of each tomb were also all recorded and drawn at the graveside. The burials and objects which were in their original position were drawn on the plan, and a scale drawing of each object was also made in the field notes, as well as a written description of each item. The burial was examined and sex and age determined (see below, **Human remains**) and recorded. The contents of the tomb were then removed and each piece numbered in ink. Photographic recording of the objects was conducted separately. The remainder of the fill of each grave was then sifted for anything that may have escaped attention.

Following the excavation of the whole cemetery, a plot plan of each numbered grave stone was surveyed, and the cemetery plan extrapolated from a combination of that and the field notes of each grave. Graves which had not been excavated were not numbered and were not included in the survey. Finally, the ground was inspected to ascertain that nothing had been missed.

Human Remains

The determination of the age and the sex of human skeletal remains is a matter requiring considerable expertise, and this note is by way of being a caveat to those who wish to make use of the physical anthropological data noted by the excavators of the Qaṣr Ibrîm cemeteries. Briefly, the main problem is that the physical characteristics of a single population need not particularly resemble or coincide with those of another. Particularly, the physical characteristics which help to distinguish male and female skeletal remains from one another are based upon the comparison of the features of each sex, rather than on some absolute norm. Because of genetically inherited differences between individuals in a given population, there is usually a fairly complete spectrum of sexual anomalies. On a broader plane, the characteristics which describe one population will not apply to another. This means that unless a good general anatomical description of the 'normal' characteritics and the specific anomalies of a population can be formulated, it is not readily possible to differentiate the sex of individuals. In the area of the Nile Valley the fine-boned Beja's skeleton, when compared with that of the much heavier-set *fellah*, would show the general characteristics of a female, although both were male specimens. Populations differ so much that in fact the identification of males and females could be reversed. An added complication is that it seems there is a definite bias towards the identification of individuals as males.[1]

The matter of age determination is slightly more secure, as much depends on specific aspects of maturation and the body's ageing process. The major uncertainty that intrudes itself is that different populations mature at varying ages and within a single population there are also variations. Again, the basic description of the population is the best tool for understanding the age of any individual.

At Qaṣr Ibrîm, an attempt to determine the sex of most individuals was made, using the criteria of the general size and rugosity of the specimens and upon the shape of the pelvis. The age of each individual was only determined on the most general level—of infant, child, or adult—based on the size of the skeleton and the dentition and suture closure of the skull. These data must be used bearing in mind that no professional physical anthropologist was involved in the expedition.

The Pottery

As it is always useful to have a single, standard reference for a subject, this present volume has

[1] K. M. Weiss, 'On the Systematic Bias in Skeletal Sexing', in *Amer. Jour. of Phys. Anthro.* 37 (1972), 239–47.

adopted the pottery typology of W. Y. Adams. Since its original appearance in 1962,[1] this typology has been constantly enlarged and refined and kept current. It is comprehensive inasmuch as it includes material found by past excavators in Lower Nubia as well as the results of the Nubian Salvage Campaign of the 1960s. The final form of the typology will be published as *Ceramic Industries of Medieval Nubia*, volumes I and II of the *Memoirs of the Archaeological Survey of Sudanese Nubia*. The description of each ceramic vessel in this present report gives a reference to the work of Adams, viz. Adams R.1.

Occasionally, reference is made to the corpus of shapes found in *The Royal Tombs of Ballana and Qustul*, pls. 111–14. This usually occurs when a fragment of a vessel was found which could be assigned to one or another type and which was not drawn in the field records.

During the course of the excavation, the industry of Mrs Smith produced, in addition to the normal field recording, a set of facsimile copies of the painted decoration so commonly found on X-group pottery vessels. These copies are now reproduced on pls. LXXVII–LXXX. It is interesting to note that although the general impression one has of ceramic decoration during the Ballâna phase is one of stylization, conventionality, and rather hasty application, there is in fact considerable variation in form and in detail in this decoration. There are four basic colours in the various elements: black, white, red, and yellow, which are used in various combinations depending upon the surface colour of the vessel and the motif. Black and white are signified in the drawings as solid colours, red is diagonally hatched and yellow is filled in dots. Again, Adams, in his *Ceramic Industries of Medieval Nubia*, deals exhaustively with decoration in all its aspects and there is no need to dwell on the subject here.

Grave Typology

Within the Meroïtic and X-group cemeteries at Qaṣr Ibrîm, six individual grave types were noted. There are three distinct types of grave pit: the simple rectangular pit; the rectangular pit with a sloping entrance ramp; and, thirdly, the lateral-niche type. The roofing or blocking of these pits was made either with local stone, which readily fractures into fairly flat slabs, or with sun-dried mud-bricks. Almost all of the tombs at Ibrîm had a single chamber, but there were two double-chamber graves (192.2 and 192.23) which were richer in contents but not noticeably more elaborate than the rest. For the most part, the graves were dug into the fossil alluvium ground of the areas of the cemeteries, although occasionally bedrock was excavated and one or two rock ledges were utilized. These are essentially the types presented by Emery,[2] with the further elaboration of the types of roofing and the addition of the double-chamber type.

The graves without exception bore the remains of superstructures. The Meroïtic graves recorded had square or rectangular structures with battered sides which were probably all pyramidal originally. The X-group graves were all covered with rubble tumuli. The field records show that most of these were stone-covered at the time of their discovery, but whether this condition was an accident of the weathering process, which would remove lighter sand particles most easily, or whether the original intention was to cover the tumulus with stones is uncertain. Although the Christian graves situated at the western side of Cemetery 193 were not recorded, it is worth mentioning the fact that a great number of them did have rectangular superstructures built of rough boulder stones, standing in many cases to well over a metre in height. A Muslim cemetery was encountered at the north end of the concession, but here no superstructures were observed. None of the X-group tumuli contained objects as did those at Quṣṭul.

In terms of the similarity of the types of tombs and superstructures there is no doubt that the X-group burials at Qaṣr Ibrîm belong to the

---

[1] *Kush* 10 (1962), 245 ff.
[2] W. B. Emery, *The Royal Tombs of Ballana and Qustul*, i, figs. 1, 2, 3.

same culture as those at Ballâna and Qustul. The Meroïtic tombs are of sufficient similarity to those at various sites both in Lower Nubia and further south that they are certainly not exceptional.

The six types of graves, then, are:

I. A rectangular pit, roofed with slabs of local stone. Frequently, the blocking stones rest on ledges cut along the sides and ends of the grave pit, although they can also be placed right on the surface of the ground. (pl. XL, 192A.5.)

II. A rectangular pit, roofed with mud-bricks which are built into a leaning barrel vault. Frequently, the bricks rest on ledges cut along the sides of the grave pit, and, if the vault protrudes much above the surface of the ground, a wall is built at the end of the grave for the vault to lean against. Blocking is effected with stones and bricks. (pl. XIII, 192.7.)

III. A rectangular pit with a sloping entrance ramp leading down to the entrance at one end. Roofing is with stone slabs, as in type I, and these often rest upon ledges. (pl. LVIII, 193.54.)

IV. A rectangular pit with a sloping entrance ramp at one end. A leaning barrel vault of mud-bricks rests on ledges cut along the sides of the pit. The entrance is blocked with stones and bricks. (pl. IV, 192.1.)

V. A large rectangular pit with a sloping entrance ramp at one end. The pit is divided into two chambers by a central wall of mud-brick and both chambers are roofed with mud-brick vaults. (pl. VI, 192.2.)

VI. The lateral-niche type, which consists of a subterranean, rectangular chamber, entered laterally from the bottom of a vertical, rectangular shaft. The entrance of the tomb was blocked with stones, and the shaft filled in. (pl. XLVI, 192B.9.)

Of these types of tombs, there are only two examples of V, and VI is not frequently found. This latter is particularly significant as the lateral-niche type of tomb is quite common

further south in the Second Cataract area and in Upper Nubia, and perhaps points to some distinction between Ballâna rulers and other peoples in the area at the same time. Types I to IV are by far the commonest at Ibrîm.

The dimensions of each grave are given in a standard order; the first dimension is that of the long axis of the pit, the second is at right angles to that, and the third is the depth of the pit, or, in the case of an underground chamber, the height of the tomb.

Distribution of the Finds

Following the closing of the excavation of the Ibrîm cemeteries, the finds were divided in the usual manner with the Egyptian Antiquities Service. The generous portion allocated to the Egypt Exploration Society by the Egyptian officials enabled a wide distribution of finds to be made to museums in Britain and abroad. The following list includes those institutions which received objects from the Qaṣr Ibrîm cemeteries. In the section of this report where each object is described in detail, the current location and accession number of each object has been included. Unfortunately, in some cases, the location has been lost. Some unnumbered glass fragments were sent to Sheffield and the Corning Museum.

Egyptian Museum, Cairo.
The British Museum, London.
University College London, The Petrie Museum.
Ashmolean Museum, Oxford.
Anthropological Museum, Marischal College, Aberdeen.
Birmingham City Museum and Art Gallery.
Blackburn Museum and Art Gallery.
Fitzwilliam Museum, Cambridge.
Museum of Archaeology and Ethnology, Cambridge.
Gulbenkian Museum of Oriental Art and Archaeology, Durham.
Royal Scottish Museum, Edinburgh.
Leeds University.

Liverpool City Museum.
Liverpool University, School of Archaeology and Oriental Studies.
Manchester Museum.
Reading Museum and Art Gallery.
Sheffield Museum.
Department of Archaeology, Queen's University, Belfast.
Nicholson Museum, Sydney, Australia.
Otago Museum, Dunedin, New Zealand.
Royal Ontario Museum, Toronto, Canada.
Rijksmuseum van Oudheden, Leiden, The Netherlands.
Musée du Louvre, Paris, France.
Corning Glass Museum, Corning, N.Y., U.S.A.

Acknowledgements

It is a pleasure to be able to record here my appreciation to a number of people. First, to Professor H. S. Smith, who encouraged me to compile this report, who has carefully read the manuscript and who has kindly written the Preface, I am most grateful. I also thank Professor Bunting and Dr Steele, Mr King, and Dr Brill for allowing me to include their reports on various technical matters in the Appendix, and Dr Millet and Dr Meltzer for their chapters on the Meroïtic and Coptic inscriptions. Professor W. Y. Adams, with his customary kindness, helped place the ceramics in his typology. I am also grateful to those colleagues in museums around the world who responded so quickly and courteously to my enquiries about objects from this site. Finally, to those in the Egyptian Department of the Royal Ontario Museum— N. B. Millet, for much valuable discussion, Mrs R. Gilchrist, for compiling the indexes, and Mrs A. Gromow, for patiently typing the manuscript—I extend my sincere thanks.

A substantial grant towards the printing of this volume by the Royal Ontario Museum has greatly assisted its appearance in its present form. For this generous help I and the Egypt Exploration Society are deeply grateful.

CEMETERY 192

THIS site, originally numbered in 1935,[1] is located to the north of the hill upon which the citadel of Qaṣr Ibrîm is situated. It covers an area of over 400 × 250 m. and the site is marked by the numerous earthen tumuli which serve as the above-ground element for almost every grave in the cemetery (pl. LXXXIV. 1). The soil into which the graves were dug is a fossil alluvium, and the limits of the site are those of this plateau of fossil soil, bounded on the north and south by wâdis, by the base of the sandstone hills on the east and by the sandstone outcrops that overlook the Nile on the west. This sandstone underlies the whole site and some of the graves were partly cut into it.

Almost every grave in the cemetery had been plundered in antiquity and many of them seemed to contain later, Christian, burials. Fortunately for the expedition, the two largest graves, nos. 2 and 23, had only been partially disturbed. Presumably, the burial chamber of each had been entered by someone who failed to realize that one of the walls was made entirely of brick and that another chamber lay on the other side of that wall. The rich deposits of ceramic, glass, metal, and wooden objects (pl. LXXXIV. 4) from these two chambers attest the level of prosperity and the close ties between the residents of Ibrîm and Ballâna. It is most interesting to note that some of the objects found in these two graves, particularly the horse-head lamp (192.23.32), the spouted beaker (192.2.13), and the cauldron with duck-head handles (192.23.39), are earlier in date than the X-group Period.[2] The lamp must be dated to the first and second centuries A.D. as the body is very similar to lamps from Pompeii and Herculaneum, which were destroyed in A.D. 79,

and is a common Roman type.[3] The beaker also has Roman prototypes in the first century[4] as well as Nubian Meroïtic parallels.[5] The cauldron's duck-head handles do not occur at Ballâna or Quṣṭul, although handles ornamented in such a fashion are found throughout the Roman Empire. Perhaps some of the Ballâna people's funerary richness at Ibrîm was obtained from the adjacent Meroïtic cemetery areas (192A, 192C).

A total of a hundred and thirty-three graves was excavated in Cemetery 192. This figure probably represents about 60 per cent of the total number of graves in the site. Only those graves excavated have been plotted on the plan (pl. LXXXI). That they are securely dated within the general X-group Period is beyond doubt, as the material so closely parallels that of Ballâna and Quṣṭul. It could be further argued that the proximity of earlier, Meroïtic remains in three adjacent sites (192A, 192B, and 192C) indicates an early use of this area by the Ballâna culture, while the post-X-group Christian burial ground is connected with Cemetery 193.[6]

Grave 192.1

Superstructure: A stone-covered rubble tumulus, 12.7 m. diam. and 3.3 m. high. On the top of the mound there were two small intrusive graves, built of brick and situated side by side. Both have a NE–SW (53° E. of N.) orientation. Both are rectangular and have stone slab roofing.

GRAVE A is 1.35 × 0.25 × 0.42 m. and contained the articulated body of an adult male, lying wrapped in a shroud, on the right side in a slightly flexed position with the head to the SW. (pl. IV.)

GRAVE B is 1.3 × 0.2 × 0.25 m. and contained the articulated body of an adult female, also wrapped in a yellow cloth, lying dorsally extended, hands on the

[1] W. B. Emery and L. P. Kirwan, *The Excavations and Survey between Wadi es-Sebua and Adindan 1929–1931*, 268.

[2] I am indebted to Miss K. Bard for the information concerning these pieces and a discussion of them.

[3] Cf. particularly S. Loeschcke, *Lampen aus Vindonissa*

(Zürich, 1919), 68–70.

[4] For example, British Museum 29179.

[5] Such as those excavated at Faras by Griffith and dated by Kirwan (*Firka*, pl. 34) to the second and third centuries A.D.
[6] See p. 48, below.

pelvis, head SW. (pl. IV.) No objects were found in association with these two burials. They are most probably Christian in date.

Grave: Type IV, 1.87×0.98×1.1 m. The entrance is 0.74 m. long. Only the lower 0.6 m. of the grave is dug into the ground, the upper portion being built within the tumulus. Orientation is ENE–WSW (63° E. of N.). (pl. IV.)

Burial: The scattered bones of an adult female.

Objects: 1. A red ware jar with white painted decoration, 27 cm. high×18 cm. max. diam. (pl. V.) Adams R.1. Nicholson Museum 63.182.

2. A red ware jar with yellow and black painted decoration, 24.9 cm. high×18 cm. max. diam. (pls. V, LXXVII.) Adams R.1. Location uncertain.

3. A red amphora with matt cream slip and black painted decoration, 37.5 cm. high×19.8 cm. max. diam. (pl. IV.) Adams W.30. Ashmolean Museum 1962.938.

4. The iron hasps, hinge, handle and fittings from a leather bag or box. (pl. IV.) Piece *a* is the handle, which was probably mounted on the edge of the lid with the three hasps hanging down to fit into the lock (missing), which would have been held in place by piece *d*. Piece *b* is the hinge for the lid and would have been mounted opposite the handle. The exact purpose of piece *c* is uncertain. The container may have been as large as 35 cm. across and probably at least 20 cm. deep. The bend in the hasps indicates that the mouth was probably flanged or flared outwards. Location uncertain.

5. A red ware cup, 9 cm. high×9.6 cm. max. diam. (pl. IV.) Adams R.1. Birmingham Museum 123.63.

6. A rectangular ivory plaque, 8.3×9.6 cm., with the incised figure of a nude woman (? Venus). This was probably originally inlaid into a wooden casket, but no trace of this remained. (pl. V.) Royal Ontario Museum 963.15.24.

Grave 192.2

Superstructure: A stone-covered rubble tumulus, 19 m. diam. and 2.5 m. high. There were four burials dug into the mound subsequent to the original burial:

GRAVE A is type II, 2.5×1.55×0.8 m. Orientation is ENE–WSW (60° E. of N.). It contained the scattered bones of five adults. (pl. V.) The grave contained three objects:

1. A grey ware goblet with impressed dot decoration. The mouth is missing. 17.4 cm. high×14.6 cm. max. diam. (pl. V.) Location uncertain.

2. A crop or stick 70 cm. long. It is made of horn, bound in several places with bronze wire and has a braided loop-in-loop chain attached to the larger end by means of two iron rings. (pl. V.) Location uncertain.

3. An iron bangle bracelet, 6.3 cm. diam. and 0.3 cm. wide. (pl. V.) Location uncertain.

GRAVE B is also type II, and is 2.7×2×0.95 m. It was completely plundered.

GRAVE C, again type II, is 2.4×0.96×0.6 m., and is orientated ENE–WSW (63° E. of N.). The burial remains consisted of the articulated body of an adult, lying extended on the right side, head WSW. Beneath the head were the remains of a straw pillow.

GRAVE D, again type II, is 2.6×1.1×0.8 m. high. The interior was white plastered.

Burial: The scattered bones of six adults.

Objects: The remains of four straw pillows; a natural fossil which possibly had been used as a pendant or amulet.

Grave: Type V. The pit, which is cut into bedrock, is 2×1.7×1.75 m. deep. Orientation is NE–SW (55° E. of N.). The pit was divided into two chambers by a brick wall 0.2 m. thick. Chamber A, which contained the burial, measured 1.2×1.7 m. This chamber had been entered by the plunderers and had been largely ransacked, disturbing the burial and leaving some common goblets, taking whatever else may have been with the burial. Chamber B, 0.6×1.7 m., was left intact by the robbers and contained over fifty objects, many of them of wood, glass, and metal. (pls. VI, VII.)

Burial: The scattered remains of an old adult male in Chamber A. The head and upper part of the thorax were articulated and indicated that the body had been placed on the right side in a flexed position with the head to the SW. The body lay on a wooden bier, of which only traces remained.

Objects: 6. A brass lamp, cast in the shape of a camel. The saddle is hinged to cover the oil-filler hole and there are two wick holes in panniers slung over the withers. The total height is 14.4 cm. (pls. IX, LXXXVII. 1.) Cairo, Egyptian Museum 89670. This lamp was found hanging from an iron hook embedded into the brick of the vault of chamber B. (pls. VI, LXXXIV. 5.)

NOTE:

The following objects were found in Chamber B, apparently undisturbed. For their relative positions within this locus, see the plan of the chamber. (pl. VII.)

7. A brass ladle. The cup is 4.1 cm. diam. and the handle, made of a twisted strip of metal, is 56.1 cm. long, and has a crook at the end for hanging the ladle on the lip of a jar. (pl. X.) It was found hanging on the lip of 192.2.59, and would probably have been used for dipping into it. Otago Museum E62.29.

8. A brass ladle. The bowl, 6.9 cm. diam., and the

handle, 39 cm. long, are formed of a single piece. There is a hanging crook at the end of the handle. (pl. X.) This piece was found together with the above hanging on the rim of 192.2.59. Nicholson Museum 63.209.

9. A brass lamp, cast in the form of a human (? male) face. The oil-filler hole at the top of the head was probably originally covered by a hinged lid, but this was not found. Total length is 17 cm. (pls. IX, LXXXVI. 2, 3.) Liverpool City Museum 1962.333.1.

10. A stone pestle, 7.5 cm. high × 6.1 cm. max. diam., of a truncated conical form, University College London 19559; and a stone mortar, the hollow being 21.6 cm. diam. and 3.2 cm. deep, with four lug handles at the rim, Birmingham Museum 142′63. These were found beside one another and, as both are made of (? grey) granite, it is probable that they belong together. (p. X.) A quantity of grain had been placed in the mortar. This has now been examined by Professor A. H. Bunting and found to be mostly a combination of sorghum and millet. (Cf. below, p. 86–7, for his report on this sample.)

11. A wooden (? ebony) circular toilet container, 20.5 cm. high × 6.2 cm. diam. There are three panels of carved relief decoration running around the box—the upper register has a series of double plumes with the sun disc; the middle register bears a series of cartouches in each of which is a winged cobra with the sun disc on her head; the bottom register has a series of these winged cobras, but not in cartouches. Considerable attention has been paid to the internal detail of the figures and the carving is of excellent quality. The lid of the container is missing. (pls. VI, LXXXVII. 1.) Cairo, Egyptian Museum 89671.

12. A small (? toilet) vessel of either blue faience, or blue-glazed pottery, 14 cm. high × 10.8 cm. max. diam. There is a panelled floral decoration, moulded in relief. Holes, pierced just below the rim, indicate that the vessel was designed to be suspended. (pls. VI, LXXXVII. 1.) Cairo, Egyptian Museum 89672.

13. A bronze beaker, 9.2 cm. high × 11 cm. rim diam. The pouring lip is large and angular. There are two horizontal incised bands around the body. (pl. VIII.) Cairo, Egyptian Museum 89673.

14. A glass dish with a low hollow foot. The dish is 6.1 cm. high × 21.9 cm. max. diam. It is a very thin and light vessel. (pls. VII, LXXXVII. 2.) Nicholson Museum 63.208.

15. A bronze *kohl* stick, 21.6 cm. long. The main decorative element is the cobra on the handle. (pls. VI, LXXXVII. 1.) As this was found in proximity to 192.2.11, the toilet tube, it was probably a companion to it. Otago Museum E62.31.

16. A hollow-footed glass cup, 5.4 cm. high × 9.8 cm. max. diam. Like 192.2.12, this piece is thin and fine. (pls. VII, LXXXVII. 3.) Ashmolean Museum 1962.945.

17. A circular, ivory toilet box, 5.4 cm. high × 9.8 cm. diam. It is fitted with a lid, 0.9 cm. high. Decoration is rather crudely incised and consists of a bird standing beneath a bunch of fruit that hangs from the branch of a tree. (pl. VII.) The lattice-work filling of the body of the bird and of the hanging object is a common element in decoration of this type. Queen's University, Belfast QAD/7/130.

18. A red ware cup with white painted splash decoration, 12.9 cm. high × 13.2 cm. max. diam. (pl. V.) Adams R.1. Queen's University, Belfast QAD/7/120.

19. A small wooden box, 8.6 × 5.5 × 4.5 cm. high. The four sides of the box are of a hard wood, the bottom was of a softer wood and has perished, the sliding lid is also made of this softer wood, but has an ivory plaque fixed to the upper side. The sides and ends of the box are decorated with relief carving. On one side are two birds (? doves) and the other side has a pair of floral elements. One end has two rosettes and a knot, and the other end has a dove, which has been largely covered by a bronze lock face, which is circular with a scalloped edge and is held in place by three round-headed nails. The sliding lid is decorated with an ivory plaque with a relief carving of a figure of Dionysus holding a staff(?) and carrying a dead animal. (pls. VII, LXXXVII. 1.) Fitzwilliam Museum E.1.1962.

20. An iron spoon, 15 cm. long. The end of the handle appears to have been broken off. (pl. VIII.) University College London 19537.

21. A bronze, hollow-footed dish with a beaded rim and fluted sides, 5 cm. high × 13 cm. max. diam. The bowl of the dish is 3.5 cm. deep. Concentric rings have been incised on the interior. (pl. IX.) Location uncertain.

22. The remains of a largely decayed wooden casket which was decorated with ivory plaques and small diamond-shaped pieces of ivory set in patterns. The original size of the base of the box was 23 × 26 cm. and it had bronze and iron fittings. Six plaques from this object were recovered. Five of them, each about 6.8 × 2.2 cm. and rectangular, bear the figure of a naked female, two in left profile, two in right and the fifth frontal. The sixth plaque is smaller, 3.8 × 1.8 cm., and shows the face and bust, clothed, of a figure. (pl. VII.) Ashmolean Museum 1962.946; inlays 1962.947 a–e, 1962.948.

23. A broken, fine glass chalice, 7.2 cm. high × 10 cm. max. diam. (pl. VII.) It is identical with 192.2.27 and 33. Liverpool City Museum 1962.333.3.

24. A two-handled, footed bronze chalice, 12 cm. high × 17.6 cm. max. diam. The rim and the base of the foot are beaded and the handles are made in a formalized vegetable design. (pl. VIII.) Cairo, Egyptian Museum 89674.

25. An iron knife blade, 11.8 cm. long × 3.3 cm. wide with the vestigial remains of a tang. (pl. VIII.) University College London 19531.

26. A schist(?) hone or whetstone, 15.3×3.8×1.3 cm. thick. (pl. IX.) University College London 19530.

27. A broken, fine glass chalice, 7.2 cm. high×10 cm. max. diam. (pl. VII.) Location uncertain.

28. A large, bronze pedestal bowl, 17.4 cm. high×36 cm. max. diam., the foot being 5.4 cm. high. (pl. X.) The vessel was crushed *in situ*, in the grave. Royal Ontario Museum 963.15.27a–b.

29. An iron cooking pan. The pan is 19.8 cm. diam. and 2.9 cm. deep, and the attached handle is 17.7 cm. long and 2.9 cm. wide, and has a ring at the end for hanging up the pan. (pl. VIII.) University College London 19534.

30. The remains of a small iron cooking pan, the pan being 12 cm. diam and 1.6 cm. deep and the handle 7.8 cm. long and shaped like that of 192.2.29. (pl. VIII.) University College London 19535.

31. A bronze cup, 8.8 cm. max. diam. and 5 cm. high, with horizontal incised lines on the exterior surface. (pl. VIII.) This is identical to 192.2.36, 42, and 46. Durham GM 1964 581.

32. A red ware jar, 25.5 cm. high × 20.4 cm. max. diam., with black and white painted horizontal bands. (pl. XI.) Adams R.1. University College London 19565.

33. Fragments of several fine glass vessels. Reconstructed height is 7.3 cm. and max. diam. is 10.1 cm. (pl. VII.) Location uncertain.

34. A red ware jar, 24.6 cm. high×18.6 cm. max. diam., with black and white painted horizontal bands. (pl. XI.) Adams R.1. Nicholson Museum 63.183.

35. A red ware flask, 26.4 cm. high × 18 cm. max. diam., decorated with black and white painted horizontal bands. (pl. XI.) Adams R.1. British Museum 66548.

36. A bronze cup, 8.8 cm. max. diam. and 5 cm. high, with horizontal incised lines on the exterior surface. (pl. VIII.) British Museum 66577.

37. A red ware amphora, 32.7 cm. high × 16.8 cm. max. diam. (pl. IX.) Adams R.25. Reading Museum 83:67/6.

38. A red ware flask, 27 cm. high×18.6 cm. max. diam., with black and white painted stripes. (pl. XI.) Adams R.1. Birmingham Museum 133′63.

39. A bronze cup or bowl, 12.5 cm. max. diam. and 7.1 cm. high. (pl. VIII.) This vessel is identical with 192.2.44, 48, 49, and 54. Rijksmuseum, Leiden F1963/8. 28.

40. A red ware flask, 24 cm. high×19.2 cm. max. diam., with black and white painted decoration. (pl. XI.) Adams R.1. Aberdeen Anthropological Museum 1109².

41. A bronze flagon, 18 cm. high×13.3 cm. max. diam. A lid with a scalloped edge is hinged to the handle. (pl. VIII.) Cairo, Egyptian Museum 89675.

42. A bronze cup, 8.8 cm. max. diam. and 5 cm. high. (pl. VIII.) Queen's University, Belfast QAD/7/115.

43. A red ware flask, 27 cm. high × 18 cm. max. diam., with black and white painted horizontal bands. (pl. XI.) Adams R.1. Aberdeen Anthropological Museum 1109².

44. A bronze cup, 12.5 cm. max. diam. and 7.1 cm. high. (pl. VIII.) Otago Museum E62.30.

45. A red ware flask, 27.6 cm. high × 18 cm. max. diam., with black and white painted stripes. (pl. XI.) Adams R.1. Manchester Museum.

46. A bronze cup, 8.8 cm. max. diam. and 5 cm. high. (pl. VIII.) Blackburn Museum.

47. A red ware flask, 26.7 cm. high × 18.6 cm. max. diam., with black and white horizontal stripes. (pl. XI.) Adams R.1. Royal Ontario Museum 963.15.7.

48. A bronze cup or bowl, 12.5 cm. max. diam. and 7.1 cm. high. (pl. VIII.) Liverpool University E1500.

49. A bronze cup or bowl, 12.5 cm. max. diam. and 7.1 cm. high. (pl. VIII.) Liverpool City Museum 1962. 333.2.

50. A red ware amphora, 30.6 cm. high × 17.4 cm. max. diam. (pl. IX.) Adams R.25. Ashmolean Museum 1962.944.

51. A red ware flask, 27.6 cm. high × 19.2 cm. max. diam., with black and white painted parallel bands. (pl. XI.) Adams R.1. Cambridge Museum of Arch. and Eth. 63.180.

52. A large bronze pan, 42.6 cm. max. diam. and 15.9 cm high. There are two free-swinging handles, which are attached to the pan by a metal strip which is folded rather like a cotter-pin to form a loop which holds the handle and is then inserted through a hole in the pan and folded back against the inner wall. (pl. X.) Royal Ontario Museum 963.15.25.

53. A large red ware jar, 51 cm. high × 33 cm. max. diam. (pl. X.) Adams R.1. University College London 19569.

54. A bronze cup or bowl, 12.5 cm. max. diam. and 7.1 cm. high. (pl. VIII.) Nicholson Museum 63.207.

55. A red ware jar, 25.8 cm. high × 19.2 cm. max. diam., with black and white horizontal bands. (pl. XI.) Adams R.1. Leeds University.

56. A glass, single-handled bottle or flask, 24.8 cm. high×11.9 cm. max. diam. (pls. VII, LXXXVII. 4.) Sheffield Museum 1966.293.

57. A cube of sandstone, 10.6 × 10.8 × 9 cm. high. Four sides have been decorated with relief carving of floral designs. The top and bottom have had a square hole, 6.2 × 6.2 × 1.9 cm. deep, cut into each, the top one being somewhat more regular in shape and more carefully cut. This piece was probably a stand or plinth for some object which has since perished. (pl. IX.) Cairo, Egyptian Museum 89676.

58. A red ware amphora, 41.1 cm. high×18 cm. max. diam. (pl. XI.) Adams R.1. British Museum 66545.

59. A large red ware amphora, 86.4 cm. high × 40.8 cm. max. diam. (pl. X.) Adams U.9. In association with this jar was a conical mud seal bearing the impression of the 'ritual bouquet of Isis', painted red. (pl. X.) Location uncertain.

NOTE:

The following objects were found in the disturbed fill of Chamber A.

60. A red ware cup, 11.1 cm. high × 12 cm. max. diam., with black and white painted 'festoon' decoration. (pl. V.) Adams R.1. Rijksmuseum, Leiden F1963/8.5.

61. A red ware cup, 12.6 cm. high × 12.6 cm. max. diam., with black and white painted 'festoon' decoration. (pl. V.) Adams R.1. Cairo, Egyptian Museum 89677.

62. A red ware cup, 12.6 cm. high × 10.8 cm. max. diam. (pl. V.) Adams R.1. Aberdeen Anthropological Museum 1109².

63. A red ware cup, 9.9 cm. high × 10.2 cm. max. diam., with black and white painted decoration. (pl. V.) Adams R.1. Fitzwilliam Museum E.6.1962.

64. A red ware cup, 12.6 cm. high × 10.8 cm. max. diam. (pl. V.) Adams R.1. Birmingham Museum 130′63.

65. A silver finger ring, 1.6 cm. diam × 0.7 cm. wide. (pl. VIII.) Nicholson Museum 63.218.

Grave 192.3

Superstructure: A stone-covered tumulus, 6.5 m. diam. and 1.1 m. high. An intrusive grave was dug into the mound. It is type II and is 2.9 × 1.1 × 1.07 m., orientated ENE–WSW (57° E. of N.). Within the chamber were the scattered remains of three adults. No objects were found.

Grave: Type II, 2.65 × 1.20 × 1.03 m. deep. The orientation is NE–SW (40° E. of N.) (pl. XII.)

Burial: None remained.

Objects: 1. A red ware cup, 9.6 cm. high × 9 cm. max. diam. (pl. XII.) Adams R.1. Otago Museum E62.27.
   There were also found portions of:
   2. A red ware amphora with a matt cream slip, Adams W.30, and
   3. Another cup similar to 192.3.1. (pl. XII.)

Grave 192.4

Superstructure: A stone-covered tumulus, 5 m. diam. and 0.5 m. high. Near the surface of the mound was an intrusive grave, type II, 2.55 × 1.2 × 0.78 m. It was orientated NE–SW (45° E. of N.).

BURIAL: The scattered bones of three adults.

OBJECTS: 1. A translucent blue glass phial, 12.5 cm. high. It was broken and incomplete when found. (pl. XII.) Rijksmuseum, Leiden F1963/8.30.
   2. A finger(?) ring, made from a silver wire, 0.1 cm.

thick, coiled nearly twice around in a loop 1.9 cm. diam. (pl. XII.) Nicholson Museum 63.219.

Grave: Type I, 2.1 × 0.7 × 0.7 m. The orientation is NNE–SSW (20° E. of N.).

Burial: None remained.

Objects: None found.

Grave 192.5

Superstructure: A stone-covered tumulus, 5 m. diam. and 0.9 m. high. There is a burial near the surface of the mound. The rectangular pit has a rectangular super-structure of brick, 2.3 × 0.6 × 0.5 m. high. The inhumation was that of an adult, lying extended on the right side with the head to the SW. No objects were associated with this burial.

Grave: Type II, 2.1 × 0.95 × 0.93 m., orientated NNW–SSE (26° W. of N.). (pl. XII.)

Burial: The scattered bones of an adult.

Objects: 1. A red ware bottle with a black slip, 10.2 cm. high × 10.2 cm. max. diam. (pl. XII.) Adams R.4. University College London 19561.
   2. A red ware jar, 30.2 cm. high × 20.9 cm. max. diam. (pl. XII.) Adams R.1. British Museum 66542.
   3. A cream biscuit-ware cup with light brown painted decoration, 7.8 cm. high × 9.1 cm. max. diam. (pls. XII, LXXX.) Adams W.30. Leeds University.

Grave 192.6

Superstructure: A stone-covered mound, 7.5 m. diam. and 0.5 m. high.

Grave: Type I. It is 2.2 × 0.6 × 0.75 m. deep. The orientation is N.–S. (10° E. of N.).

Burial: Only the skull of an adult was found.

Objects: 1. A red ware cup, 9.2 cm. high × 4.8 cm. max. diam. (pl. XII.) Adams R.1. Liverpool University E6312.
   2. A red ware flask with cream slip, 15.6 cm. high × 12.4 cm. max. diam. (pl. XII.) Adams W.28. Reading Museum 83:67/5.
   3. A red ware goblet with black and white painted 'splash' decoration, 13.3 cm. high × 12.8 cm. max. diam. (pl. XII.) Adams R.1. Liverpool University E6328.
   4. A red ware cup, 9.6 cm. high × 8.8 cm. max. diam. (pl. XII.) Adams R.1. Rijksmuseum, Leiden F1963/8.4.
   5. A red ware goblet with painted black and white 'festoon' decoration, 12.3 cm. high × 12.5 cm. max. diam. (pl. XII.) Adams R.1. Ashmolean Museum 1962.920.

Grave 192.7

Superstructure: A stone-covered tumulus, 5.8 m. diam. and 1 m. high.

Grave: Type II. It is 2.45×0.87×0.85 m. and is orientated ENE–WSW (65° E. of N.). (pl. XIII.)

Burial: The undisturbed body of an adult male, lying slightly flexed on the right side, wrapped in a yellow linen shroud. This body is not the original burial as below it were found the scattered bones of an adult male.

Objects: 1. A red ware flask, 28.6 cm. high×19.3 cm. max. diam. (pl. XIII.) Adams R.1. University College London 19568.

Grave 192.8

Superstructure: A stone-covered mound, 6 m. diam. and 0.5 m. high.

Grave: Type I, 2.6×1.1×0.7 m. The orientation is NW–SE (38° W. of N.).

Burial: None remained.

Objects: 1. A brown ware cup with a cream slip, 7.6 cm. high×4.8 cm. max. diam. (pl. XIII.) Adams W.30. Liverpool University E6327.

Grave 192.9

Superstructure: A stone-covered mound, 4 m. diam. and 0.3 m. high.

Grave: Type I, 1.35×0.78×0.4 m. deep. It is orientated NNW–SSE (21° W. of N.).

Burial: None remained.

Objects: None were found.

Grave 192.10

Superstructure: A stone-covered mound, 4 m. diam. and 0.4 m. high.

Grave: Type I, cut or built partly into bedrock, one side of the grave being built or lined with bricks. The grave is 2.4×0.8×0.62 m. deep and is orientated WNW–ESE (57° W. of N.).

Burial: None remained.

Objects: None were found.

Grave 192.11

Superstructure: A stone-covered mound, 11.75 m. diam. and 0.8 m. high. Within the tumulus were two intrusive graves:

INTRUSIVE GRAVE A. There was a rectangular superstructure built of brick and stones. The grave, type II, was 2.8×1.3×0.5 m. In it was the extended burial of an adult, lying on the right side, head due west. There were no objects.

INTRUSIVE GRAVE B. Also a brick and stone superstructure; the type II grave was 2.1×0.7×0.5 m. It contained the undisturbed body of a child, lying extended on the right side, head west. No objects.

Grave: Type IV, 2.65×1.3×1 m., with an entrance pit 0.95 m. long. Orientation is NW–SE (42° W. of N.).

Burial: The undisturbed body of an adult female, lying extended on the right side, head to the SE.

Objects: 1. A red ware cup with painted decoration in black and white, 8.1 cm. high×9.3 cm. max. diam. (pl. XIII.) Adams R.2. Otago Museum E62.5.

2. A buff ware cup with a matt cream slip and black painted rim, 8.1 cm. high×9.8 cm. max. diam. (pl. XIII.) Adams W.2. Liverpool University E6334.

3. A red ware cup with black and white painted decoration, similar to 192.11.1, 8.4 cm. high×9.6 cm. max. diam. (pl. XIII.) Adams R.2. Location uncertain.

4. A red ware cup, 9 cm. high×8.8 cm. max. diam. (pl. XIII.) Adams R.1. Rijksmuseum, Leiden F1963/8.6.

5. A red ware cup, 9.5 cm. high×8.8 cm. max. diam., similar to 192.11.4. (pl. XIII.) Adams R.1. Ashmolean Museum 1962.916.

6. A red ware cup, 9.3 cm. high×9.1 cm. max. diam., similar to 192.11.4. (pl. XIII.) Adams R.1. Ashmolean Museum 1962.917.

7. A red ware goblet with white painted 'festoon' decoration, 12.1 cm. high×11.9 cm. max. diam. (pl. XIII.) Adams R.1. Durham GM 1964 570.

8. A red ware goblet with white painted decoration, 12 cm. high×11 cm. max. diam. (pl. XIII.) Adams R.1. Cairo, Egyptian Museum 89678.

9. A red ware goblet with black and white painted 'festoon' decoration, 12.9 cm. high×11.2 cm. max. diam. (pl. XIII.) Adams R.1. Liverpool University E6316.

10. A red ware goblet with black and white painted decoration, 9.3 cm. high×10.6 cm. max. diam. (pl. XIII.) Adams R.1. British Museum 66560.

11. A red ware goblet with black and white painted 'festoon' decoration, 11.9 cm. high×11.4 cm. max. diam. (pl. XIII.) Adams R.1. Leeds University.

Grave 192.12

Superstructure: A stone-covered tumulus, 14.1 m. diam. and 0.7 m. high, in which there are two intrusive graves:

INTRUSIVE GRAVE A. A rectangular brick superstructure over a grave 2.8×0.7×0.2 m. at the surface of the mound. Neither burial nor objects were found.

INTRUSIVE GRAVE B. Again with a brick superstructure, the grave is 2.2×0.7×0.2 m. In it was the articulated body of an adult, lying extended on the right side, head west. No objects were found.

Grave: Type IV, 2.45×1.6×1.4 m. deep. The orientation is NE–SW (38° E. of N.).

Burial: The scattered bones of an adult in the fill.

Objects: 1. A red ware goblet with white painted decoration, 13.5 cm. high×11.9 cm. max. diam. (pl. XIII.) Adams R.1. Aberdeen Anthropological Museum 1109².

2. A red ware jar with black and white painted decoration, 25.2 cm. high×16.1 cm. max. diam. (pl. XIII.) Adams R.1. Ashmolean Museum 1962.931.

3. A red ware goblet with white painted decoration, 13.5 cm. high×11.9 cm. max. diam. (pl. XIII.) This piece is similar to 192.12.1. Adams R.1. Aberdeen Anthropological Museum 1109².

Also found were fragments of two other red ware jars similar in shape to 192.12.2. One of them had a cream slip and painted black decoration and the other was plain.

Grave 192.13

Superstructure: A stone-covered tumulus, 12.5 m. diam. and 1.3 m. high. In it were two intrusive burials.

INTRUSIVE BURIAL A. This was near the surface of the mound. The grave was type IV and measured 2.65× 0.87×0.95 m. deep. The orientation was NE–SW (54° E. of N.). No burial was recovered. The only object found was:

11. A wooden stick, notched in three places. It is round, 2.1 cm. diam., and the preserved length is 39 cm. (pl. XIV.) University College London 19540.

INTRUSIVE BURIAL B. Again near the surface, this grave is type I, and is 2.7×0.75×0.4 m. deep and orientated ENE–WSW (63° E. of N.). The burial was articulated and was that of an adult male, lying in an extended position, head to the WSW. No objects were found.

Grave: Type IV, 3.2×1.6×1.6 m. with an entrance pit a further 0.75 m.

Burial: The articulated body of an adult female, lying extended on the back.

Objects: 1. A red ware goblet with white painted decoration, 12 cm. high×10.2 cm. max. diam. (pl. XIV.) Adams R.1. The decoration on this vessel is similar to 192.13.2, 3, 6, and 10. Leeds University.

2. A red ware goblet with white painted decoration, 11.8 cm. high×11.3 cm. max. diam. (pl. XIV.) Adams R.1. Durham GM 1964 568.

3. A red ware goblet with white painted decoration, 12.8 cm. high×11 cm. max. diam. (pl. XIV.) Adams, R.1. Durham GM 1964 567.

4. A red ware footed cup, 9.5 cm. high×8.5 cm. max. diam. (pl. XIV.) Adams R.1. Nicholson Museum 63.224.

5. A brown ware footed cup with a matt cream slip, 8.2 cm. high×7.1 cm. max. diam. (pl. XIV.) Adams W.30. Durham GM 1964 549.

6. A red ware goblet with white painted decoration, 11.9 cm. high×11.3 cm. max. diam. (pl. XIV.) Adams R.1. Liverpool University E6315.

7. A red ware ribbed amphora, 62.7 cm. high×18 cm. max. diam. (pl. XIV.) Adams U.4. British Museum 66539.

8. A red ware flask, 26.3 cm. high×16.8 cm. max. diam. (pl. XIV.) Adams R.1. Rijksmuseum, Leiden F1963/8.7.

9. A red ware flask similar to 192.13.8, 26.6 cm. high× 17.3 cm. max. diam. (pl. XIV.) Adams R.1. Leeds University.

10. A red ware goblet with white painted decoration, 12 cm. high×10.9 cm. max. diam. (pl. XIV.) Adams R.1. Royal Ontario Museum 963.15.8.

Also within the fill of the grave was a mud sealing with an impression comprising three equal panels—the end ones have a diagonal cross on each and the centre panel has an ostrich (?). (pl. XIV.)

Grave 192.14

Superstructure: A stone-covered tumulus, 14 m. diam. and 1.25 m. high. There are three intrusive graves in the surface of the mound:

INTRUSIVE GRAVE A contained the articulated body of a young adult, lying extended on the right side, head west, in a grave 2.6×1.05×0.4 m. deep.

INTRUSIVE GRAVE B is 1.55×0.9×0.65 m. and contains the body of an adult lying extended on the right side, head west.

INTRUSIVE GRAVE C is 2.5×0.8×0.45 m. and contains the undisturbed body of an adult, lying extended on the right side, head west.

No objects were found with any of these three graves.

Grave: Type IV, 3.1×2×1.32 m. It is orientated E.–W. (79° E. of N.).

Burial: Only the scattered bones of an adult were recovered.

Objects: 1. A red ware ribbed amphora with a cream slip, 52.5 cm. high×28.2 cm. max. diam. (pl. XIV.) Adams U.2. Liverpool University E6336.

2. A red ware goblet, 12.8 cm. high×12.5 cm. max. diam., with black and white painted decoration. (pl. XIV.) Adams R.1. This is one of three identical vessels, the others being 192.14.9 and 10. Queen's University, Belfast QAD/7/122.

3. A brown ware jar with a white slip and red and black painted decoration, 29.9 cm. high×18.7 cm. max. diam. (pls. XIV, LXXVII.) Adams W.30. This is one of four identical flasks in this grave, the others being 192.14.4, 5, and 6. Blackburn Museum.

4. A brown ware jar with a white slip and red and black painted decoration, 29.9 cm. high×18.7 cm. max. diam. (pls. XIV, LXXVIII.) Adams W.30. Cairo, Egyptian Museum 89679.

5. A brown ware jar with a white slip and red and black

painted decoration, 29.9 cm. high×18.7 cm. max. diam. (pls. XIV, LXXIX.) Adams W.30. British Museum 66549.

6. A brown ware jar with a white slip and red and black painted decoration, 29.9 cm. high×18.7 cm. max. diam. (pls. XIV, LXXVIII.) Adams W.30. Fitzwilliam Museum E.7.1962.

7. A brown ware cup with a white slip and red and black painted decoration, 7.2 cm. high×8.7 cm. max. diam. (pl. XIV.) Adams W.30. Durham GM 1964 580.

Fragments of the following were also recovered from the fill of this grave:

8. A cream biscuit ware cup, 9.4 cm. high×8.1 cm. max. diam. (pl. XIV.) Adams W.30. Location uncertain.

9. A red ware goblet with black and white painted decoration, 12.8 cm. high×12.5 cm. max. diam. (pl. XIV.) Adams R.1. Location uncertain.

10. A red ware goblet with black and white painted decoration, 12.8 cm. high×12.5 cm. max. diam. (pl. XIV.) Adams R.1. Location uncertain.

11. A brown ware jar with cream slip, 25 cm. high× 12.1 cm. max. diam. (pl. XIV.) Adams W.30. Location uncertain.

12. Fragments of three glass footed cups, 8.5 cm. tall×8 cm. max. diam. (pl. XIV.) Location uncertain.

13. A mud jar sealing depicting the 'bouquet of Isis' and coloured red. (pl. XIV.) Location uncertain.

Grave 192.15

Superstructure: A stone-covered mound, 9 m. diam. and 1.3 m. high. Near the surface was an intrusive grave with a rectangular brick superstructure, 2.5×1.5 m., orientated ENE–WSW. Neither burial nor objects were found.

Grave: Type II, 2×1.27×0.6 m., orientated NE–SW (47° E. of N.). There is another grave (B) of the same type built against the NE end of the former. It is 2.1× 1.27×0.42 m. deep. The orientation of this second grave is also exactly the same as the first. That grave B was added secondarily is inferred from the fact that the burial in it was articulated, whereas the other had been disturbed. (pl. XV.)

Burial: The scattered bones of an adult were found in grave A. In grave B was the articulated body of an adult female, lying dorsally extended with the head to the NE. This latter is, to all appearances except the orientation, a Christian burial.

Objects: The location within the complex of graves and mound of the following objects is unrecorded, except the fifth.

1. A red ware cup, 9.3 cm. high×9.8 cm. max. diam. (pl. XV.) Adams R.1. British Museum 66568.

2. A red ware bottle with painted 'splash' decoration in white, 3 cm. high×19.8 cm. max. diam. (pl. XV.) Adams R.1. Cairo, Egyptian Museum 89680.

3. A red ware bottle with white painted decoration, 33.3 cm. high×15.6 cm. max. diam. (pl. XV.) Adams R.1. Cambridge Museum of Arch. and Eth. 63.178.

4. A cream biscuit ware cup with brown painted decoration, 9 cm. high×7.8 cm. max. diam. (pls. XV, LXXX.) Adams W.30. Nicholson Museum 63.185.

5. A silver ring, 2 cm. diam., with a rectangular bezel, 1.3×1.5 cm. (pl. XV.) There is a series of apparently intentional marks, including two pairs of parallel lines on the bezel. Their significance is uncertain. This ring was recovered from the fourth finger of the right hand of the burial in grave B. Nicholson Museum 63.214.

Grave 192.16

Superstructure: A stone-covered mound, 7 m. diam. and 1.15 m. high. In the mound were two intrusive graves. The first was type I, 2.5×1×0.3 m., and contained the scattered bones of an adult and no objects. The second, again type I, was 2.3×0.8×0.4 m. and contained the articulated body of an adult male, lying extended on the right side with the head to the west.

Grave: Type I, 2.75×1.37×0.7 m., orientated NE–SW (45° E. of N.).

Burial: The articulated body of an adult, lying extended on the right side, head SW.

Objects: None were found.

Grave 192.17

Superstructure: A stone-covered rubble tumulus, 10 m. diam. and 1.75 m. high. There were two surface burials in the mound. Both are type I. The first is 2.2×0.85× 0.4 m., and contained the articulated body of an adult, lying extended on the right side, head to the west. The second was 2.53×0.8×0.4 m., and contained the articulated body of a young adult, lying extended on the right side, head west. No objects were found in either grave.

Grave: Type IV. It is 3.12×1.45×1.5 m. and the entrance pit is a further 1.1 m. long. Orientation is ENE–WSW (59° E. of N.). In addition to each end wall being raised above the level of the top of the vault, there is a third construction in brick which rests on top of the vaulting and is built up to the level of the ends. The purpose of this is unclear.

Burial: The scattered bones of an adult male.

Objects: 1. A red ware cup, 9.9 cm. high×9.6 cm. max. diam. (pl. XVI.) Adams R.1. Ashmolean Museum 1962.915.

2. A red ware cup, 9.9 cm. high×9.6 cm. max. diam., identical with 192.17.1. (pl. XVI.) Adams R.1. Leeds University.

3. A red ware cup, 12.9 cm. high × 12 cm. max. diam. (pl. XVI). Adams R.1. University College London 19562.

4. A red ware cup with black and white painted decoration, 13.5 cm. high × 12 cm. max. diam. (pl. XVI.) Adams R.1. Reading Museum 83:67/7.

5. A red ware cup with black and white painted decoration, 13.5 cm. high × 12.0 cm. max. diam. (pl. XVI.) This cup is identical with 4, above. Adams R.1. Ashmolean Museum 1962.914.

6. A red ware jar with black and white painted decoration, 25.2 cm. high × 15.6 cm. max. diam. (pls. XVI, LXXVIII.) Royal Ontario Museum 963.15.9.

7. A brown ware jar with a cream slip and black painted 'splash' decoration, 27 cm. high × 18 cm. max. diam. (pl. XVI.) Adams W.30. Otago Museum E62.15.

8. Fragments of mud jar sealings on which are the impression of the 'Isis bouquet' with indentations painted red. (pl. XVI.) Location uncertain.

Grave 192.18

Superstructure: A stone-covered rubble tumulus, 8.25 m. diam. and 0.35 m. high. There is an intrusive grave in the mound. It is type II and is 3.2 × 1.1 × 0.62 m. deep and orientated NE–SW (53° E. of N.). It contained the articulated body of an elderly adult male, lying extended on the right side, head to the SW. With this burial was found the following object:

1. A brown ware flask with a cream slip, 25.8 cm. high × 15.6 cm. max. diam. (pl. XVI.) Adams W.28. Rijksmuseum, Leiden F1963/8.8.

Grave: Type II, 3.2 × 0.95 × 0.78 m., orientated NE–SW (54° E. of N.). This grave directly underlies the intrusive grave in the mound. (pl. XVI.)

Burial: The scattered bones of an adult female.

Objects: 2. A red ware cup with painted decoration in white, 12.9 cm. high × 12 cm. max. diam. (pl. XVI.) Adams R.1. Birmingham Museum 127'63.

3. A red ware cup with white painted decoration, 11.7 cm. high × 10.8 cm. max. diam. (pl. XVI.) Adams R.1. Cambridge Museum of Arch. and Eth. 63.181.

4. A brown ware jar with a cream slip, 23.7 cm. high × 13.8 cm. max. diam. (pl. XVI.) Adams W.28. Ashmolean Museum 1962.934.

There was also part of a red ware cup, Adams R.1., of Ballâna/Qusṭul type 87B.

Grave 192.19

Superstructure: A stone-covered mound, 6.75 m. diam. and 0.25 m. high.

Grave: Type I, 2.65 × 1.08 × 0.45 m., orientated ENE–WSW (60° E. of N.) (pl. XVII.)

Burial: The articulated body of an adult, lying dorsally extended. The head was missing, but was originally at the WSW end of the grave.

Objects: 1. A pair of sandals was found on the feet. (pl. XVII.) Location uncertain.

Grave 192.20

Superstructure: A stone-covered rubble mound, 12.5 m. diam. and 0.6 m. high. Within the tumulus were three intrusive graves:

INTRUSIVE GRAVE A. Type II, 2.5 × 1.5 × 0.2 m. and orientated NE–SW (50° E. of N.). It was completely empty.

INTRUSIVE GRAVE B. Type II, 3.55 × 2 × 1 m. It contained only a few scattered bones.

INTRUSIVE GRAVE C. Type II, 2.48 × 0.7 × 0.5 m., orientated ENE–WSW (64° E. of N.). It contained the articulated body of an adult female, lying extended with head to the WSW. High in the fill was:

3. An iron bangle bracelet, 6.5 cm. diam. and 2 mm. thick. (pl. XVII.) Nicholson Museum 63.211.

Grave: Type IV, 2.85 × 1.08 × 1.1 m. orientated NE–SW (50° E. of N.). The entrance pit was another 1 m. long.

Burial: The articulated body of an adult female, lying in an extended position with the head to the NE.

Objects: 1. A red ware jar, 27 cm. high × 19.8 cm. max. diam. (pl. XVII.) Adams R.1. University College London 19567.

2. A red ware jar with yellow and black painted decoration, 28.5 cm. high × 18 cm. max. diam. (pls. XVII, LXXIX.) Adams R.1. Cairo, Egyptian Museum 89681.

Grave 192.21

Superstructure: A stone-covered rubble tumulus, 10.8 m. diam. and 1 m. high.

Grave: Type II, 2.25 × 1.4 × 1.15 m. (pl. XVIII.)

Burial: The articulated body of an adult male, lying somewhat flexed on the right side.

Objects: 1. A cream biscuit ware cup with brown and red painted decoration, 10.5 cm. high × 9 cm. max. diam. (pls. XVIII, LXXX.) Adams W.30. Cairo, Egyptian Museum 89682.

2. An iron pick with a short wooden handle. The blade of the tool is 17.6 cm. long, and is fashioned into a loop at one end for hafting the handle, which is 4.3 cm. diam. and remains to a length of 43.5 cm. (pl. XVIII.) Location uncertain.

3. A brown ware jar with cream slip and black and red painted decoration, 24.6 cm. high × 19.8 cm. max. diam. (pl. XVIII.) Adams W.30. Nicholson Museum 63.186.

4. A red ware cup, 9.3 cm. high×9 cm. max. diam. (pl. XVIII.) Adams R.1. Nicholson Museum 63.187.

5. A red ware cup, 9.3 cm. high×9 cm. max. diam. (pl. XVIII.) Adams R.1. University College London 19564.

6. A cream biscuit ware cup with black and red painted decoration, 7.8 cm. high×9 cm. max. diam. (pl. XVIII.) Adams W.30. Ashmolean Museum 1962.926.

7. A red ware jar, 28.8 cm. high×18 cm. max. diam. (pl. XVIII.) Adams R.1. Queen's University, Belfast QAD/7/134.

8. A red ware cup with black and white painted decoration, 12.6 cm. high×11.4 cm. max. diam. (pl. XVIII.) Adams R.1. Royal Ontario Museum 963.15.10.

9. A red ware cup, 12.3 cm. high×11.4 cm. max. diam. (pl. XVIII.) Adams R.1. Queen's University, Belfast QAD/7/121.

10. A cream biscuit ware cup with red painted decoration, 10.5 cm. high×8.4 cm. max. diam. (pl. XVIII.) Adams W.30. University College London 19563.

11. A red ware jar with black painted decoration, 24 cm. high×18 cm. max. diam. (pl. XVIII.) Adams R.1. Queen's University, Belfast QAD/7/136.

Grave 192.22

Superstructure: A stone-covered rubble tumulus, 9.5 m. diam. and 1 m. high. In the mound was an intrusive grave of type II, 2.9×1×0.4 m., which contained only the articulated body of a female adult, lying in an extended position.

Grave: Type IV, 2.15×1.48×1.07 m., orientated ENE–WSW (61° E. of N.). The entrance pit, at the WSW end, adds a further 0.65 m. to the length. (pl. XVII.)

Burial: None remained.

Objects: The remains of a wooden bier, which was probably originally 1.48 m. long×0.78 m. wide, were found on the floor of the grave. Only fragments were recovered, but it appears to have been constructed of four pieces of wood, each about 8 cm. wide, with butt joints at the corners. The centre space was presumably filled with cloth or rope, which has since completely perished.

Grave 192.23

Superstructure: A stone-covered rubble tumulus, 10.75 m. diam. and 2 m. high. An intrusive grave, type II, 2.5× 1.2×1 m., near the surface of the mound, contained only the scattered bones of two bodies.

Grave: Type V. The total length of the pit is 3.97 m., of which the grave occupies 2.12 m.; the total width is 2.50 m. and the depth is 1.47 m. Chamber A, which was the one used for the grave goods, was 1.15 m. wide and Chamber B, the burial chamber, was 1.35 m. wide. Each was roofed with its own vault. The pit is partly dug into bedrock. Orientation is ENE–WSW (57° E. of N.). (pls. XIX, LXXXIV. 3.)

Burial: The original burial is uncertain. The burial chamber, B, contained the bodies of eleven male adults, twelve female adults, and two children, all lying in extended positions and all with their heads WSW. It is unlikely that these all belong to the original burial in this grave, for even the royal tombs of Ballâna do not contain as many inhumations as this. Probably this was a single mass burial at some date subsequent to the original burial.

Objects: The following objects were *in situ* in Chamber A:

1. A red ware jar, 39 cm. high×28.2 cm. max. diam. (pl. XXII.) Adams R.1. Ashmolean Museum 1962.939.

2. A red ware flask with white painted neck, 28.2 cm. high×18.6 cm. max. diam. (pl. XXIII.) Adams R.1. Liverpool University E6325.

3. A cream biscuit ware cup with a brown rim stripe, 10.8 cm. high×9 cm. max. diam. (pl. XXII.) Adams W.30. British Museum 66561. This piece is identical with numbers 7, 10, and 15 from this tomb.

4. A brown ware flask with a cream slip and black painted decoration, 28.8 cm. high×21 cm. max. diam. (pl. XX.) Adams W.30. Aberdeen Anthropological Museum 1109^2.

5. A red ware flask with a cream slip and red and black painted decoration, 27.3 cm. high×18.6 cm. max. diam. (pls. XXIII, LXXIX.) Adams W.30. Cairo, Egyptian Museum 89683.

6. A brown ware flask with cream slip and black painted decoration, 25.8 cm. high×18.6 cm. max. diam. (pl. XXII.) Adams W.30. Otago Museum E62.2.

7. Cream biscuit ware cup, with a black rim stripe, 10.8 cm. high×9 cm. max. diam. (pl. XXII.) Adams W.30. Leeds University

8. A brown ware cup with a cream slip and a brown painted rim stripe, 8.4 cm. high×9 cm. max. diam. (pl. XX.) Adams W.30. Liverpool University E6332.

9. A brown ware jar with cream slip and black painted 'splash' decoration, 27 cm. high×19.8 cm. max. diam. (pl. XXIII.) Adams W.30. Leeds University. This piece is identical with no. 23, below.

10. A cream biscuit ware cup with a black painted rim stripe, 10.8 cm. high×9 cm. max. diam. (pl. XXII.) Adams W.30. British Museum 66566.

11. A red ware jar with a cream slip, 22.8 cm. high× 16.8 cm. max. diam. (pl. XX.) Adams R.1. University College London 19566.

12. A stone mortar, 6.8 cm. high×18 cm. interior diam., with four lug handles, one of which has been broken off; together with a pestle of the same stone, 7 cm. high×4.5 cm. max. diam. (pl. XXIII.) The mortar is now at University College London 19559, and the pestle is at Birmingham Museum 142'63.

13. A cream biscuit ware cup with brown painted decoration, 8.7 cm. high×8.4 cm. max. diam. (pl. XXIII.) Adams W.30. Nicholson Museum 63.188. This piece is identical with nos. 20 and 24, below.

14. A brown ware flask with cream slip, 27.3 cm. high×19.8 cm. max. diam. (pl. XXII.) Adams W.30. Reading Museum 83:67/8.

15. A cream biscuit ware cup with brown painted rim stripe, 10.8 cm. high×9 cm. max. diam. (pl. XXII.) Adams W.30. Cairo, Egyptian Museum 89684.

16. A red ware flask with a cream slip, 27 cm. high× 18.6 cm. max. diam. (pl. XX.) Adams W.30. Nicholson Museum 63.189.

17. A red ware two-handled amphora, 31.5 cm. high× 15 cm. max. diam. (pl. XXII.) Adams R.1. Cairo, Egyptian Museum 89685.

18. A large, red ware amphora with white painted decoration, 47.1 cm. high×24 cm. max. diam. (pl. XX.) Adams R.1. University College London 19595.

19. A cream biscuit ware cup with brown painted decoration, 8.1 cm. high×9.6 cm. max. diam. (pl. XX.) Adams W.30. Cambridge Museum of Arch. and Eth. 63.183.

20. A cream biscuit ware cup with brown painted decoration, 8.7 cm. high×8.4 cm. max. diam. (pls. XXIII, LXXX.) Adams W.30. British Museum 66563.

21. A brown ware flask with a cream slip, 27.6 cm. high×18.6 cm. max. diam. (pl. XXIII.) Adams W.30. British Museum 66546.

22. A cream biscuit ware cup with brown painted decoration, 7.2 cm. high×9.6 cm. max. diam. (pl. XX.) Adams W.30. Royal Ontario Museum 963.15.11.

23. A brown ware flask with a cream slip and red and black painted 'splash' decoration, 27 cm. high×19.8 cm. max. diam. (pl. XXIII.) Adams W.30. Aberdeen Anthropological Museum 1109².

24. A cream biscuit ware cup with brown painted decoration, 8.7 cm. high×8.4 cm. max. diam. (pl. XXIII.) Adams W.30. Queen's University, Belfast QAD/7/129.

25. A brown ware flask with a cream slip and red and black painted decoration, 28.8 cm. high×21 cm. max. diam. (pls. XX, LXXIX.) Adams W.30. Nicholson Museum 63.190.

26. A red ware cup with a cream slip, 9 cm. high×9.6 cm. max. diam. (pl. XXII.) Adams W.30. Otago Museum E62.19.

27. A red ware cup, 12.6 cm. high×12.6 cm. max. diam. (pl. XXIII.) Adams R.1. Queen's University, Belfast QAD/7/119.

28. An iron balance rod, 31 cm. long×1.6 cm. max. diam. It is tapered at both ends. (pl. XXI.) University College London 19532.

29. An iron pan, 25.4 cm. rim diam. and 4.4 cm. deep, with a pair of twisted loop handles riveted to opposite sides. (pl. XXI.) University College London 19533.

30. A ladle. The bronze cup is 4 cm. diam. and 4.8 cm. deep. Soldered to the side of this is an iron handlle, 0.3 cm. diam., which was broken but was at least 40.6 cm. long and has a crook at the end for hanging on the lip of a jar. (pl. XXIII.) Queen's University, Belfast QAD/7/116.

31. A glass chalice, 10.9 cm. high×7.5 cm. max. diam., the foot being 3.3 cm. high. (pl. XXII.) British Museum 66578.

32. A bronze hand lamp with a loop handle terminating in a horse's head. The lamp is 17.5 cm. long×8 cm. max. wide×4.8 cm. high, and the handle brings the max. height to 10.4 cm. (pls. XXI, LXXXVI. 4.) British Museum 66576.

33. A long-necked glass flask or bottle, 19.5 cm. high×11.4 cm. max. diam. There is a 'dimple' base and a rib running around the shoulder. (pls. XXII, LXXXVII. 5.) Birmingham Museum 141'63.

34. A pointed iron knife blade, 16.2 cm. long×2.5 cm. wide. It was hafted on a tang, 3.2 cm. long, through which a rivet hole has been drilled and held firm by means of an iron band or ring, 1.9 cm. diam. and 1.4 cm. wide. (pl. XXI.) University College London 19522.

35. An iron spoon, the bowl of which is 9.6 cm. diam.×3.1 cm. deep, and the handle 19.6 cm. long×1.5 cm. wide and flat. The whole appears to have been fashioned from one piece. (pl. XXIII.) University College London 19521.

36. An iron trivet or tripod, constructed by riveting three legs to a ring of iron. The ring is 15 cm. diam. and 2.6 cm. wide and each leg is 2 cm. wide and turned out at the base into a foot. The whole stands 13.9 cm. high. The top of each leg piece is bent forward towards the centre of the ring, thus forming a seat for the vessel. It is presumed that this was used for cooking, although no trace of carbon or burning are present on the trivet. (pl. XXIII.) University College London 19519.

37. A square, glass, one-handled flask, 17.9 cm. high× ×9.6 cm. wide. The sides and the bottom are all 'dimpled' (pl. XXII.) Cairo, Egyptian Museum 89686.

38. A blue faience (? glazed pottery), two-handled jar, 9.6 cm. high×9.2 cm. max. diam. (pl. XXI.) Location uncertain.

39. A large bronze bowl or pan, 32 cm. rim diam. and 6.1 cm. high, with a pair of side handles the mountings of which are fashioned in the shape of a duck's or a goose's head. The interior of the vessel is decorated with a fine embossed ribbing which radiates from an imaginary circle around the centre of the bottom. (pl. XXIII.) Cairo, Egyptian Museum 89687.

40. Two iron arrowheads, 7 and 8.4 cm. long. The single barb and the point of each has disappeared. (pl. XIX.) University College London 19523.

41. A wood disc, 11 cm. diam. and 0.4 cm. thick, with a round hole in the centre 1.6 cm. diam. The upper surface is convex and is covered with a bronze plate on which are embossed four heads of Isis alternating with four elements which resemble crowns of the complicated Meroïtic type, but which could be floral motifs instead. A stick, 1.6 cm. diam., of unknown length, which was inserted in the hole in the centre of the disc, was decorated with four separate bands of bronze, 2.7 cm. wide, on which is embossed a series of arches supported by pillars. (pl. XXI.) Rijksmuseum, Leiden F1963/8.29.

42. A red ware cup with white painted 'festoon' decoration, 12.6 cm. high × 13.2 cm. max. diam. (pl. XXII.) Adams R.1. Royal Ontario Museum 963.15.12.

43. A red ware cup with white painted 'festoon' decoration, 12.9 cm. high × 11.4 cm. max. diam. (pl. XXII.) Adams R.1. Liverpool University E6320.

44. A red ware cup with white painted 'festoon' decoration, 12.6 cm. high × 13.2 cm. max. diam. (pl. XXII.) Adams R.1. Reading Museum 118:65/1.

45. A square glass one-handled flask, more squat than no. 37, but similar to it. It is 16 cm. wide, and has 'dimpled' sides and base (pl. XXII.) Sheffield Museum 1966.297.

46. A circular, wooden toilet box, 21 cm. high, of which the lid comprises 4.8 cm., and 5.6 cm. diam. Most of the surface of the box has been destroyed (by white ant), but one band of carved decoration, consisting of a series of *uadjet*-eyes surmounting detailed *nb* baskets, still remains around the top. The sides of the lid are plain, but the top is decorated with a pattern of concentric circles and radiating lines. The inner hole of the lid is 3.2 cm. diam. and 2.5 cm. deep and is lined with a 0.4 cm. thickness of lead. This is designed to fit over the mouth of the box, which is 2 cm. diam. and protrudes 1.5 cm. above the body. The box has a hole bored out of the centre, 1.5 cm. diam. and probably about 17 cm. deep. The lid is attached to the body by means of a bronze bead chain. (pl. XXI.) Location uncertain.

47. The remains of a wooden box with bronze and iron fittings. The box had been destroyed by white ant, but the exterior dimensions were ascertained to have been 32 cm. long × 16.9 cm. wide × 17.8 cm. high. The lid rested on top and was 32 × 16.9 × 2 cm. high. (pl. XXI.) Several strips of bronze fittings, all about 2.5 cm. wide, were recovered. They were attached to the box with iron nails and have embossed decoration. Many of the pieces are rather indistinct now, but those with discernible features are reproduced on pl. XCII. 4. One vertical and two horizontal fragments bear profile bust representations which probably have their origin in coinage and may represent emperors. Motifs on other pieces are floral—an

undulating vine stem with grapes in one and with grape leaves in another.[1] Similar but not parallel motifs can be found in Samian Ware vessels and as architectural decoration. Birmingham Museum.

48. An ivory, tubular toilet vessel, 5.6 cm. high × 2.9 cm. max. diam. It is decorated with a series of ribs at the top and at the base. The base is a separate piece, glued in place. (pl. XIX.) Durham GM 1964 562.

49. A plano-convex disc, 5.4 cm. diam. and 0.7 cm. max. thickness, of a fine white stone. The convex side has engraved decoration in the form of four straight fronds which divide the circle into quadrants and in each of which are four small circles. The disc is pierced in the centre with a hole 0.25 cm. diam., presumably for hafting. (pl. XIX.) Durham GM 1964 564.

The following objects were recovered from the burial chamber, B.

50. A brown ware, hand-made cooking vessel, 20.4 cm. high × 27.6 cm. max. diam. (pl. XX.) University College London 19597.

51. A red ware flask, the mouth of which is missing, 21 cm. high × 9.6 cm. max. diam. (pl. XX.) Adams U.2. Royal Ontario Museum 963.15.15.

52. A red ware footed dish, 6.6 cm. high × 18.6 cm. max. diam. (pl. XX.) Adams R.4. British Museum 66557.

Grave 192.24

Superstructure: A stone-covered mound.

Grave: Type II, 3.15 × 0.6 × 0.6 m.

Burial: The scattered bones of an adult female.

Objects: 1. A red ware amphora, 33.9 cm. high × 15.6 cm. max. diam. (pl. XXIV.) Adams R.25. Royal Ontario Museum 963.15.13.

2. A red ware flask with cream slip and black and white painted decoration, 23.7 cm. high × 15 cm. max. diam. (pl. XXIV.) Adams W.30. University College London 19574.

3. A red ware flask with black and white painted stripes, 27.6 cm. high × 18 cm. max. diam. (pl. XXIV.) Adams R.1. Cairo, Egyptian Museum 89688.

4. A red ware cup, 8.5 cm. high × 9.6 cm. max. diam. (pl. XXIV.) Adams R.1. Rijksmuseum, Leiden F1963/8.9.

5. A red ware flask with white painted decoration, 24.6 cm. high × 16.8 cm. max. diam. (pl. XXIV.) Adams R.1. Cairo, Egyptian Museum 89689.

Grave 192.25

Superstructure: A stone-covered rubble tumulus, 8.5 m. diam. and 1.8 m. high.

---

[1] Mr John Ruffle informs me that an interesting parallel is to be found in a group of bronze decorative fittings from a trinket box found at Wroxeter and now in the Birmingham Museum. The vine and grape motifs in that case are rather more elaborately worked.

Grave: Type IV, 2.6×1.37×1.25 m., the entrance pit being another 0.75 m. long. The orientation is WNW–ESE (74° W. of N.).

Burial: The scattered bones of three adult males, probably all intrusive.

Objects: 1. A red ware flask, 27.9 cm. high×20.4 cm. max. diam. (pl. XXIV.) Adams R.1. Aberdeen Anthropological Museum 1109².

2. A red ware flask with a cream slip, 30 cm. high×21 cm. max. diam. (pl. XXIV.) Adams W.30. Royal Ontario Museum 963.15.14.

3. A cream ware cup with brown painted decoration, 7.5 cm. high×8.7 cm. max. diam. (pl. XXIV.) Adams W.30. Cairo, Egyptian Museum 89690.

4. A cream ware cup with brown painted decoration, 8.7 cm. high×9 cm. max. diam. (pls. XXIV, LXXX.). Adams W.30. Aberdeen Anthropological Museum 1109².

5. A cream biscuit ware cup with brown painted decoration, 7.9 cm. high×9 cm. max. diam. (pl. XXIV.) Adams W.30. Cairo, Egyptian Museum 89691.

Grave 192.26

Superstructure: A stone-covered rubble tumulus, 5 m. diam. and 0.7 m. high.

Grave: Type I, 2.25×1.3×0.55 m., orientated NE–SW (50° E. of N.).

Burial: A few scattered bones of two adults.

Objects: 1. A pink ware cup with a cream slip and black and red painted decoration, 8.1 cm. high×9 cm. max. diam. (pl. XXIV.) Adams W.30. Birmingham Museum 129'63.

2. A red ware cup, 9.3 cm. high×10.8 cm. max. diam. (pl. XXIV.) Adams R.1. Reading Museum 83:67/9.

3. A red ware flask with black and white painted decoration, 27 cm. high×17.4 cm. max. diam. (pl. XXV.) Adams R.1. Reading Museum 83:67/10.

4. A red ware flask with yellow and black painted decoration. The neck is broken and the preserved height is 24.6 cm., max. diam. is 20.4 cm. (pls. XXV, LXXIX.) Adams R.1. Ashmolean Museum 1962.932.

5. A red ware, ribbed amphora, 35.1 cm. high×21.6 cm. max. diam. (pl. XXIV.) Adams R.25. Aberdeen Anthropological Museum 1109².

Grave 192.27

Superstructure: A stone-covered rubble mound, 6.5 m. diam. and 1 m. high.

Grave: Type I, 2.55×0.87×0.65 m., orientated NNE–SSW (27° E. of N.). (pl. XXV.)

Burial: A. The articulated body of an adult male, lying dorsally extended, head SSW. Probably intrusive.

B. The articulated body of an adult male, lying slight-ly flexed on the left side, head to the NNE. This body lies at the side of the grave and was probably also intrusive.

C. The original(?) burial, now only some scattered bones of an adult.

Objects: 1. A red ware flask with yellow, white, and black painted decoration, 30.9 cm. high×19.2 cm. max. diam. (pl. XXV.) Adams R.1. Cairo, Egyptian Museum 89692.

2. A red ware, ribbed amphora, 36.6 cm. high×19.8 cm. max. diam. (pl. XXV.) Adams R.25. Queen's University, Belfast QAD/7/138.

Fragments of two decorated biscuit ware cups were also recovered.

Grave 192.28

Superstructure: A stone-covered rubble mound, 9 m. diam. and 2 m. high.

Grave: Type II, 3.55×1.65×1.75 m., orientated WNW–ESE (60° W. of N.).

Burial: None remained.

Objects: 1. A brown ware flask with a white slip and a black and red painted decoration, 29.1 cm. high×18 cm. max. diam. (pls. XXV, LXXVIII.) Adams W.30. Cairo, Egyptian Museum 89693.

2. A red ware cup, 8.7 cm. high×8.4 cm. max. diam. (pl. XXV.) Adams R.1. This piece is identical with nos. 3, 5, and 6. Durham GM 1964 550.

3. A red ware cup, 8.7 cm. high×8.4 cm. max. diam. (pl. XXV.) Adams R.1. Nicholson Museum 63.191.

4. A red ware cup, 9.3 cm. high×8.4 cm. max. diam. (pl. XXV.) Adams R.1. Queen's University, Belfast QAD/7/117.

5. A red ware cup, 8.7 cm. high×8.4 cm. max. diam. (pl. XXV.) Adams R.1. Queen's University, Belfast QAD/7/117.

6. A red ware cup 8.7 cm. high×8.4 cm. max. diam. (pl. XXV.) Adams R.1. British Museum 66559.

7. A red ware cup with white painted decoration, 12.9 cm. high×10.8 cm. max. diam. (pl. XXV.) Adams R.1. Ashmolean Museum 1962.919.

Also found were: an iron nail, 9 cm. long; fragments of two cups similar to nos. 2, 3, 5, and 6, and of one similar to no. 7; and fragments of several glass vessels.

Grave 192.29

Superstructure: A stone-covered tumulus.

Grave: Type I, 3.35×1.40×1.27 m. A secondary burial (A) was made in this grave at a depth of 0.75 m. below the surface. Orientation is NE–SW (54° E. of N.). (pl. XXVI.)

Burial: A. The articulated body of an adult female, lying extended on the right side, head to the SW.

B. The articulated body of an adult male, lying dorsally extended, head SW.

Objects: All were found *in situ* with burial B.

1. A red ware flask with white painted decoration, 27.6 cm. high × 19.2 cm. max. diam. (pl. XXVI.) Adams R.1. Cambridge Museum of Arch. and Eth. 63.179.

2. A red ware flask with black and white painted decoration, 33.6 cm. high × 21 cm. max. diam. (pl. XXVI.) Adams R.1. Cairo, Egyptian Museum 89694.

3. A red ware cup with a grey slip and brown painted decoration, 7.2 cm. high × 8.7 cm. max. diam. (pls. XXVI, LXXX.) Adams W.30. Cairo, Egyptian Museum 89695. This cup was found overturned on the mouth of no. 2.

4. A brown ware flask with a cream slip and black painted decoration, 28.8 cm. high × 18.6 cm. max. diam. (pl. XXVI.) Adams W.30. University College London 19573.

5. A cream biscuit ware cup with brown rim stripe, 8.4 cm. high × 8.4 cm. max. diam. (pl. XXVI.) Adams W.30. Birmingham Museum 119′63.

6. An iron adze blade, 16.4 cm. long, 12.6 cm. of which is the blade, the remaining length having been turned into a ring for hafting, and 5.4 cm. max. wide. There is no trace of the handle, but the hole is only 3.6 cm. diam. and from this one can safely assume a short handle of probably no more than 45 cm. (pl. XXVI.) University College London 19520.

7. A curved iron sickle blade, 13.6 cm. max. length, with a tang 3 cm. long. The hafting was made secure by means of a rivet passing through a hole in the tang and the handle, and with a ring of iron, 1.1 cm. wide × 2.6 cm. outside diam. The cutting edge is denticulated. (pls. XXVI, LXXXVI. 5.) University College London 19524.

Grave 192.30

Superstructure: A stone-covered rubble mound, 6.5 m. diam. and 0.55 m. high.

Grave: Type I, 2.5 × 1.08 × 0.78 m. Orientation is NE–SW (40° E. of N.). (pl. XXVII.)

Burial: The articulated body, apart from the head which was missing altogether, of an adult, lying dorsally extended, head NE.

Objects: 1. A leather quiver, 51.7 cm. long and 17.8 cm. wide. It is plain, apart from some flowers tooled near the mouth of the bag. It was made from a single piece of leather, folded once and stitched along the bottom and one side with leather thonging. The shoulder strap is now missing, but was attached to the quiver with braided leather thongs at the corner of the mouth and half-way along the same side of the bag. (pl. XXVII.) Ashmolean Museum 1962.953.

2. Also found in the area of the feet was a pair of leather sandals and a crumpled-up leather garment.

Grave 192.31

Superstructure: A stone-covered tumulus, 4.75 m. diam. and 0.6 m. high.

Grave: Type I, 2.24 × 0.75 × 0.95 m., orientated ENE–WSW (59° E. of N.).

Burial: The articulated body of an adult male, lying dorsally extended, head WSW.

Objects: 1. A grey ware crucible/cup, 4.5 cm. high × 6.6 cm. max. diam. (pl. XXVII.) Location uncertain.

Grave 192.32

Superstructure: A stone-covered rubble mound, 4.9 m. diam. and 0.5 m. high.

Grave: Type IV, 2.5 × 1 × 0.87 m., the entrance being an additional 0.98 m. long. Orientation is ENE–WSW (63° E. of N.).

Burial: The articulated body of an adult female, lying dorsally extended, head WSW. This is probably an intrusive burial, because there were also some scattered bones and a skull in the fill.

Objects: 1. A silver ear-ring, 1.5 cm. diam., set with a blue faience bead. (pl. XXVII.) Location uncertain.

Grave 192.33

Superstructure: A stone-covered rubble mound, 4.5 m. diam. and 0.25 m. high.

Grave: Type II, 2.62 × 1.60 × 0.8 m., orientated ENE–WSW (60° E. of N.).

Burial: A. The articulated body of an adult, lying extended on the front, head WSW. This body is at a slightly higher level than burial B, and is supposed to have been intrusive.

B. The articulated body of an adult, lying dorsally extended, head WSW.

Objects: A necklet, consisting of a thin leather strap and one large white bead, was found on the neck of burial A.

Grave 192.34

Superstructure: A stone-covered tumulus, 8 m. diam. and 0.75 m. high.

Grave: Type II, 2.65 × 1.42 × 1.23 m., orientated NE–SW (36° E. of N.).

Burial: None remained.

Objects: 1. A red ware flask with white and black painted decoration, 30.9 cm. high × 18 cm. max. diam. (pl. XXVII.) Adams R.1. Birmingham Museum 134′63.

2. A brown ware flask with a cream slip and black

painted 'splash' decoration, 25.2 cm. high×15.6 cm. max. diam. (pl. XXVII.) Adams W.30. Manchester Museum.

3. A red ware flask with black and white 'splash' decoration 27.9 cm. high×17.4 cm. max. diam. (pl. XXVII.) Adams R.1. Birmingham Museum 135'63.

4. A red ware cup with white and black painted 'splash' decoration, 13.5 cm. high×12.6 cm. max. diam. (pl. XXVII.) Adams R.1. Birmingham Museum 118'63.

5. A red ware cup with black painted 'splash' decoration, 12.0 cm. high×10.2 cm. max. diam. (pl. XXVII.) Adams R.1. Birmingham Museum 128'63.

6. A red ware cup with a cream slip, 9 cm. high×8.4 cm. max. diam. (pl. XXVII.) Adams W.30. Cambridge Museum of Arch. and Eth. 63.182.

Also found were the fragmentary remains of a leather quiver.

Grave 192.35

Superstructure: A stone-covered rubble mound, 6.5 m. diam. and 0.3 m. high.
Grave: Type II, 2.3×1.5×0.55 m. orientated ENE–WSW (67° E. of N.).
Burial: The articulated body of an adult lying extended on the right side, head WSW.
Objects: None found.

Grave 192.36

Superstructure: A stone-covered rubble mound, 6.4 m. diam. and 0.4 m. high.
Grave: Type II, 2.9×1.08×1.02 m., orientated NE–SW (46° E. of N.).
Burial: The scattered bones of an adult female.
Objects: 1. A red ware cup, 5.5 cm. high×7 cm. max. diam. (pl. XXVII.) Adams R.1. Liverpool University E6322.

2. A red ware ribbed flagon with incised decoration, 10 cm. high×8 cm. max. diam. (pl. XXVII.) Adams R.31. Location uncertain.

3. A red ware cup with a cream slip, 8.7 cm. high× 9.6 cm. max. diam. (pl. XXVII.) Adams W.30. Fitzwilliam Museum E.5.1962.

4. A red ware flask, 25.5 cm. high×17.4 cm. max. diam. (pl. XXVII.) Adams R.1. Birmingham Museum 137'63.

Grave 192.37

Superstructure: A stone-covered rubble mound, 5 m. diam. and 0.25 m. high.
Grave: Type I, 2.4×1×0.98 m., orientated ENE–WSW (62° E. of N.). (pl. XXVII.)
Burial: A. The articulated body of an adult, lying extended on the right side, head WSW. This burial lies 0.32 m.

above the bottom of the grave and is presumed to be intrusive.

B. The original(?) burial. The articulated body of an adult, lying in a crouched position at the ENE end of the grave. The small size and crouched position lead one to suspect that this was a cripple.
Objects: None were found.

Grave 192.38

Superstructure: A stone-covered mound, 4.5 m. diam. and 0.4 m. high.
Grave: Type I, 3.2×0.95×0.75 m., orientated ENE–WSW (73° E. of N.).
Burial: A. The articulated body of an adult lying in an extended position on the left side, head ENE. This body was some 0.2 m. above the bottom of the grave and was probably secondary.

B. The articulated body of an adult, lying dorsally extended, head ENE, on the floor of the grave.
Objects: 1. A red ware cup, 8.4 cm. high×10.2 cm. max. diam. (pl. XXVIII.) Adams R.1. Royal Ontario Museum 963.15.16.

2. A red ware flask with white painted decoration, 27 cm. high×19.2 cm. max. diam. (pl. XXVIII.) Adams R.1. British Museum 66543.

Grave 192.39

Superstructure: A stone-covered rubble mound, 4.75 m. diam. and 0.2 m. high.
Grave: Type I, 2.37×0.98×0.62 m., orientated NNE–SSW (32° E. of N.).
Burial: The articulated body of an adult, lying dorsally extended, head SSW.
Objects: None found.

Grave 192.40

Superstructure: A stone-covered mound, 3.75 m. diam. and 0.45 m. high.
Grave: Type I, 1.98×1×0.87 m., orientated E.–W. (90° E. of N.).
Burial: The articulated bodies of two infants, lying side by side dorsally extended at the east end of the grave, heads both west.
Objects: None found.

Grave 192.41

Superstructure: A stone-covered rubble tumulus, 7.3 m. diam. and 0.9 m. high.
Grave: Type I, 2.25×1×0.5 m., orientated ENE–WSW (72° E. of N.).

Burial: The articulated body of an adult female, lying dorsally extended, head WSW.

Objects: 1. A ribbed red ware cup, 6.6 cm. high×8.4 cm. max. diam. (pl. XXVIII.) Adams R.1. Leeds University

2. A ribbed red ware amphora with a cream slip, 25.5 cm. high×15 cm. max. diam. (pl. XXVIII.) Adams W.28. Location uncertain.

3. A red ware bowl, 7.2 cm. high×16.2 cm. max. diam. (pl. XXVIII.) Adams R.1. Nicholson Museum 63.192.

4. A red ware flask with black and white painted decoration. The mouth is missing—preserved height is 21 cm. and max. diam. is 14.4 cm. (pl. XXVIII.) Adams R.1. Birmingham Museum 139′63.

5. A string of shell beads. Location uncertain.

6. A pair of leather sandals, 23 cm. long. The upper side of the soles is decorated with tooled parallel lines and a border. There is a single toe strap and heel straps. (pl. XXVIII.) Ashmolean Museum 1962.956a, b.

Grave 192.42

Superstructure: A stone-covered rubble mound, 4.75 m. diam.

Grave: Type I, 2×1.57×0.62 m., orientated NNW–SSE (21° W. of N.).

Burial: The articulated body of an adult, lying dorsally extended, head NNW.

Objects: None found.

Grave 192.43

Superstructure: A stone-covered rubble tumulus, 7.5 m. diam. and 0.35 m. high.

Grave: Type IV, 2.6×1.27×1.12 m. deep, orientated NW–SE (55° W. of N.).

Burial: None remained.

Objects: 1. A pair of opaque white glass ear studs, 0.9 cm. max. diam. (pl. XXVIII.) University College London 19525.

Grave 192.44

Superstructure: A stone-covered rubble mound, 5 m. diam. and 0.3 m. high.

Grave: Type II, 1.9×0.8×0.5 m. orientated NNW–SSE (29° W. of N.).

Burial: The scattered bones of a child.

Objects: None found.

Grave 192.45

Superstructure: A stone-covered rubble tumulus, 4.5 m. diam. and 0.55 m. high.

Grave: Type I, 1.85×0.85×0.73 m. deep, orientated

N.–S. (8° W. of N.). The grave was dug in somewhat crumbly soil and the sides were buit up with large stone slabs standing on edge.

Burial: None remained.

Objects: 1. A red ware, hand-made jar with white painted decoration, 15.3 cm. high×14.4 cm. max. diam. (pl. XXVIII.) Adams H.13. Birmingham Museum 117′63.

2. A brown ware dish, 5.4 cm. high×13.6 cm. max. diam. (pl. XXVIII.) Adams R.1. Durham GM 1964 576.

Grave 192.46

Superstructure: A stone-covered mound, 8 m. diam. and 0.6 m. high.

Grave: Type I, 1.85×1.35×0.53 m. One side of the pit was built up with vertically standing stone slabs.

Burial: None remained.

Objects: 1. A red ware bowl, 6.9 cm. high×12.6 cm. max. diam. (pl. XXVIII.) Adams R.1. Leeds University. This bowl is identical with no. 3.

2. A red ware cup, the bottom half of which has been fired black, 11.4 cm. high×9.6 cm. max. diam. (pl. XXVIII.) Adams R.1. Blackburn Museum.

3. A red ware bowl, 6.9 cm. high×12.6 cm. max. diam. (pl. XXVIII.) Adams R.1. Birmingham Museum 131′63.

Grave 192.47

Superstructure: A stone-covered rubble tumulus, 6 m. diam. and 0.65 m. high.

Grave: Type I, 2.3×0.95×0.9 m., orientated NW–SE (45° W. of N.). All the four sides of this grave pit were built up with stone slabs standing on edge.

Burial: The scattered bones of an adult.

Objects: None found.

Grave 192.48

Superstructure: A stone-covered rubble tumulus, 6.1 m. diam. and 0.4 m. high.

Grave: Type IV, 2.5×0.95×0.58 m., orientated NW–SE (45° W. of N.). There is an entrance pit at each end, making the total length of the pit 4.25 m. The sides of the grave were built of bricks.

Burial: The articulated body of an adult female, lying dorsally extended, head NW. In addition there were some scattered bones of another previous (?), interment.

Objects: None found.

Grave 192.49

Superstructure: A stone-covered mound, 6 m. diam. and 0.3 m. high.

Grave: Type II, 3.02×1.15×0.9 m., orientated WNW–ESE (58° W. of N.).

Burial: The scattered bones of an adult.

Objects: 1. A red ware cup with black and white painted decoration, 7.2 cm. high×6.6 cm. max. diam. (pl. XXVIII.) Adams R.1. Birmingham Museum 126′63.

2. A red ware ribbed amphora with a cream slip, 26.7 cm. high×15 cm. max. diam. (pl. XXVIII.) Adams W.28. Birmingham Museum 124′63.

Grave 192.50

Superstructure: A stone-covered rubble mound, 6 m. diam. and 0.45 m. high.

Grave: Type I, 2.25×1.1×0.77 m., orientated NE–SW (41° E. of N.).

Burial: A. An intrusive body of an adult in an extended position, wrapped in linen and well preserved.

B. The articulated body of an adult female, lying dorsally extended, head SW, on the floor of the grave.

Objects: Fragments of a red ware flask, Adams R.1, Ballâna/Quṣṭul corpus type 57.

Fragments of a red ware cup, Adams R.1, Ballâna/Quṣṭul corpus type 87.

Fragments of a red ware flask, Adams R.1.

Grave 192.51

Superstructure: A stone-covered tumulus, 8 m. diam. and 2 m. high.

Grave: Type IV, 2.65×1.25×1.45 m., orientated NE–SW (35° E. of N.). The entrance pit is a further 0.8 m. long.

Burial: The scattered bones of an adult male.

Objects: 1. A red ware flask with black and white painted decoration, 27.3 cm. high×20.4 cm. max. diam. (pls. XXVIII, LXXVII.) Adams R.1. Ashmolean Museum 1962.937.

2. A red ware flask with white painted decoration, 29.4 cm. high×20.4 cm. max. diam. (pl. XXIX.) Adams R.1. Cairo, Egyptian Museum 89706.

3. A red ware flask with white painted decoration, 18.6 cm. high×15.6 cm. max. diam. (pl. XXVIII.) Adams R.1. Cairo, Egyptian Museum 89707.

4. A red ware cup, 8.4 cm. high×10.2 cm. max. diam. (pl. XXVIII.) Adams R.1. Nicholson Museum 63.196.

5. A red ware cup with black and white painted decoration, 8.1 cm. high×8.4 cm. max. diam. (pl. XXVIII.) Adams R.1. Durham GM 1964 577.

Grave 192.52

Superstructure: A stone-covered rubble tumulus, 6.75 m. diam. and 0.80 m. high.

Grave: Type III, 1.85×0.75×0.75 m., orientated NNE–SSW (29° E. of N.). The entrance pit is another 0.77 m. in length.

Burial: The scattered bones of an adult.

Objects: 1. A red ware cup with white painted decoration, 9.3 cm. high×9 cm. max. diam. (pl. XXIX.) Adams R.1. Leeds University.

Grave 192.53

Superstructure: A stone-covered mound, 4.7 m. diam. and 0.5 m. high.

Grave: Type IV, 1.8×0.7×0.75 m., the entrance being a further 0.72 m. long. The orientation is NNE–SSW (22° E. of N.).

Burial: None remained.

Objects: 1. A red ware cup with black and white painted decoration, 9 cm. high×9.6 cm. max. diam. (pl. XXIX.) Adams R.1. Durham GM 1964 578.

Grave 192.54

Superstructure: A stone-covered rubble tumulus, 6 m. diam. and 0.35 m. high.

Grave: Type I, 2.87×1.24×0.75 m., orientated ENE–WSW (69° E. of N.).

Burial: The scattered bones of an adult.

Objects: 1. A red ware flask with a cream slip, 19.5 cm. high×15.6 cm. max. diam. (pl. XXIX.) Adams W.28. Liverpool University E6314.

Grave 192.55

Superstructure: A stone-covered mound, 4 m. diam. and 0.5 m. high.

Grave: Type I, 2.7×0.95×1 m., orientated NE–SW (55° E. of N.).

Burial: The scattered bones of an adult male.

Objects: None found.

Grave 192.56

Superstructure: A stone-covered rubble mound, 8 m. diam. and 0.65 m. high.

Grave: Type I, 2.49×1.12×0.65 m., orientated NE–SW (55° E. of N.).

Burial: The scattered bones of an adult.

Objects: 1. A red ware flask with a cream slip, 28.8 cm. high×19.2 cm. max. diam. (pl. XXIX.) Adams W.30. Nicholson Museum 63.197.

Grave 192.57

Superstructure: A rubble mound, 4 m. diam. and 0.6 m. high.

Grave: Type I, 2.2×0.5×0.85 m., orientated ENE–WSW (63° E. of N.).

Burial: A few scattered bones.

Objects: 1. A red ware flask with a cream slip and black painted 'splash' decoration, 32.4 cm. high×18.6 cm. max. diam. (pl. XXIX.) Adams W.30. Rijksmuseum, Leiden F1963/8.13.

  2. Another, identical, red ware flask with a cream slip and black painted 'splash' decoration, 32.4 cm. high× 18.6 cm. max. diam. Adams W.30. Queen's University, Belfast QAD/7/135.

Grave 192.58

Superstructure: A stone-covered rubble mound, 4 m. diam. and 0.45 m. high.

Grave: Type I, 2.35×0.95×0.5 m., orientated N.–S. (8° W. of N.).

Burial: The scattered bones of an adult.

Objects: 1. A red ware cup, 9 cm. high×8.4 cm. max. diam. (pl. XXIX.) Adams R.1. Reading Museum 83:67/14.

Grave 192.59

Superstructure: A rubble mound, 6 m. diam. and 0.8 m. high.

Grave: Type I, 2.65×0.92×0.87 m., orientated NNE– SSW (14° E. of N.). (pl. XXIX.)

Burial: The articulated pelvis and legs of an adult female, the position of which indicates that the burial lay dorsally extended, head NNE.

Objects: 1. A red ware flask with a yellow slip, 22.5 cm. high×15.6 cm. max. diam. (pl. XXIX.) Adams W.30. Cairo, Egyptian Museum 89709.

  2. A red ware cup with white painted decoration, 11.4 cm. high×10.8 cm. max. diam. (pl. XXIX.) Adams R.1. Reading Museum 83:67/15.

Grave 192.60

Superstructure: A rubble mound, 5 m. diam. and 0.6 m. high.

Grave: Type III, 2.25×1×0.62 m., the entrance pit adding another 0.5 m. to the length. The orientation is N.–S. (9° E. of N.).

Burial: A few scattered bones.

Objects: 1. A red ware flask with black and white painted 'splash' decoration 24 cm. high×16.8 cm. max. diam. (pl. XXIX.) Adams R.1. Reading Museum 83:67/16.

Grave 192.61

Superstructure: A rubble mound, 6.5 m. diam. and 0.7 m. high.

Grave: Type IV, 2.48×1.35×1.15 m., the entrance being a further 0.9 m. long. Orientation is E.–W. (79° E. of N.).

Burial: The articulated body of an adult, lying dorsally extended, head east.

Objects: None were found.

Grave 192.62

Superstructure: A rubble tumulus, 5.5 m. diam. and 0.8 m. high.

Grave: Type IV, 1.92×1.18×1.25 m., orientated NNE– SSW (18° E. of N.). The entrance pit adds another 0.55 m. to the length of the pit.

Burial: None remained.

Objects: None found.

Grave 192.63

Superstructure: A rubble mound, 4.5 m. diam. and 0.8 m. high.

Grave: Type I, 2.15×0.5×1 m., orientated E.–W. (85° W. of N.).

Burial: The disturbed remains of three skeletons.

Objects: None found.

Grave 192.64

Superstructure: An oval stone-covered rubble tumulus, 3.50×4.50 m., and 0.50 m. high.

Grave: Type III, 1.75×1.15×0.80 m., the entrance being 0.60 m. longer. The orientation is E.–W. (81° W. of N.). (pl. XXX.)

Burial: The articulated torso and legs of an adult female, originally lying dorsally extended, head to the west.

Objects: 1. A red ware cup with a white slip and black painted decoration, 8.7 cm. high×9.0 cm. max. diam. (pl. XXX.) Adams W.30. Liverpool University E6329.

  2. A red ware flask with a white slip and black painted decoration, 25.2 cm. high×18 cm. max. diam. (pls. XXX, LXXX.) Adams W.30. Rijksmuseum, Leiden F1963/8.14.

  3. A red ware flask with black and white painted decoration, 24.1 cm. high×17.4 cm. max. diam. (pl. XXIX.) Adams R.1. Liverpool University E6309.

Grave 192.65

Superstructure: A rubble mound, 5 m. diam. and 0.8 m. high.

Grave: Type IV, 2.73×1.15×0.95 m., with the entrance pit a further 0.80 m. long. The orientation is N.–S. (8° W. of N.).

Burial: The articulated legs and pelvis of an adult male, originally lying dorsally extended, head north.

Objects: None remained.

Grave 192.66

Superstructure: A rubble mound, 4.5 m. diam. and 0.5 m. high.

Grave: Type I, 2.31×1.02×0.75 m., orientated E.–W. (88° E. of N.).

Burial: None remained.

Objects: None found.

Grave 192.67

Superstructure: A stone-covered rubble mound, 8.75 m. diam. and 1.05 m. high.

Grave: Type I, 3.2×1.2×0.8 m. deep, orientated NE–SW (40° E. of N.). (pl. XXX.)

Burial: The skull of an adult.

Objects: 1. A red ware cup with white painted decoration 12.6 cm. high×11.4 cm. max. diam. (pl. XXX.) Adams R.1. Durham GM 1964 569. This cup is identical with nos. 5 and 7 from this grave.

2. A red ware cup with white and black painted 'festoon' decoration, 12 cm. high×12 cm. max. diam. (pl. XXX.) Adams R.1. Rijksmuseum, Leiden F1963/8.15. This cup is identical with no. 6 from this grave.

3. A red ware flask with a black painted rim, 18.6 cm. high×14.4 cm. max. diam. (pl. XXX.) Adams R.1. Otago Museum E62.4.

4. A red ware cup, 9 cm. high×9 cm. max. diam. (pl. XXX.) Adams R.1. Liverpool University E6318.

5. A red ware cup with white painted decoration, 12.6 cm. high×11.4 cm. max. diam. (pl. XXX.) Adams R.1. Reading Museum 83:67/18.

6. A red ware cup with white and black painted 'festoon' decoration, 12 cm. high×12 cm. max. diam. (pl. XXX.) Adams R.1. Queen's University Belfast QAD/7/118.

7. A red ware cup with white painted decoration, 12.6 cm. high×11.4 cm. max. diam. (pl. XXX.) Adams R.1. Blackburn Museum.

8. A red ware cup, 9.9 cm. high×10.8 cm. max. diam. (pl. XXX.) Adams R.1. Queen's University Belfast QAD/7/118.

Also found were fragments of another flask similar to no. 3.

Grave 192.68

Superstructure: A stone-covered rubble tumulus, 3 m. diam. and 0.25 m. high.

Grave: Type I, 2.30×0.75×0.65 m., orientated NE–SW (56° E. of N.).

Burial: The articulated skeleton of an adult, lying extended on the right side, head SW.

Objects: None remained.

Grave 192.69

Superstructure: A stone-covered rubble mound, 5.5 m. diam. and 0.4 m. high.

Grave: Type I, 2.72×0.98×0.65 m., orientated NW–SE (47° W. of N.).

Burial: None remained.

Objects: 1. A red ware flask with black and white painted 'splash' decoration, 24.6 cm. high×18 cm. max. diam. (pl. XXX.) Adams R.1. Blackburn Museum.

Grave 192.70

Superstructure: None remained.

Grave: Type I with one side and the two ends built up with rough stones, 2.70×1×0.5 m., orientated NW–SE (34° W. of N.). (pl. XXX.)

Burial: A few scattered bones of an adult.

Objects: None were found.

Grave 192.71

Superstructure: A stone-covered rubble tumulus, 5.75 m. diam. and 0.65 m. high.

Grave: Type III, 2.45×1.1×0.82 m. with an additional 0.55 m. in the entrance pit. The sides are partly shored up with stones. The orientation is ENE–WSW (67° E. of N.).

Burial: The articulated bodies of three adults were found, apparently having been shoved into the grave after the original burial, which was missing its head, but otherwise complete and articulated. It seems originally to have been lying in a dorsally extended position, head WSW.

Objects: 1. A brown ware flask with a cream slip, 26.1 cm. high×22.2 cm. max. diam. (pl. XXXI.) Adams W.30. Ashmolean Museum 1962.930.

2. A red ware flask with black and white painted 'splash' decoration, 22.1 cm. high×19.2 cm. max. diam. (pl. XXXI.) Adams R.1. Rijksmuseum Leiden F1963/8.16.

3. A red ware cup, 10.2 cm. high×9.6 cm. max. diam. (pl. XXXI.) Adams R.1. University College London 19571.

Grave 192.72

Superstructure: A stone-covered mound, 6.5 m. diam. and 0.35 m. high.

Grave: Type III, 2.5×1.26×0.5 m. with the entrance adding another 0.65 m. to the length. The orientation of the grave is NNW–SSE (22° W. of N.).

Burial: The articulated body of an adult, lying in a flexed position on the right side, head NNW.

Objects: 1. A red ware flask, 26.1 cm. high×17.4 cm. max.

diam. (pl. XXXI.) Adams R.1. Rijksmuseum, Leiden F1963/8.17.

Grave 192.73

Superstructure: A stone-covered rubble mound.

Grave: Type III, 2.80×1.4×0.98 m. with the entrance pit an additional 0.8 m. long. The orientation is NE–SW (46° E. of N.). (pl. XXXI.)

Burial: None remained.

Objects: 1. A brown ware flask with a cream slip and brown painted decoration, 25.2 cm. high×19.2 cm. max. diam. (pls. XXXI, LXXX.) Adams W.30. Cairo, Egyptian Museum 89710.

2. A brown ware flask with a cream slip and brown painted decoration, 24.6 cm. high×16.2 cm. max. diam. (pls. XXXI, LXXX.) Adams W.30. Birmingham Museum 132′63.

3. A red ware cup, 9.3 cm. high×8.4 cm. max. diam. (pl. XXXI.) Adams R.1. Rijksmuseum, Leiden F1963/8.18.

4. A cream ware flask with red painted decoration, 7.2 cm. high×6 cm. max. diam. (pl. XXXI.) Adams W.30. Royal Ontario Museum 963.15.17.

5. Part of a wood *koḥl*(?) stick. One end was broken off and the remaining length is 14 cm. and max. diam. 0.5 cm. (pl. XXXI.) Location uncertain.

6. A pair of leather sandals of approximately 23 cm. in length. The upper sides of the soles were decorated with tooled or stamped stars or rosettes. (pl. XXXI.) Location uncertain.

Grave 192.74

Superstructure: A rubble mound, 5 m. diam. and 0.5 m. high.

Grave: Type IV, 1.87×1×0.6 m., the entrance adding another 0.95 m. to the length. The orientation is NNE–SSW (29° E. of N.).

Burial: A few scattered bones of an adult.

Objects: 1. A red ware cup, 8.4 cm. high×9.6 cm. max. diam. (pl. XXXII). Adams R.1. Rijksmuseum, Leiden F1963/8.19.

2. A small, red ware two-handled ribbed flask, 14.1 cm. high×9 cm. max. diam. (pl. XXXII.) Adams W.28. British Museum 66567.

Fragments of another red ware cup, similar to no. 1.

Grave 192.75

Superstructure: A stone-covered mound, 3.5 m. diam. and 0.25 m. high.

Grave: Type I, 2.49×1.25×0.59 m., orientated NE–SW (51° E. of N.).

Burial: None remained.

Objects: None were found.

Grave 192.76

Superstructure: A rubble mound, 6 m. diam. and 0.8 m. high.

Grave: Type IV, 2×0.98×0.87 m., with the entrance another 0.75 m. The orientation is NNE–SSW (20° E. of N.).

Burial: A few scattered bones of an adult.

Objects: 1. A red ware flask, with white and black painted decoration, 29.7 cm. high×19.2 cm. max. diam. (pl. XXXII.) Adams R.1. Rijksmuseum, Leiden F1963/8.20.

2. A red ware flask with white and black painted decoration, 30.3 cm. high×20.4 cm. max. diam. (pl. XXXII.) Adams R.1. Queen's University, Belfast QAD/7/137.

Grave 192.77

Superstructure: A stone-covered rubble mound, 3.75 m. diam. and 0.3 m. high.

Grave: Type I, 1.7×0.9×0.52 m., orientated NE–SW (45° E. of N.).

Burial: None remained.

Objects: 1. A red ware flask, 17.1 cm. high×1.5 cm. max. diam. (pl. XXXII.) Adams R.1. Nicholson Museum 63.199.

2. A red ware cup, 8.1 cm. high×9.6 cm. max. diam. (pl. XXXII.) Adams R.1. Nicholson Museum 63.200.

Grave 192.78

Superstructure: A stone-covered tumulus, 4.5 m. diam. and 0.7 m. high.

Grave: Type IV, 1.97×0.8×0.75 m., with an additional 0.75 m. in the entrance. The orientation is NE–SW (42° E. of N.).

Burial: The scattered bones of an adult.

Objects: 1. A red ware flask with black and white painted 'splash' decoration, 23.1 cm. high×16.4 cm. max. diam. (pl. XXXII.) Adams R.1. Reading Museum 83:67/19.

2. A red ware cup with black and white painted decoration, 9 cm. high×9 cm. max. diam. (pl. XXXII.) Adams R.1. British Museum 66564.

3. A red ware cup with black and white painted decoration, 9.6 cm. high×8.4 cm. max. diam. (pl. XXXII.) Adams R.1. Otago Museum E62.21.

Grave 192.79

Superstructure: A rubble mound, 5 m. diam. and 0.5 m. high.

Grave: Type II, 2.75×1×1 m., orientated ENE–WSW (69° E. of N.). (pl. XXXII.)

Burial: The articulated body of an adult female, lying in an extended position on the right side, head to the WSW.

Objects: 1. A red ware flask with black and white painted decoration, 27.6 cm. high×20.4 cm. max. diam. (pl. XXXII.) Adams R.1. University College London 19572.

Also found were fragments of a red ware cup, Adams R.1, Ballâna and Quṣṭul corpus type 87D, and a bracelet made of shells.

Grave 192.80

Superstructure: A stone-covered mound, 6 m. diam. and 0.65 m. high.

Grave: Type IV, 2.5×1.08×1.05 m., the entrance pit being a further 0.5 m. long. The orientation is ENE–WSW (59° E. of N.).

Burial: None remained.

Objects: 1. A red ware flask with white and black painted decoration, 27.3 cm. high×18.6 cm. max. diam. (pls. XXXII, LXXX.) Adams R.1. British Museum 66555.

2. A red ware cup, 9 cm. high×9.6 cm. max. diam. (pl. XXXII.) Adams R.1. Royal Ontario Museum 963.15.18.

3. A red ware cup, 8.4 cm. high×9.6 cm. max. diam. (pl. XXXII.) Adams R.1. Nicholson Museum 63.201.

Grave 192.81

Superstructure: A stone-covered rubble tumulus, 5 m. diam. and 0.4 m. high.

Grave: Type II, 1.7×0.95×0.8 m., orientated ENE–WSW (69° E. of N.).

Burial: None remained.

Objects: 1. A red ware jar, 15.3 cm. high×13.2 cm. max. diam. (pl. XXXIII.) Adams R.1. Manchester Museum.

Grave 192.82

Superstructure: A rubble mound, 5 m. diam. and 0.45 m. high.

Grave: Type II, 1.98×0.95×0.7 m., orientated NW–SE (34° W. of N.). (pl. XXXIII.)

Burial: A few scattered bones of an adult.

Objects: 1. A red ware amphora with white painted 'splash' decoration, 39.6 cm. high×19.2 cm. max. diam. (pl. XXXIII.) Adams R.1. University College London 19570.

2. A red ware jar, 22.2 cm. high×17.6 cm. max. diam. pl. XXXIII.) Adams R.1. Liverpool University E6310.

3. Part of a leather sandal, probably originally about 23 cm. long. (pl. XXXIII.) Location uncertain.

4. A group of beads (pl. XXXIII) which include the following:

(*a*) black stone, long square cylinder bead with one convex side. This may in fact be an amulet stone or perhaps a weight as no perforation is indicated;

(*b*) a series of bronze standard tubular beads,

(*c*) drop-shaped blue glass pendants;

(*d*) bone short cylinder beads;

(*e*) black stone and white stone keeled drop pendants;

(*f*) blue glass bead, which resembles a mulberry in shape;

(*g*) red glass ball bead;

(*h*) blue glass long tubular bead.

Location uncertain.

Grave 192.83

Superstructure: A stone-covered mound, 5 m. diam. and 0.7 m. high.

Grave: Type I, 3.05×0.77×0.82 m., orientated NW–SE (45° W. of N.). (pl. XXXIII.)

Burial: The articulated body of an adult female, lying dorsally extended, head NW.

Objects: 1. A red ware cup, 8.7 cm. high×11.1 cm. max. diam. (pl. XXXIII.) Adams R.1. Leeds University.

2. A short part of a string of green faience beads. The stringing order is preserved and consists of sections of one large ball and three smaller ball beads. (pl. XXXIII.) Location uncertain.

Grave 192.84

Superstructure: A rubble mound, 4 m. diam. and 0.5 m. high.

Grave: Type I, 2×0.9×0.8 m., orientated WNW–ESE (57° W. of N.).

Burial: A few scattered bones.

Objects: None remained.

Grave 192.85

Superstructure: A rubble mound, 5 m. diam. and 0.45 m. high.

Grave: Type I, 1.5×0.35×0.57 m., orientated NE–SW (46° E. of N.). (pl. XXXIII.)

Burial: The skull and a few other bones of a child, scattered in the grave.

Objects: 1. A red ware flask, 16.8 cm. high×13.2 cm. max. diam. (pl. XXXIII.) Adams R.1. Rijksmuseum, Leiden F1963/8.21.

Grave 192.86

Superstructure: A rubble mound, 6 m. diam. and 0.55 m. high.

Grave: Type III, 2.24×0.85×0.98 m., the entrance adding

another 0.35 m. to the length. The orientation is NNW–SSE (31° W. of N.).

Burial: The scattered bones of one body and the articulated bones of another, this latter lying dorsally extended, head NNW.

Objects: None remained.

Grave 192.87

Superstructure: A stone-covered rubble mound, 6.25 m. diam. and 0.8 m. high.

Grave: Type I, 3.35×1.12×0.72 m. deep, orientated NNW–SSE (17° W. of N.).

Burial: The articulated body of an adult male, lying dorsally extended, head NNW.

Objects: Part of a red ware amphora with a cream slip and red and black painted decoration. Adams W.30. Ballâna/Qusṭul corpus type 40D.

Grave 192.88

Superstructure: A stone-covered rubble mound, 5.5 m. diam. and 0.45 m. high.

Grave: Type II, 3×0.6×0.95 m., orientated NNW–SSE (17° W. of N.).

Burial: None remained.

Objects: None remained.

Grave 192.89

Superstructure: A stone-covered mound, 6.5 m. diam. and 0.4 m. high.

Grave: Type II, 3.03×1×0.8 m., orientated NW–SE (54° W. of N.).

Burial: The intrusive body of an adult, lying extended, wrapped in a shroud.

Objects: None remained.

Grave 192.90

Superstructure: A stone-covered mound, 6 m. diam. and 0.5 m. high.

Grave: Type II, 2.7×0.8×1 m. deep, orientated NW–SE (45° W. of N.).

Burial: Only the leg bones of an adult.

Objects: Fragments of a red ware flask.

Grave 192.91

Superstructure: A stone-covered mound, 4 m. diam. and 0.5 m. high.

Grave: Type I, 1.8×0.7×1.15 m., orientated NW–SE (44° W. of N.). The stone blocking slabs rest on side ledges that are only 0.4 m. above the bottom of the grave.

Burial: The scattered bones of an adult.

Objects: None remained.

Grave 192.92

Superstructure: A stone-covered mound, 3.75 m. diam. and 0.3 m. high.

Grave: Type IV, 1.3×0.75×0.9 m., with an extension at the NW end of the pit of 0.5 m. The orientation is NW–SE (47° W. of N.).

Burial: The scattered bones of a child.

Objects: None remained.

Grave 192.93

Superstructure: A stone-covered rubble mound, 9 m. diam. and 1.15 m. high.

Grave: Type I, 2.72×1.1×1.1 m., orientated NW–SE (55° W. of N.).

Burial: The scattered bones of an adult.

Objects: 1. A red ware jar, 30 cm. high×23.4 cm. max. diam. (pl. XXXIV.) Adams R.1. Cairo, Egyptian Museum 89711.

Grave 192.94

Superstructure: A stone-covered mound, 4 m. diam. and 0.7 m. high.

Grave: Type II, 1.51×0.6×0.87 m. deep., orientated NW–SE (46° W. of N.).

Burial: The scattered bones of a child.

Objects: 1. A red ware flask with white painted decoration, 19.5 cm. high×15.6 cm. max. diam. (pl. XXXIII.) Adams R.1. Aberdeen Anthropological Museum 1109[2].
2. A red ware cup with painted black and white decoration, 9.9 cm. high×8.4 cm. max. diam. (pl. XXXIII.) Adams R.1. Reading Museum 83:67/20.

Grave 192.95

Superstructure: A rubble tumulus, 3 m. diam. and 0.5 m. high.

Grave: Type I, 1.18×0.75×0.24 m., orientated NW–SE (47° W. of N.).

Burial: None remained.

Objects: None remained.

Grave 192.96

Superstructure: A stone-covered rubble mound, 6 m. diam. and 0.7 m. high.

Grave: Type II, 2.73×0.9×1.25 m., orientated NE–SW (38° E. of N.).

Burial: A female adult.

Objects: 1. A red ware cup, 9 cm. high×11.4 cm. max. diam. (pl. XXXIV.) Adams R.1. British Museum 66562.

Grave 192.97

Superstructure: A stone-covered rubble mound, 6.3 m. diam. and 0.35 m. high.

Grave: Type I, 2.4×0.9×0.72 m., orientated NW–SE (46° W. of N.).

Burial: None remained.

Objects: 1. A cream ware flask with red painted decoration, 8.8 cm. high×7.8 cm. max. diam. (pl. XXXIV.) Adams W.30. Cairo, Egyptian Museum 89714.

Grave 192.98

Superstructure: A rubble mound, 4.5 m. diam. and 0.5 m. high.

Grave: Type II, 1.75×0.4×0.8 m., orientated NW–SE (48° W. of N.) (pl. XXXIV.)

Burial: The articulated body of a child lying dorsally extended. The head was missing.

Objects: 1. A red ware flask with a cream slip and red painted decoration, 22.5 cm. high×18 cm. max. diam. (pl. XXXIV.) Adams W.30. Cairo, Egyptian Museum 89712.

2. A red ware cup, 8.4 cm. high×10.2 cm. max. diam. (pl. XXXIV.) Adams R.1. Aberdeen Anthropological Museum 1109[2].

3. A bracelet of bone short cylinder beads. Found on the right wrist of the skeleton. (pl. XXXIV.) Location uncertain.

Grave 192.99

Superstructure: A rubble mound, 5 m. diam. and 0.4 m. high.

Grave: Type II, 2.55×0.87×0.76 m., orientated NNW–SSE (14° W. of N.).

Burial: The scattered bones of an adult male.

Objects: None remained.

Grave 192.100

Superstructure: A rubble mound, 3 m. diam. and 0.25 m. high.

Grave: Type I, 1.22×0.35×0.45 m., orientated NW–SE (37° W. of N.).

Burial: None remained.

Objects: None were found.

Grave 192.101

Superstructure: A stone-covered tumulus, 5 m. diam. and 0.7 m. high.

Grave: Type II, 2.6×0.8×1 m., orientated NNW–SSE (31° W. of N.).

Burial: The scattered bones of an adult male.

Objects: None remained.

Grave 192.102

Superstructure: A rubble mound, 4.5 m. diam. and 0.5 m. high.

Grave: Type IV, 1.5×0.65×0.82 m., with the entrance pit another 0.48 m. long. The orientation is WNW–ESE (61° W. of N.).

Burial: The scattered bones of an adult.

Objects: 1. Part of a bracelet of bone short cylinder beads. (pl. XXXIV.) Location uncertain.

2. The base of a glass vessel. Location uncertain.

Grave 192.103

Superstructure: A rubble mound, 7 m. diam. and 1 m. high.

Grave: Type I, 2.75×0.77×0.70 m., orientated NW–SE (54° W. of N.). (pl. XXXIV.)

Burial: The articulated body of an adult female, lying dorsally extended, head SE.

Objects: None remained.

Grave 192.104

Superstructure: A rubble mound, 4 m. diam. and 0.5 m. high.

Grave: Type I, 1.52×0.5×0.68 m., orientated WNW–ESE (64° W. of N.).

Burial: None remained.

Objects: 1. The remains of a multi-coloured woollen rug. Location uncertain.

Grave 192.105

Superstructure: A rubble mound, 7 m. diam. and 0.7 m. high.

Grave: Type I, 2×0.87×0.87 m., orientated WNW–ESE (57° W. of N.).

Burial: The articulated body of an adult female, lying in a flexed position on the left side, head WNW.

Objects: 1. A brown ware flask with a cream slip and black painted decoration, 27.6 cm. high×22.2 cm. max. diam. (pls. XXXIV, LXXVIII.) Adams W.30. Cairo, Egyptian Museum 89713.

2. There were the remains of leather sandals on the feet. Location uncertain.

Grave 192.196

Superstructure: A rubble mound, 5 m. diam. and 0.5 m. high.

Grave: Type IV, 2.23×0.75×0.70 m., with the entrance

pit an additional 0.2 m. Orientation is NW–SE (40° W. of N.). (pl. XXXIV.)

Burial: The articulated body of an adult female, lying dorsally extended, head NW.

Objects: a. Sherds of a red ware amphora with a cream slip and black painted 'splash' decoration. (pl. XXXIV.) Adams W.30.

Grave 192.107

Superstructure: A stone-covered rubble mound, 5.25 m. diam. and 0.45 m. high.

Grave: Type II, 2 m. × 0.6 × 0.5 m., orientated NW–SE (47° W. of N.).

Burial: None remained.

Objects: None remained.

Grave 192.108

Superstructure: A rubble mound, 3.5 m. diam. and 0.55 m. high.

Grave: Type I, 1.3 × 0.62 × 0.5 m., orientated NW–SE (44° W. of N.).

Burial: None remained.

Objects: None were found.

Grave 192.109

Superstructure: A rubble mound, 7 m. diam. and 0.55 m. high.

Grave: Type II, 2.6 × 1 × 0.52 m., orientated NW–SE (44° W. of N.).

Burial: None remained.

Objects: None remained.

Grave 192.110

Superstructure: A pile of stones, 4 m. diam. and 0.6 m. high.

Grave: Type I, 1.98 × 0.87 × 0.5 m., orientated NW–SE (44° W. of N.). (pl. XXXIV.)

Burial: The scattered bones of a child.

Objects: 1. A red ware jar with black and white painted decoration, 22.2 cm. high × 16.2 cm. max. diam. (pl. XXXIV.) Adams R.1. Reading Museum 118:65/2.

Grave 192.111

Superstructure: A stone-covered rubble mound, 6.75 m. diam. and 0.75 m. high.

Grave: Type II, 2.75 × 0.75 × 0.87 m., orientated NW–SE (48° W. of N.).

Burial: None remained.

Objects: 1. A red ware flask with black painted decoration, 19.2 cm. high × 17.4 cm. max. diam. (pl. XXXV.) Adams R.1. Cairo, Egyptian Museum 89715.

   2. A brown ware amphora with a cream slip, 37.5 cm. high × 19.8 cm. max. diam. (pl. XXXV.) Adams W.28. Durham GM 1964 548.

   3. A red ware cup, 8.4 cm. high × 10.2 cm. max. diam. (pl. XXXV.) Adams R.1. University College London 19579.

   4. A red ware flask, 23.4 cm. high × 18.6 cm. max. diam. (pl. XXXV.) Adams R.1. Rijksmuseum, Leiden F1963/8.22.

Grave 192.112

Superstructure: A stone-covered rubble mound, 2.2 m. diam.

Grave: Type I, 2.05 × 1.1 × 0.5 m., orientated NW–SE (48° W. of N.). (pl. XXXV.)

Burial: None remained.

Objects: 1. A small red ware cup with black and white painted decoration, 8.4 cm. high × 8.6 cm. max. diam. (pl. XXXV.) Adams R.1. Cairo, Egyptian Museum 89716.

   2. A ribbed, red ware amphora, 39.9 cm. high × 18 cm. max. diam. (pl. XXXV.) Adams R.1. Rijksmuseum, Leiden F1963/8.23.

Grave 192.113

Superstructure: A stone-covered rubble mound, 3.75 m. diam. and 0.4 m. high.

Grave: Type II, 1.98 × 0.75 × 0.73 m., orientated NNW–SSE (31° W. of N.).

Burial: None remained.

Objects: 1. A red ware spouted two-handled flask with white painted decoration, 21 cm. high × 12 cm. max. diam. (pl. XXXV.) Adams R.1. Cairo, Egyptian Museum 89717.

Grave 192.114

Superstructure: A stone-covered mound, 6 m. diam. and 0.35 m. high.

Grave: Type II, 2.5 × 0.75 × 0.62 m., orientated NW–SE (46° W. of N.).

Burial: The disturbed body of an adult female.

Objects: None remained.

Grave 192.115

Superstructure: A stone-covered mound, 3.25 m. diam. and 0.25 m. high.

Grave: Type I, 1.5 × 0.62 × 0.5 m., orientated NNE–SSW (16° E. of N.).

Burial: None remained.

Objects: None were found.

Grave 192.116

Superstructure: A rubble mound, 6 m. diam. and 0.5 m. high.

Grave: Type IV, 2.27×0.75×0.8 m., the entrance pit being another 0.35 m. long. The orientation is NNW–SSE (30° W. of N.).

Burial: The scattered bones of an adult male.

Objects: 1. A red ware flask, 24.3 cm. high×19.8 cm. max. diam. (pl. XXXV.) Adams R.1. Otago Museum E62.6.

2. A red ware cup, 8.1 cm. high×10.8 cm. max. diam. (pl. XXXV.) Adams R.1. Blackburn Museum. This cup is identical with the following one.

3. A red ware cup, 8.1 cm. high×10.8 cm. max. diam. (pl. XXXV.) Adams R.1. University College London 19578.

Grave 192.117

Superstructure: A stone-covered rubble mound, 5 m. diam. and 0.4 m. high.

Grave: Type IV, 2.05×0.7×0.60 m., the entrance pit adding 0.3 m. to the length. The orientation is NNW–SSE (21° W. of N.). (pl. XXXVI.)

Burial: A few scattered bones.

Objects: 1. A red ware amphora, 38.4 cm. high×18.6 cm. max. diam. (pl. XXXVI.) Adams R.1. Ashmolean Museum 1962.933.

2. A buff-yellow ware cup with dark brown painted decoration, 7.5 cm. high×8.4 cm. max. diam. (pls. XXXVI, LXXX.) Adams W.30. British Museum 66565.

Grave 192.118

Superstructure: A stone-covered rubble mound, 5 m. diam. and 0.5 m. high.

Grave: Type II, 1.62×0.57×0.6 m., orientated NNW–SSE (16° W. of N.).

Burial: The disturbed body of a young woman.

Objects: None remained.

Grave 192.119

Superstructure: A rubble mound, 5 m. diam. and 0.6 m. high.

Grave: Type IV, 2.08×0.75×0.75 m., the entrance adding 0.48 m. to the length. The orientation is NW–SE (44° W. of N.).

Burial: The scattered remains of two skeletons.

Objects: 1. A red ware cup with black and white painted decoration, 8.4 cm. high×9.6 cm. max. diam. (pl. XXXVI.) Adams R.1. Royal Ontario Museum 963.15.19.

2. A red ware flask, 13.8 cm. high×10.2 cm. max. diam. (pl. XXXVI.) Adams R.1. British Museum 66570.

3. A red ware flask with a white painted neck, 24.3 cm. high×17.4 cm. max. diam. (pl. XXXVI.) Adams R.1. Nicholson Museum 63.202.

4. A red ware amphora with a cream slip, 38.1 cm. high×17.4 cm. max. diam. (pl. XXXVI.) Adams W.28. Cambridge Museum of Arch. and Eth. 63.185.

5. Also found was a red ware oil flask, Ballâna/Qusṭul corpus type 50A, Adams R.1, the neck of which was missing. Preserved height is 16 cm., max. diam. is 10.9 cm. (pl. XXXVI.) Location uncertain.

Grave 192.120

Superstructure: A stone-covered rubble mound, 4 m. diam.

Grave: Type I, 2.62×0.57×0.7 m., orientated ENE–WSW (57° E. of N.).

Burial: The disturbed bodies of an adult female and an adult male.

Objects: 1. A red ware jar, 20.1 cm. high×13.2 cm. max. diam. Adams R.1. Cairo, Egyptian Museum 89718.

Grave 192.121

Superstructure: A stone-covered rubble mound, 4.2 m. diam.

Grave: Type IV, 2.98×1.7×1 m. deep, the entrance adding another 1.5 m. to the length. The orientation is NNE–SSW (31° E. of N.). (pl. XXXVII.)

Burial: The articulated body of an adult male, lying dorsally extended, head SSW. There were also a few scattered bones of an adult female in the grave.

Objects: 1. A red ware cup, 7.2 cm. high×10.2 cm. max. diam. (pl. XXXVII.) Adams R.1. Durham GM 1964 571. This and the following cup are identical.

2. A red ware cup, 7.2 cm. high×10.2 cm. max. diam. (pl. XXXVII.) Adams R.1. Liverpool University E6333.

Grave 192.122

Superstructure: A stone-covered mound, 5.25 m. diam. and 0.35 m. high.

Grave: Type I, 2.25×1×0.74 m., orientated NE–SW (45° E. of N.).

Burial: None remained.

Objects: None were found.

Grave 192.123

Superstructure: A stone-covered rubble mound, 6 m. diam. and 0.4 m. high.

Grave: Type I, 2.51×1×1 m. (pl. XXXVI.)

Burial: The scattered bones of an adult female.

Objects: 1. A red ware flask, 19.2 cm. high×14.4 cm. max. diam. (pl. XXXVI.) Adams R.1. Cambridge Museum of Arch. and Eth. 63.184.

2. A red ware cup, 4.9 cm. high×9.3 cm. max. diam. (pl. XXXVI.) Adams R.1. Liverpool University E6331.

Grave 192.124

Superstructure: A stone-covered rubble tumulus, 8 m. diam. and 0.85 m. high.

Grave: Type III, 3×1.25×0.85 m., the entrance being an additional 0.74 m. long. The orientation is NE–SW (50° E. of N.).

Burial: The scattered bones of three adults, one male and two females.

Objects: None remained.

Grave 192.125

Superstructure: A stone-covered mound, 3.5 m. diam. and 0.35 m. high.

Grave: Type I, 1.98×0.55×0.58 m., orientated NNE–SSW (17° E. of N.).

Burial: The articulated body of an infant, lying dorsally extended, head SSW, in the middle of the grave.

Objects: None remained.

Grave 192.126

Superstructure: A stone-covered rubble mound, 6.5 m. diam.

Grave: Type I, 2.72×1.25×0.75 m.

Burial: The skull only, of an adult.

Objects: 1. A wooden spindle whorl, 5.8 cm. diam. and 1.4 cm. thick (pl. XXXVII.) Durham GM 1964 563.

2. The fragments of a cream biscuit ware cup with brown painted decoration, 10.5 cm. high×8.1 cm. max. diam. (pl. XXXVII.) Adams W.30. Location uncertain.

Grave 192.127

Superstructure: A stone-covered rubble mound, 2.7 m. diam.

Grave: Type I, 2.75×0.7×0.82 m., orientated ENE–WSW (67° E. of N.).

Burial: There were the remains of three bodies in this grave. There is an articulated body of an adult male, lying dorsally extended, head WSW. This is probably not the original burial as the body is longer than the grave and the head rests upright against one end. The other

remains were the disturbed body of an adult female and that of a child.

Objects: None remained.

Grave 192.128

Superstructure: A stone-covered rubble mound, 4.5 m. diam.

Grave: Type I, 2.45×0.6×0.78 m., orientated NE–SW (54° E. of N.).

Burial: None remained.

Objects: None remained.

Grave 192.129

Superstructure: A stone-covered rubble mound, 4.5 m. diam. and 0.4 m. high.

Grave: Type I, 2.5×0.98×0.68 m., orientated NW–SE (36° W. of N.).

Burial: A few scattered bones.

Objects: 1. A red ware flask with cream and black painted decoration, 25.8 cm. high×19.2 cm. max. diam. (pl. XXXVII.) Adams R.1. Cairo, Egyptian Museum 89719.

Grave 192.130

Superstructure: A rubble mound, 7 m. diam. and 1 m. high.

Grave: Type II, 3.05×1×1.12 m., orientated NE–SW (40° E. of N.).

Burial: The scattered bones of two adults.

Objects: None remained.

Grave 192.131

Superstructure: A stone-covered rubble mound, 6.5 m. diam. and 0.5 m. high.

Grave: Type II, 2.48×1.2×1.2 m., orientated NE–SW (40° E. of N.).

Burial: None remained.

Objects: None remained.

Grave 192.132

Superstructure: A stone-covered rubble mound, 4 m. diam. and 0.5 m. high.

Grave: Type I, 2.25×0.65×0.68 m., orientated NNW–SSE (26° W. of N.).

Burial: None remained.

Objects: None were found.

Grave 192.133

Superstructure: A rubble mound, 5 m. diam. and 0.5 m. high.

Grave: Type I, 2.33×0.62×0.88 m., orientated WNW–ESE (62° W. of N.).

Burial: The scattered bones of an adult.

Objects: 1. A red ware cup with black and white painted decoration, 8.6 cm. high×9.6 cm. max. diam. (pl. XXXVII.) Adams R.1. Aberdeen Anthropological Museum 1109². This cup is identical with no. 3, below.

2. A two-handled red ware amphora with white painted decoration, 35.1 cm. high×21.6 cm. max. diam. (pl. XXXVII.) Adams R.1. British Museum 66540.

3. A red ware cup with black and white painted decoration, 8.6 cm. high×9.6 cm. max. diam. (pl. XXXVII.) Adams R.1. Liverpool University E6321.

CEMETERY 192A

THIS cemetery, which lies to the north of Cemetery 192, is one of the Meroïtic areas of the Qaṣr Ibrîm cemeteries. The excavation in the area was carried out during the first four days of November and, after evidence was gained concerning the dating of the area to the Meroïtic and Ballâna phases and of the general condition of the area, the site was abandoned for other work.

The Meroïtic elements are found in graves 1, 2, and 3, which are clustered together at the north-west corner of the site (see pl. XLIV). That these tombs are Meroïtic is supported by their architectural similarity to Karanog type A tombs[1] and the objects and ceramics from them all belong to the Late Meroïtic Period. The general size and quality of these tombs reveal that the Meroïtic occupation here at Ibrîm was not simply one of a small outpost or agricultural settlement, but contained elements of socially or economically stratified population. This assessment is further supported by the tombs in Cemetery 192C, q.v.

The remainder of this cemetery, graves 4 to 25, is readily identified with the Ballâna culture and ought, perhaps, to date to the third century AD. Of particular interest, here, are the iron tools and weapons from graves 7 and 25.

The area occupied by this cemetery is roughly 140 × 100 m., and the growth of this particular area was inhibited by the amount of fossil alluvial soil available for digging the graves. In view of theories which lay emphasis on the most prominent and convenient parts of a cemetery for dating internal sequences of graves, it is difficult to account for the obviously very early use of this somewhat insignificant area furthest away from the hilltop settlement at Ibrîm.

Three stone objects were recovered from the surface of this area. All are sandstone and Meroïtic and were quite possibly locally produced.

1. Part of a sandstone offering table, 36 × 32 × 11 cm. thick, bearing a relief of two water jars and four loaves. A single line of inscription in Meroïtic linear script runs around the rim. (pl. LXXXVIII. 2.) British Museum 66585. This piece is fully described below, p. 78.

2. A rectangular sandstone block 15 × 35 cm., upon one end of which a representation of an offering table has been crudely cut by scratching. (pl. LXXXVIII. 3.) British Museum 66580.

3. A fragment of the edge of a sandstone offering table, inscribed in the Meroïtic linear script. (pl. LXXXVIII. 4.) University College London 19560. This piece is fully described below, p. 78.

Grave 192A.1

Superstructure: A rectangular structure, 6 × 6.4 m., of dressed stone with an earth-filled core. It was preserved to a maximum of three courses, 0.55 m., and there is no indication that the sides were battered. It was centrally located over the pit of the grave.

Grave: Type IV, 2.9 × 2 × 1.75 m. The entrance is 0.9 m. long. The orientation is NW–SE (42° W. of N.). (pl. XXXVIII.)

Burial: None remained.

Objects: 1. Fragments of a turned ivory handle, 1.4 cm. diam. and 4.5 cm. remaining length, decorated with carved representations of uraei. (pl. XXXVIII.) Ashmolean Museum 1962.949.

2. Fragment of an ivory object, 2.7 cm. preserved length and 0.9 cm. max. width, decorated with carved representations of uraei. (pl. XXXVIII.) Ashmolean Museum 1962.918.

Grave 192A.2

Superstructure: A rectangular structure, 4.75 × 4.25 m., of dressed stone with an earth-filled core. Preservation was only two courses high and there was no indication of any battering. It was centrally located over the grave pit.

Grave: Type IV, 2.32 × 1.72 × 1.25 m. The entrance is 0.55 m. long, and orientation is NW–SE (40° W. of N.).

Burial: None remained.

Objects: 1. An iron *kohl* stick, 13.6 cm. long × 0.6 cm. max. diam. (pl. XXXVIII.) Location uncertain.

2. An iron ring, 2.3 cm. outside diam. and 0.4 cm. thick. (pl. XXXVIII). Location uncertain.

---

[1] C. L. Woolley and D. R. MacIver, *Karanog: The Romano-Nubian Cemetery*, 22–3.

Grave 192A.3

Superstructure: A rectangular structure, 4.9×5.35 m., built of dressed stone with an earth-filled core. It was not completely preserved.

Grave: Type II, 2.3×2×0.65 m., orientated NNW–SSE (31° W. of N.).

Burial: A skull.

Objects: 1. A red ware, ribbed jar, 30 cm. high×26.4 cm. max. diam. (pl. XXXVIII.) Adams R.32. Location uncertain.

   2. A three-legged red ware cup, 4.6 cm. high×7.6 cm. max. diam. (pl. XXXVIII.) Adams R.32. British Museum 66558.

   3. A red ware cup, 6.9 cm. high×6.6 cm. max. diam. (pl. XXXVIII.) Adams R.32. University College London 19575.

   4. The sandstone head of a Ba statue, with a total height of 28 cm. The head is surmounted by a rather oval disc and, apart from the tips of the ears and the nose, is complete. It was found on the surface of the ground very near grave 3 and is considered as having belonged to it. (pls. XXXVIII, XC. 6.) Cairo, Egyptian Museum 89696.

Grave 192 .4

Superstructure: A stone-covered tumulus, 6.75 m. diam. and 0.4 m. high.

Grave: Type I, 2.75×0.97×1.2 m. The orientation is ENE–WSW (60° E. of N.). (pl. XXXIX.)

Burial: The pelvis, legs, and feet, all articulated, of an adult, probably originally lying dorsally extended, head WSW. There were also the scattered bones of another adult, presumably subsequently intruded, at a higher level in the fill of the grave.

Objects: 1. A red ware jar, 22.2 cm. high×16.8 cm. max. diam., with black and white painted decoration. (pl. XXXIX.) Adams R.1. Liverpool University E6313.

   2. A pink ware amphora with a cream slip, 35.1 cm. high×19.2 cm. max. diam. (pl. XXXIX.) Adams W.28. University College London 19576.

   3. A red ware cup, 9 cm. high×9 cm. max. diam. (pl. XXXIX.) Adams R.1. Cambridge Museum of Arch. and Eth. 63.186.

   4. A small red ware, one-handled flask, 13.5 cm. high ×9.6 cm. max. diam. (pl. XXXIX.) Adams R.1. Cambridge Museum of Arch. and Eth. 63.187.

   5. A red ware, two-handled flask, 19.5 cm. high×11.4 cm. max. diam. (pl. XXXIX.) Adams R.1. Durham GM 1964 558.

   6. A silver finger ring, 1.8 cm. diam., with beaded decoration around the band and a garnet stone set in the bezel. (pl. XXXIX.) Nicholson Museum 63.215.

   7. Blue faience ball and white faience short barrel beads. (pl. XXXIX.) University College London 19558.

Grave 192A.5

Superstructure: A stone-covered rubble mound, 6 m. diam. and 0.35 m. high.

Grave: Type I, 2.7×0.74×1 m. It is orientated N.–S. (6° W. of N.). (pl. XL.)

Burial: The scattered bones of an adult.

Objects: 1. A red ware jar, 29.7 cm. high×20.4 cm. max. diam. (pl. XL.) Adams R.1. Durham GM 1964 552.

Grave 192A.6

Superstructure: A stone-covered rubble tumulus, 6.5 m. diam. and 0.5 m. high.

Grave: Type I, 2.65×1×1 m. It was orientated N.–S. (2° W. of N.).

Burial: None remained.

Objects: 1. A red ware jar, 23.4 cm. high×18 cm. max. diam. (pl. XXXVIII.) Adams R.1. Durham GM 1964 555.

   2. A red ware cup, 8.7 cm. high×10.8 cm. max. diam. (pl. XXXVIII.) Adams R.1. Durham GM 1964 574.

   3. A red ware cup, 8.4 cm. high×10.8 cm. max. diam. (pl. XXXVIII.) Adams R.1. Fitzwilliam Museum E.4.1962.

Grave 192A.7

Superstructure: A rubble tumulus, 5 m. diam. and 1 m. high.

Grave: Type I, 2.52×0.9×0.93 m. The orientation is NNE–SSW (21° E. of N.). (pl. XL.)

Burial: None remained.

Objects: 1. An iron spear with bronze fittings on the grip, a wooden haft, and an iron spike butt. The blade is 51 cm. long×8.4 cm. max. wide. The total length of the spear was 2.35 m. The haft was not preserved, but sufficient traces remained in the grave floor to enable the entire weapon to be reconstructed. (pl. XL, LXXXVI. 6.) University College London 19527.

   2. A red ware cup, 8.4 cm. high×8.4 cm. max. diam. (pl. XL.) Adams R.1. Otago Museum E62.18.

   3. A red ware cup, 7.5 cm. high×9.6 cm. max. diam. (pl. XL.) Adams R.1. Aberdeen Anthropological Museum 1109².

   4. An archer's finger loose of black and white porphyritic rock, 4.2 cm. long×3.9 cm. max. diam. (pl. XL.) Cambridge Museum of Arch. and Eth. 63.188.

   5. An iron hammer, the handle having been made separately and subsequently hafted. The total length is 24.3 cm. (pl. XL.) University College London 19528.

   6. An iron knife blade, 11.1 cm. long, with a straight

back and convexly curved cutting edge. There were traces of a wooden handle, hafted in the usual manner with a ring and nails. (pl. XL.) University College London 19529.

Also found in the fill of the grave were (a) a few fragments of a wooden casket with iron fittings; (b) fragments of an amber, thin-walled glass cup with a coiled blue foot. (pl. XL.) Corning Museum of Glass 353. See p. 89 below.

Grave 192A.8

Superstructure: A stone-covered rubble tumulus, 3.4 m. diam. and 0.55 m. high.

Grave: Type I, 2.55×0.92×0.9 m. The orientation is NW–SE (38° W. of N.).

Burial: None remained.

Objects: None were found.

Grave 192A.9

Superstructure: A stone-covered tumulus, 5.25 m. diam. and 0.6 m. high.

Grave: Type II, 2.57×1.12×1.3 m., orientated ENE–WSW (57° E. of N.). (pl. XLI.)

Burial: The scattered bones of an adult.

Objects: 1. A red ware flask, 23.4 cm. high×16.2 cm. max. diam., with white and black painted decoration. (pls. XLI, LXXIX.) Adams R.1. Durham GM 1964 557.

Grave 192A.10

Superstructure: A rubble mound, 4.5 m. diam. and 0.4 m. high.

Grave: Type I, 2.49×1×0.75 m., orientated ENE–WSW (74° E. of N.).

Burial: The scattered bones of an adult.

Objects: Fragments of two cream biscuit ware ribbed cups with red painted bands of decoration. Adams W.26.

Grave 192A.11

Superstructure: A stone-covered rubble tumulus, 4.25 m. diam. and 0.55 m. high.

Grave: Type I, 2.87×0.91×0.95 m., orientated ENE–WSW (70° E. of N.).

Burial: The scattered bones of an adult.

Objects: 1. A red ware jar, 27.8 cm. high×19.8 cm. max. diam. (pl. XLI.) Adams R.1. Otago Museum E62.22.
2. A red ware cup, 8.1 cm. high×9 cm. max. diam. (pl. XLI.) Adams R.1. Durham GM 1964 575.

Also found was part of a red ware flask, similar to Ballâna/Qusṭul Corpus no. 57A.

Grave 192A.12

Superstructure: A rubble tumulus, 6 m. diam. and 0.7 m. high.

Grave: Type IV, 1.52×0.76×1 m. The entrance is a further 0.87 m. long. The orientation is NE–SW (40° E. of N.). (pl. XLII.)

Burial: The articulated body of an adult male, lying dorsally extended, head SW.

Objects: 1. A small red ware amphora, 36 cm. high×21 cm. max. diam. (pl. XLI.) Adams R.1. Manchester Museum 20955.
2. A red ware cup, 7.5 cm. high×6.6 cm. max. diam., decorated with painted bands of black and white. (pl. XLI.) Adams R.1. Liverpool University E6311.

Grave 192A.13

Superstructure: A rubble tumulus, oval in shape, 2.5 m.× 1.5 m. and 0.5 m. high.

Grave: Type II, cut into bedrock, 2.5×1.03×0.77 m. The orientation is NW–SE (41° W. of N.).

Burial: None remained.

Objects: None were found.

Grave 192A.14

Superstructure: A rubble tumulus, 4 m. diam. and 0.7 m. high.

Grave: Type I, 2.1×0.92×0.6 m., orientated NE–SW (34° E. of N.).

Burial: None remained.

Objects: None were found.

Grave 192A.15

Superstructure: A rubble mound, 4 m. diam. and 0.65 m. high.

Grave: Type I, 1.92×0.75×0.7 m., orientated NW–SE (35° W. of N.).

Burial: The articulated body of an adult male, lying dorsally extended, head SE, at the entrance to the tomb chamber.

Objects: 1. An iron, single-tanged arrow head, 4.9 cm. long. (pl. XLI.) Location uncertain.

Grave 192A.16

Superstructure: A rubble mound, 3 m. diam. and 0.5 m. high.

Grave: Type III, 2×0.95×0.7 m. It was orientated ENE–WSW (65° E. of N.).

Burial: The scattered bones of an adult.

Objects: 1. A red ware cup, 8.4 cm. high×9.6 cm. max. diam. (pl. XLII.) Adams R.1. Manchester Museum 20185.

2. A red ware cup, exactly similar to no. 1, above, 8.4 cm. high×9.6 cm. max. diam. (pl. XLII.) Adams R.1. Durham GM 1964 572.

Grave 192A.17

Superstructure: An oval rubble mound, 4×6 m. and 0.5 m. high.

Grave: Type II, 2×0.81×0.7 m., orientated NW–SE (52° W. of N.). (pl. XLII.)

Burial: The articulated pelvis, legs, and feet of an adult male, lying extended with the legs crossed, the head originally to the NW. The position indicated on the plan of the grave may not be the original one for this burial, as there is hardly enough room for the upper half of the body. Presumably, it was displaced during the plundering.

Objects: 1. A red ware jar, 22.2 cm. high×15 cm. max. diam., with a white painted neck. (pl. XLII.) Adams R.1. Location uncertain.

2. A red ware, two-handled flask, 16.5 cm. remaining height×12 cm. max. diam., decorated with black painted bands. The mouth is missing. (pl. XLII.) Adams R.1. Location uncertain.

3. A red ware cup, 8.4 cm. high×10.2 cm. max. diam. (pl. XLII.) Adams R.1. Cambridge Museum of Arch. and Eth. 63.189.

Grave 192A.18

Superstructure: A stone-covered rubble tumulus, 5.5 m. diam. and 0.45 m. high.

Grave: Type II, 2.8×0.87×1 m., orientated NW–SE (36° W. of N.).

Burial: The scattered bones of an adult.

Objects: 1. A red ware cup with matt cream slip, 4.6 cm. high×7.2 cm. max. diam. (pl. XLII.) Adams W.30 (?). Queen's University, Belfast QAD/7/126.

Grave 192A.19

Superstructure: A stone-covered mound, 6 m. diam. and 0.65 m. high.

Grave: Type IV, 2.7×0.7×0.87 m. The entrance is 0.55 m. long and the grave orientation is WNW–ESE (60° W. of N.).

Burial: The scattered bones of an adult.

Objects: 1. A small red ware bottle, 10.5 cm. high×10.8 cm. max. diam. (pl. XLII.) Adams R.1. Nicholson 63.184.

Grave 192A.20

Superstructure: A stone-covered rubble tumulus, 4 m. diam. and 0.3 m. high.

Grave: Type I, 2.62×0.95×0.65 m. The orientation is NW–SE (41° W. of N.).

Burial: None remained.

Objects: 1. A red ware cup similar to 192A.17.3. Location uncertain.

Grave 192A.21

Superstructure: A stone-covered tumulus, 4.75 m. diam. and 0.25 m. high.

Grave: Type II, 1.75×0.68×0.75 m., orientated N.–S. (4° E. of N.). (pl. XLII.)

Burial: The articulated body of an infant, lying slightly flexed on the back, head to the north.

Objects: None were found.

Grave 192A.22

Superstructure: A slightly oval rubble mound, 2×2.5 m. and 0.5 m. high.

Grave: Type II, 2.2×0.6×1.05 m. Instead of the usual ledges cut to hold the brick vault, there is a shelf cut into each side at a depth of 0.73 m. The orientation is NNW–SSE (27° W. of N.). (pl. XLII.)

Burial: The disturbed remains of an adult male.

Objects: None were recovered.

Grave 192A.23

Superstructure: A rubble mound, 0.6 m. high.

Grave: Type IV, 2.95×0.85×0.82 m., with the entrance an additional 1.47 m. long. The orientation is NW–SE (52° W. of N.). (pl. XLIII.)

Burial: The greatly disturbed remains of an adult.

Objects: 1. A number of beads, principally bone disc beads, but also some green faience barrel and faceted beads. (pl. XLII.) Location uncertain.

Grave 192A.24

Superstructure: A stone-covered rubble mound, 7 m. diam. and 0.75 m. high.

Grave: Type II, 2.5×0.82×1 m.

Burial: The articulated leg of an adult. It was extended.

Objects: 1. A red ware amphora, 26.1 cm. high×15.6 cm. max. diam., with a decoration of black painted bands. (pl. XLIII.) Adams R.1. Cairo, Egyptian Museum 89701.

2. A red ware, one-handled flask, 15.9 cm. high×10.8 cm. max. diam. (pl. XLIII.) Adams R.1. Leeds University.

3. A pair of leather sandals, 25 cm. long×10.4 cm. max. wide. (pl. XLIII.) Ashmolean Museum 1962.955a and 1962.955b.

Grave 192A.25

Superstructure: A rubble tumulus, 5 m. diam. and 1 m. high.

Grave: Type IV, 1.97×1.25×1 m. The entrance is 0.8 m. long and the grave pit is dug through 0.45 m. of compacted sand and into 0.55 m. of the underlying *gebel*. The orientation is NE–SW (42° E. of N.).

Burial: A disturbed skeleton.

Objects: 1. A pair of iron pincers, 28.2 cm. long, with the jaws flattened to 1.2 cm. wide. (pl. XLIII.) University College London 19526.

North End Group

Just north of Cemetery 192A is a small group of five graves adjacent to a Muslim cemetery. All are similar, and the evidence of the graves, burials, and objects leaves the dating uncertain.

Grave 1

Superstructure: A stone-covered rubble mound, 5 m. diam. and 0.45 m. high.

Grave: Type I, 3.35×0.75×0.7 m.

Burial: The articulated body of a male adult, lying dorsally extended, hands on the pelvis.

Objects: None were found.

Grave 2

Superstructure: A stone-covered mound, 5 m. diam. and 0.5 m. high.

Grave: Type I, 2×1×0.8 m.

Burial: There were some scattered bones in the fill.

Objects: None were found.

Grave 3

Superstructure: A stone-covered tumulus, 4.1 m. diam. and 0.5 m. high.

Grave: Type I, 2.2×0.9×0.80 m.

Burial: Nothing remained.

Objects: 1. A brown ware pot with a ribbed neck, 8.1 cm.

high×8.7 cm. max. diam. (pl. XLII.) Manchester Museum 20186.

Grave 4

Superstructure: A stone-covered mound, 6 m. diam. and 0.7 m. high.

Grave: Type I, 2.5×1×1.1 m.

Burial: The articulated body of a girl, lying dorsally extended, hands on the pelvis.

Objects: There was a bracelet of shell beads in the right hand of the burial.

Grave 5

Superstructure: A stone-covered tumulus, 5.4 m. diam. and 0.45 m. high.

Grave: Type I, 2.4×1×0.9 m., orientated ENE–WSW (76° E. of N.).

Burial: The articulated body of an adult male, lying dorsally extended.

Objects: 1. A red ware bowl, 3.7 cm. high×13.8 cm. max. diam. Nicholson Museum 63.198.

2. A red ware bowl, 3 cm. high×13.2 cm. max. diam. Reading Museum 83:67/17.

CEMETERY 192B

THIS site, the second of three Meroïtic areas in the northern necropolis of Qaṣr Ibrîm, is situated on a rocky promontory overlooking the Nile. It is about 400 m. north of the hill of the town of Ibrîm and some 90 m. north-west of grave 192.2.

The area covered by the site is 22 × 18 m. and consists of stone structural elements and ten graves (pl. XLV.). Surface indications of this site were traces of the well-built stone walls. A brief excavation revealed walls, standing to a maximum of 3 m. although generally rather lower, which were apparently intended to be retaining walls forming the sides of a *mastaba* or terrace (pl. LXXXIV. 2). Abutting the south side of this is a second building. Seven graves were discovered beneath the *mastaba* and three outside it to the south.

The ground upon which the structures sit is bedrock and all the graves are cut into this. Graves 1 to 6 are within the *mastaba* structure, are aligned with it, and clearly can be dated with it. Similarly, no. 7 can be attributed to the west end of the *mastaba*. Grave 8, although having the same orientation as the others, is outside the *mastaba* and is a simpler type of grave and need not necessarily have been part of the original complex. Unfortunately, the orientation of graves 9 and 10 was not recorded, nor were they included in the plan, so their association may be fortuitous. The date of these last two graves, from the evidence of their contents, is X-group. The date of the remainder is less certain and must depend to a great extent on the date of the structures.

The original structure is rectangular, 12.8 × 11 m., and is the eastern three-quarters of the *mastaba*. This was built with large stone blocks and the masonry is well fitted, although the blocks' faces have not been smoothed off. It was built around a knoll of rock and a terracing effected by filling the hollows in the interior with stones and rubble. There is no evidence of the original height of the structure, whether it was an open terrace or enclosed, or even how it was floored. There may well have been a small funerary chapel or shrine on it. Within its floor were dug graves 1 to 6, most of which were intended to receive multiple burials. Subsequently, an addition was built on to the western end of the *mastaba*, extending the whole structure to 17.3 × 11 m., and grave 7 was dug into it. The date of this *mastaba* is probably Meroïtic. In addition to the good masonry and carefully laid out structure, evidence of fragments of a life-size statue, a cavetto cornice, and the scattered remains of inhumations showing signs of mummification[1] all point to a Meroïtic rather than a later date here.

The strongest evidence for a Meroïtic origin of this site comes from grave 8, where stones, still in quite good condition, were reused as roofing slabs for the tomb.[2] The assumption is that the stones would have been obtained from as close a source as possible for the sake of convenience. It has been presumed that the *mastaba* structure was that source.

At a still later date a new structure was added to the south side of the *mastaba*. Again, the walls are built of stone, but are light and not particularly well made. A fault or cleft in the sandstone has been utilized along the south and east sides of the building and perhaps the southern wall of the *mastaba* was similarly employed. Unfortunately, this building is badly ruined and although a couple of rooms are clearly defined, most of the plan is lost. The original erroneous designation of this building as a church[3] was based upon the round wall at the eastern end and the Christian ceramic material. However,

---

[1] These interesting items of evidence are only mentioned in Emery's field diary, and not recorded in the field notes concerning this site.

[2] See below, p. 43.

[3] W. B. Emery, 'Preliminary Report on Excavations at Kaṣr Ibrîm', in *Fouilles en Nubie (1961–1963)*, 60, fig. 4.

this 'apse' is not axially located in the building, assuming that the south wall is the southern edge of the structure, nor is there enough preserved to show the usual symmetry of the early Lower Nubian churches, nor is the building orientated the normal east to west, although this would have been a simple matter with the *mastaba* right there. The sherds recorded from the site (pl. XLVIII) include Adams R.2 (no. 5), R.4 (nos. 1, 2, 3, 4, 6, 7, 8, 10, 12, 13, 16, 17, and 18), R.5 (no. 15), and H.4 (no. 11). These indicate a date of somewhere between AD 500 and 850, most probably AD 600–50, although no. 11 is later. The ceramics also appear to be more domestic than otherwise and as the dating is so early, it seems unlikely that they would be the result of a later occupation.

Six objects were collected from the surface of 192B. They are:

1. A moulded red ware lamp, 8 cm. diam. and 5.2 cm. high. (pl. XLVIII, no. 16.) Adams R.4. The handle is broken off. Ashmolean Museum 1962.941.

2. A moulded brown ware lamp, 9 cm. diam. and 4.6 cm. high, with a frog on the top. (pl. XLVIII, no. 17.) Adams R.4. Ashmolean Museum 1962.942.

3. A moulded red ware lamp, 6.6 cm. diam. and 2.8 cm. high, with four crosses in a centre panel and an inscription around the border. (pl. XLVIII, no. 18.) Adams R.4. Ashmolean Museum 1962.943.

4. An ostracon with the remains of seven lines of a Coptic inscription (see below, p. 84). British Museum 66573.

5. An ostracon with the remains of ten lines of Coptic on the interior face and eight lines on the exterior (see below, p. 84–5). British Museum 66574.

6. An ostracon with a faint inscription in Coptic (see below, p. 85). British Museum 66575.

Grave 192B.1

Grave: There is a rectangular entrance shaft, 2 × 1.07 m. and 2.2 m. deep, which leads to four separate chambers, one off each side. The northern one is 2 × 1.14 × 0.9 m.; the western 2.25 × 0.95 × 1.10 m.; the southern one 2 × 1.15 × 0.9 m.; and the eastern one 2.4 × 0.95 × 1.14 m. The orientation of the entrance shaft and all four tomb chambers is E.–W. (82° E. of N.). The southern chamber has a brick-lined, stone-roofed grave built in it.

Burial: None remained in any of the chambers.

Objects: None were found.

Grave 192B.2

Grave: There is a rectangular entrance shaft, 2 × 1.05 m. and 2.25 m. deep, which leads to two chambers, one each on the north and south sides. That to the north is 2.2 × 1 × 0.85 m., and has a mud-brick blocking. The southern chamber is 2.3 × 1.1 × 0.85 m., and also has a brick blocking. The orientation of the shaft and chambers is E.–W. (86° W. of N.).

Burial: None remained.

Objects: None were found.

Grave 192B.3

Grave: There is a rectangular entrance shaft, 1.9 × 1.15 × 1.8 m., with a rectangular chamber off each of the east and west ends. The eastern chamber is 2.15 × 0.85 × 0.9 m. and the western is 2.18 × 0.83 × 0.9 m. The orientation of all three is E.–W. (86° W. of N.).

Burial: Nothing remained.

Objects: None were found.

Grave 192B.4

Grave: There is a rectangular shaft, 1.35 × 0.62 × 1.60 m., which has a chamber 0.6 × 0.62 × 0.9 m. at the eastern end. A ledge around the shaft at a depth of 0.75 m. held blocking stones. The orientation is E.–W. (82° E. of N.). (pl. XLVI.)

Burial: The articulated bodies of two adults, lying side by side, dorsally extended, head west, hands on the pelvis.

Objects: None were found.

Grave 192B.5

Grave: A rectangular pit, 2.25 × 0.8 × 1.75 m., orientated E.–W. (81° E. of N.). (pl. XLVI.)

Burial: The articulated body of an adult, lying dorsally extended, head west, hands on the pelvis.

Objects: None were found.

Grave 192B.6

Grave: A rectangular shaft, 2.04 × 1.1 × 1.75 m., leads to three underground chambers. The one to the east is 1.98 × 1.1 × 1 m., the northern one 2.04 × 1.15 × 0.9 m., and the chamber at the west is 1.6 × 0.8 × 0.9 m. All the features are orientated E.–W. (90° E. of N.).

Burial: None remained.

Objects: None were found.

Grave 192B.7

Grave: Type VI, with the shaft 1.15 × 0.65 × 1.2 m., and the lateral chamber 1.65 × 0.8 × 0.95 m. The orientation is E.–W. (86° W. of N.).

Burial: Nothing remained.

Objects: None were found.

Grave 192B.8

Grave: Type I, 1.9×0.65×0.95 m. deep, orientated E.–W. (90° E. of N.). (pl. XLVI.)

Burial: The remains of an adult female and two infants were found.

Objects: Nothing was found with the burial, but at least three of the blocking stones had been reused from a nearby Meroïtic area. Their excellent state of preservation is accounted for by virtue of their having been placed face down into the grave and thereby protected from wind and sand. (pl. LXXXIX. 1.)

1. A sandstone stela, 50×45 cm. and 9 cm. thick, bearing fourteen lines of Meroïtic linear script. fig.1, pl. LXXXIX. 2.) Cairo, Egyptian Museum 89699. This stela is fully described below, pp. 69ff.

2. A sandstone stela, 65×38 cm. and 9 cm. thick, bearing nineteen lines of Meroïtic linear script. (fig. 2, pl. LXXXIX. 3.) Cairo, Egyptian Museum 89700. This stela is fully described below, pp. 73ff.

3. A sandstone architectural block bearing a winged disc on a cavetto cornice, 58×27 cm. (pl. LXXXIX. 4.) Ashmolean Museum 1962.950.

Grave 192B.9

Grave: Type VI, 1.27×0.45×0.47 m., with an entrance shaft 1.15×0.45×0.52 m. The blocking was with mud bricks. (pl. XLVI.)

Burial: The articulated body of a small child, lying dorsally extended, hands on the pelvis.

Objects: 1. A small glass flask, 8 cm. high×4.4 cm. max. diam. (pl. XLVII.) Cairo, Egyptian Museum 89697.

2. A brown ware amphora with a yellow slip, 22.5 cm. high×13.8 cm. max. diam. (pl. XLVII.) Adams W.28. Birmingham Museum 125'63.

3. A red ware jar, 19.8 cm. high×15.9 cm. max. diam. (pl. XLVII.) Adams R.1. Durham GM 1964 556.

4. A red ware cup, 9 cm. high×11.4 cm. max. diam. (pl. XLVII.) Adams R.1. Nicholson Museum 63.193. This cup was placed over the mouth of no. 5.

5. A red ware jar, 16.9 cm. high×17.1 cm. max. diam. (pl. XLVII.) Adams R.1. Birmingham Museum 116'63.

6. A necklace of bone disc, orange glass disc, white glass, and blue and white glass barrel beads. (pl. XLVII). Location uncertain.

7. A green glass bust of Isis (?), probably belonging to the necklace, no. 6. 1.9 cm. high×1.2 cm. wide. (pl. XLVII). Location uncertain.

8. Two iron bells, 1.8 cm. diam. The clapper and the loop handle are one piece. (pl. XLVII.) University College London 19551.

9. Fragments of a glass vessel. (pl. XLVII.) Location uncertain.

Grave 192B.10

Grave: Type I, 2.7×0.75×1.25 m., orientated WNW–ESE (60° W. of N.).

Burial: There were the scattered bones of an adult male and an adult female.

Objects: 1. A red ware flask with white and black painted decoration, 21 cm. high×18 cm. max. diam. (pl. XLVII.) Adams R.1. Otago Museum E62.9.

2. A red ware flask with white and black painted decoration, 21 cm. high×18 cm. max. diam. (pl. XLVII.) Adams R.1. Nicholson Museum 63.194.

3. A red ware flask, 18.3 cm. high×17.4 cm. max. diam. (p. XLVII.) Adams R.1. Reading Museum 83:67/11.

4. A cream biscuit ware cup with red painted decoration, 9 cm. high×9 cm. max. diam. (pl. XLVII.) Adams W.30 or W.29. Cairo, Egyptian Museum 89698.

There were also fragments of several other flasks, cups, and amphorae in the fill.

CEMETERY 192C

This Meroïtic area is a necropolis of large tombs with rectangular, mud-brick superstructures, which were probably originally pyramidal. The tombs here are, again, similar to the Karanog type A tombs, with a distinct offering place on the east side of the superstructure. In the case of grave 1 this takes the form of an offering table on a pedestal or altar, in the others the offering chapel is built of brick and abuts the pyramid. The interior of each superstructure was filled with rubble and stones. None of them stands over a few courses of brick in height. It is obvious from the plan (pl. L) that care and thought went into the planning and construction of the cemetery and that the cemetery was not in use long enough to have the ground between the tombs used up with later or poorer burials.

This cemetery was excavated for only three days. What was excavated is the northern edge of an apparently somewhat larger group of tombs most of which had been overlaid by a cemetery of the Muslim period. It was not possible to excavate in the latter area and one has had to be content with the knowledge of the quality and size of a small portion of the original. Unfortunately, the tombs were also badly plundered.

Three small cups were found on the surface of this site:

192C.o.1. A ribbed, cream biscuit ware cup with a brown painted rim, 6.3 cm. high×11.4 cm. max. diam. Adams W.25. Rijksmuseum, Leiden F1963/8.11.

192C.o.2. A brown ware cup with a cream slip, 6 cm high×10.8 cm. max. diam. Adams W.29. Cambridge Museum of Arch. and Eth. 63.190.

192C.o.3. A brown ware cup with a cream slip, 6 cm. high×10.2 cm. max. diam. Adams W.29. Rijksmuseum, Leiden F1963/8.12.

Also found on the surface of this site were the following, none of which could be associated with a specific tomb.

192C.o.4. A sandstone *ba* statue of a female, 55 cm. tall. It is broken into three pieces and the head is missing, but is otherwise in perfect condition. It is in the normal position for this type of object, the wings are smooth and without any detail, and there is no evidence that it was painted. (pl. XC. 1, 2.) Location uncertain.

192C.o.5. A small, rectangular, sandstone shrine or window, 39 cm. tall and 25 cm. wide. Such shrines, with torus moulding and cavetto cornice, are found in association with Meroïtic pyramids,[1] where they are fitted into the east face, high up on the pyramid. (pl. XC. 3.) British Museum 66583.

192C.o.6. Two fragments of a sandstone *ba* statue. One is the base, 17×47 cm., which bears only the feet of the statue on its upper surface. The other is part of the wings. This piece is 16 cm. wide and 38 cm. high and details of feathering are present in the lower half. (pl. XC. 4, 5.) Location uncertain.

Grave 192C.1

Superstructure: A rectangular, mud-brick structure, 3.1×3.1 m., (pl. L), standing four courses or 0.5 m. high. All the sides are battered at an angle of 70°, which would permit a pyramid of 3.95 m. high to be reconstructed (pl. XLIX.) The interior was filled with stone and earth rubble. In line with the long axis of the grave pit and at a distance of 0.75 m. from the SE face of the pyramid is an altar or pedestal, 0.55×0.35 m., which presumably originally held the sandstone offering table, no. 2.

Grave: Type II, 1.8×0.58×0.55 m., orientated NW–SE (40° W. of N.). The grave pit is aligned with the superstructure, but not centrally located beneath it.

Burial: Nothing remained.

Objects: 1. extra A small bronze bowl, 5.4 cm. high×12 cm. max. diam., with a single ring handle and turned grooves around the rim. (pl. XLIX.) Reading Museum 83:67/26.

2. A sandstone offering table, 25×33 cm. max. width and 11.5 cm. thick. In the centre is a plain, roughly finished, rectangular depression, 12×9 cm. and 3.8 cm. deep, and leading from it to the end of the spout is a similarly finished trough, 17 cm. long×3 cm. wide×1 cm. deep. An inscription in Meroïtic demotic runs around the top. (pl. LXXXVIII. 5.) British Museum 66584. The inscription is fully described below, p. 78.

Grave 192C.2

Superstructure: A rectangular, mud-brick structure, 4.75×

[1] N. B. Millet, 'Gebel Adda Preliminary Report for 1963', in *JARCE* 2 (1963), 161.

4.85 m., standing 0.6 m. high. Against the SE wall and directly in line with the grave pit, is a mud-brick offering chapel, 1.45 m. deep×1.35 m. wide and two courses (0.22 m.) high. The interior of the superstructure is filled with stone and earth rubble and the reconstructed pyramid is 6.6 m. high.

Grave: Type I, 2.8×1.5×0.85 m., orientated NW–SE (40° W. of N.) and aligned with the superstructure. (pl. L.)

Burial: Nothing remained.

Objects: Neither was from inside the grave pit.
   1. A pink ware cup with a matt cream slip, 6.4 cm. high×10.8 cm. max. diam. (pl. XLIX.) Adams W.29. Queen's University, Belfast QAD/7/127.
   2. A red ware cup, 5.3 cm. high×9.6 cm. max. diam. (pl. XLIX.) Adams R.32. Birmingham Museum 121′63.

Grave 192C.3

Superstructure: A rectangular, mud-brick structure, 5.25×5.1 m. and standing 1 m. high. Against the SE wall and in line with the grave pit is an offering chapel, 1.5 m. deep×1.8 m. wide, built of mud-brick. (pl. L.) The interior of the superstructure is filled with stone and earth rubble and the original pyramid was 7.45 m. high.

Grave: Type I, 1.65×1.05×0.75 m. The orientation is NW–SE (41° W. of N.) and the pit is aligned with, although not exactly centrally located under, the superstructure.

Burial: There were the headless, but otherwise complete, articulated bodies of an adult and a child, lying beside one another, dorsally extended, hands on the pelvis and heads NW. These may not be the original inhumations of this tomb.

Objects: 1. A fragment of a wooden box, 13.2 cm. long×1.1

cm. thick, decorated with a pattern of inlaid, diamond-shaped ivory pieces. (pl. XLIX.) Location uncertain.

Grave 192C.4

Superstructure: A rectangular, mud-brick structure, 6.25×6.55 m., standing 1.2 m. high. The interior is filled with stone and earth rubble and the battering of the sides indicates an original pyramid height of about 9 m. At the centre of the SE face is a brick offering chapel, 1.55 m. deep×1.4 m. wide, standing 0.5 m. high. It is slightly misaligned with the grave.

Grave: Type I, 2.4×1.3×0.85 m., orientated NW–SE (41° W. of N.). It is aligned with the superstructure, although not centrally located within it. (pl. L.)

Burial: Nothing remained.

Objects: 1. A red ware jar, 36.5 cm. high×27 cm. max. diam. (pl. XLIX.) Adams R.32. Rijksmuseum, Leiden F1963/8.10. This jar and no. 2 are identical.
   2. A red ware jar, 36.5 cm. high×27 cm. max. diam. (pl. XLIX.) Adams R.32. Birmingham Museum 136′63.

Grave 192C.5

Superstructure: A rectangular, mud-brick structure, 6.35×6.25 m., with 1.2 m. still remaining. The pyramid would have been about 9 m. tall and the interior filled with stone and rubble. At the SE side is a brick offering chapel, 1.15 m. deep×1.5 m. wide. It is at the centre of the wall and not aligned with the grave pit, which is off centre.

Grave: Type I, 1.9×1.2×0.6 m. It is orientated NW–SE (42° W. of N.) as is the superstructure, but is located towards the north corner of it.

Burial: There was a fragment of the skull of an adult.

Objects: None were found.

CEMETERY 192D

THIS sub-site consists of a group of four graves, which lie in a straight line running north to south and are about 8 m. apart from one another (pl. XLIV). The exact location of the site is not recorded, but it probably lies along the eastern edge of Cemetery 192, just at the base of a sandstone hillside. The four graves are all quite similar and their contents place them in the same date region as 192.

Grave 192D.1

Superstructure: A rubble mound, 4.8 m. diam. and 0.5 m. high.

Grave: Type IV, 1.87×1.1×1 m., the entrance being 0.68 m. long and the orientation ENE–WSW (65° E. of N.). (pl. LI.)

Burial: Nothing remained.

Objects: 1. A red ware cup, 9 cm. high×10 cm. max. diam. (pl. LI). Adams R.1. Reading Museum 83:67/12.

Grave 192D.2

Superstructure: A stone-covered rubble tumulus, 7.5 m. diam. and 0.55 m. high.

Grave: Type IV, 2.5×1.1×0.98 m., the entrance adding 0.48 m. to the length. The orientation is E.–W. (82° E. of N.).

Burial: None remained.

Objects: 1. A brown ware, ribbed amphora with a cream slip and brown painted 'splash' decoration, 37.8 cm. high ×20.2 cm. max. diam. (pl. LI.) Adams W.30. Leeds University.

2. A red ware flask with black and white painted horizontal parallel bands, 24.4 cm. high×18.8 cm. max. diam. (pl. LI.) Adams R.1. Reading Museum 83:67/13.

3. A red ware flask with black and white painted decoration, 26.8 cm. high×17.7 cm. max. diam. (pl. LI.) Adams R.1. Cairo, Egyptian Museum 89702.

4. A red ware bottle, 10.6 cm. high×10.2 cm. max. diam. (pl. LI.) Adams R.1. Cairo, Egyptian Museum 89703.

5. A small, brown ware cup 4.3 cm. high×7.6 cm. max. diam. (pl. LI.) Adams R.1. Cairo, Egyptian Museum 89704.

6. A red ware cup, 8.8 cm. high×10.2 cm. max. diam. (pl. LI.) Adams R.1. Nicholson Museum 63.195.

7. An iron *kohl* stick, 16 cm. long. (pl. LI.) University College London 19544.

Grave 192D.3

Superstructure: A rubble mound, 6 m. diam. and 0.7 m. high.

Grave: Type IV, 1.7×0.87×0.98 m. The entrance is 0.58 m. long and the grave is orientated N.–S.

Burial: Nothing remained.

Objects: 1. A red ware flask with painted decoration of black and white horizontal bands, 27 cm. high×18 cm. max. diam. (pl. LI.) Adams R.1. Aberdeen Anthropological Museum 1109².

Grave 192D.4

Superstructure: A stone-covered rubble mound, 7 m. diam. and 0.8 m. high.

Grave: Type II, 2.62×1.25×1.12 m., orientated ENE–WSW (78° E. of N.).

Burial: Only the skull of an adult was found.

Objects: The fragments of an X-group flask.

CEMETERY 193

CEMETERY 193 was originally located and numbered by Emery and Kirwan during their survey and graves 1 to 29 were excavated to confirm the similarity of the Qaṣr Ibrîm cemeteries to the Ballâna and Quṣṭul tombs. Those twenty-nine graves were published in 1935[1] and it is not the intention to reproduce that earlier report here. The reader is referred to that publication for it. The graves have, however, been included in the present site plan (pls. LXXXII, LXXXIII), although the recognition of each was done from memory and may not be accurate.

The site lies in the area immediately to the south of the hill upon which the citadel is situated. The area is large, covering about 32 ha., and fills a large plain and the two *wâdi* mouths that debouch into it. The ground is generally a fossil alluvium, which overlies the local Nubian sandstone, of which there are a number of low outcrops from place to place. The steep sandstone cliffs rise up on all the perimeter of the site except along the river side at the west. Apart from one or two places, the graves are not crowded together (pl. LXXXV.1). Presumably, this spacing out over the site is due partly to the site not having been used for a protracted period of time, partly to the relatively large superstructures (tumuli) over the graves, and partly to the fact that the available fossil alluvium was so extensive.

The dating of this cemetery in broad terms is simple and sheds some light on the attitude of the Ballâna people to their cemetery ground. The earliest graves excavated were those of the Ballâna culture.[2] These appear in the following report. There were also a large number, perhaps 150, of rectangular superstructures, built of un-

dressed, local boulder stones, standing a metre or so high and generally orientated east to west. These were clustered together at the north-west corner of the site, i.e. the area nearest to the citadel hill (pl. LXXXV. 2). There were also a few, domed, rectangular mud-brick *gubba* structures at the west side of the site, an example of which is shown on pl. LXXXV. 3. It was assumed that all these dated to the Christian period and none of them was excavated. There was in addition a number of apparently Christian burials intruded into the mounds of various graves, e.g. nos. 30, 33. Probably, also, many of the X-group tombs were reused during the Christian occupation at Ibrîm. It seems a reasonable assumption that this burial ground, at the south side of the citadel, came into use during the Ballâna habitation, after the northern cemetery, 192, became filled.

It is interesting to note an observation of Emery on the condition of this site. Some 50 per cent of the X-group tombs here had been opened during the period between his survey investigation of the site in the 1930s and the 1961 season. Most of the tombs, however, were apparently plundered anciently, either by the Ballâna people themselves or a subsequent culture.

There follows a description of the individual tombs recorded by the expedition. Although the first grave, no. 30, was published in 1967,[3] the information has been enlarged and reorganized to correspond with the present format and it is republished here.

Grave 193.30

Superstructure: A stone-covered rubble mound, 20 m. diam. and 2.5 m. high (pl. LXXXV. 4). In the mound is

[1] W. B. Emery and L. P. Kirwan, *Survey*, 268–77.

[2] The only possible exception to this is a rock-cut pit-and-end-chamber grave, cut into the south hillside of the citadel. This had a total length of 5.81 m and a depth of 1.13 m, but was completely empty. The grave had a 'Meroïtic appearance', but contained no dating evidence, and must be discounted.

[3] W. B. Emery, 'Preliminary Report . . .', in *Fouilles en Nubie (1961–1963)*, 58–9, figs. 2, 3.

an intrusive burial. The grave is rectangular and built of mud-bricks, 1.9×0.4 m. The burial was the articulated body of a young adult male, lying dorsally extended, head to the west, the hands at the sides. Beside the pelvis was:

1. A sandstone stamp seal, conical in shape, with a rectangular base, 5×3.4 cm. (pl. LIV.) Durham GM 1964 566.

Grave: Type IV, 3.39×1.5×2.08 m. The entrance, which was completely filled with stones, is an additional 1 m. long. The bottom 0.6 m. of the grave is cut into bedrock. A unique feature of this grave is a cross, 28 cm. high×24 cm. wide, carefully carved on the east end of the grave pit (pl. LXXXV. 5). Nearby is a small semicircular niche 12 cm. high, presumably intended to hold a lamp. The orientation of the grave is NW–SE (46° W. of N.). (pl. LII).

Burial: Only the scattered bones of an adult male were found.

Objects: 2. A white biscuit ware cup with brown and white parallel horizontal painted bands, 7.8 cm. high×8.1 cm. max. diam. (pl. LII.) Adams W.30. Nicholson Museum 63.179.

3. The fragmentary remains of a wooden casket with decorative inlays of four carved ivory plaques and a bronze lock. Only the ivory plaques were recovered. Three of them were vertically mounted and have rounded tops, the fourth is horizontal, rectangular, and bears a sphinx behind a cobra. The three vertical pieces are decorated individually, one with a Hathor(?) head, another with a male youth, and the third with a standing (? dancing) female figure. (pl. LIV.) Cairo, Egyptian Museum 89663.

4. A red ware jar with a white painted neck, 23.1 cm. high×19.2 cm. max. diam. (pl. LIII.) Adams R.1. Royal Ontario Museum 963.15.2.

5. A red ware jar, decorated with painted horizontal parallel black and white bands, 32.7 cm. high×19.8 cm. max. diam. (pl. LIII.) Adams R.1. Royal Ontario Museum 963.15.3.

6. A ribbed, buff ware amphora, 30.9 cm. high×18 cm. max. diam. (pl. LIII.) Adams R.1. Nicholson Museum 63.180.

7. A red ware jar with a white painted neck and red and white spots around the neck, 29.1 cm. high×19.5 cm. max. diam. (pl. LIV.) Adams R.1. British Museum 66541.

8. A red ware amphora with a white painted neck, 36.1 cm. high×20.1 cm. max. diam. (pl. LIII.) Adams R.1. Otago Museum E62.11.

9. A red ware jar with yellow and black painted horizontal parallel bands, 27 cm. high×19.2 cm. max. diam. (pl. LIII.) Adams R.1. Royal Ontario Museum 963.15.4.

10. A cream biscuit ware cup, 6 cm. high×10.8 cm. max. diam. (pl. LII.) Adams W.30(?). Queen's University, Belfast QAD/7/128.

11. A red ware ribbed amphora, 36 cm. high×19.5 cm. max. diam. (pl. LII.) Adams R.1. Liverpool University E6337.

12. A red ware jar with a white painted neck and painted decoration in black and white, 28.8 cm. high× 18 cm. max. diam. (pl. LIV, LXXVII.) Adams R.1. Otago Museum E62.7.

13. A red ware jar with a white painted neck and black and yellow painted 'splash' decoration, 30.6 cm. high× 19.9 cm. max. diam. (pl. LIII.) Adams R.1. Durham GM 1964 553.

14. A red ware jar with white painted neck, 27 cm. high×19.2 cm. max. diam. (pl. LIV.) Adams R.1. Aberdeen Anthropological Museum 1109².

15. A red ware jar with white painted decoration, 28.8 cm. high×19.2 cm. max. diam. (pl. LIV.) Adams R.1. Rijksmuseum, Leiden F1963/8:1.

16. Traces of a wooden bier, originally painted with pitch. The body had originally lain on this.

17. A cream biscuit ware cup, 5.5 cm. high×10.2 cm. max. diam. (pl. LII.) Adams W.30(?). Otago Museum E62.26.

18. A cream biscuit ware cup, 6 cm. high×9 cm. max. diam. (pl. LII.) Adams W.30(?). Reading Museum 83:67/1.

Grave 193.31

Superstructure: A stone-covered rubble tumulus, 5.35 m. diam. and 0.75 m. high.

Grave: Type I, 1.3×0.67×1 m. The orientation is NNW–SSE (15° W. of N.). There is a flat stone lying on the grave floor at the south end. (pl. LIV.)

Burial: Only the skull of an adult.

Objects: 1. A red ware flask, decorated with two incised lines below the neck. 16 cm. high×12 cm. max. diam. (pl. LIV.) Adams R.1. Royal Ontario Museum 963.15.1.

Grave 193.32

Superstructure: A stone-covered rubble tumulus.

Grave: Type II, 3.1×1.5×1.5 m. The lower 0.95 m. is cut into bedrock and the crown of the vault lies partly within the tumulus. The orientation is NNW–SSE (26° W. of N.).

Burial: A few scattered bones.

Objects: 1. An iron nail, 10.6 cm. long. (pl. LV.) University College London 19543.

2. Eleven single-barb arrowheads, varying in length from 3.1 cm. to 6 cm. (pl. LV.) University College London 19538.

Grave 193.33

Superstructure: A rubble tumulus, 23 m. diam. and 5.5 cm. high. Within this mound were three intrusive graves:

INTRUSIVE GRAVE A is a vaulted chamber, 2.27 × 0.68 × 0.32 m. high, within a square, mud-brick enclosure, which was probably originally 3 m. along each side and which remained standing 0.87 m. Neither burial nor objects were associated with this grave.

INTRUSIVE GRAVE B is a surface burial of a child, lying extended on the right side, head to the east, facing north. Found on the right ankle was:

1. An iron anklet, 4.5 cm. diam. and 0.4 cm. thick, made by twisting an iron bar several times and then forming it into a ring. The ends are looped back. (pl. LV.) Location uncertain.

INTRUSIVE GRAVE C is a vaulted chamber, 2.78 × 0.87 m., within a rectangular structure, 3.48 × 2.1 m., constructed of mud-brick and partly of stone. No burial or objects are associated with this grave.

In addition, two inscriptions were found on the top of this mound, which were most probably placed there in association with the intrusive graves, although this could not be definitely determined.

2. Part of a small, rectangular, sandstone plaque, 20.5 × 20 × 5.5 cm. thick, with eight incised horizontal lines of Coptic text. (pls. LXXVI, XCI. 1.) Durham GM 1964 560. This text is fully described below on p. 82 f.

3. A small, round-topped, sandstone stela, 37.5 × 15.5 × 8.5 cm. thick. The Coptic inscription, which is not completely preserved, is in sixteen, horizontal, incised lines. The stela was broken in two. (pls. LXXV, XCI. 2.) British Museum 66582. This text is fully described below on p. 83.

Grave: Type IV, 2.65 × 1.75 × 1.5 m., with the entrance an additional 2.35 m. long. (pl. LV.)

Burial: The scattered bones of an adult.

Objects: Traces of a linen shroud and three iron nails.

Grave 193.34

Superstructure: A stone-covered rubble mound, 8 m. diam. and 0.55 m. high.

Grave: Type IV, 2.6 × 1.15 × 1 m. The orientation is ENE–WSW (66° E. of N.). (pl. LV.)

Burial: The articulated skeleton of an adult female, lying dorsally extended, head facing SE.

Objects: 1. A red ware flask, decorated with incised parallel lines and alternating black and white painted parallel lines. 24 cm. high × 16.2 cm. max. diam. (pl. LV.) Adams R.1. Cairo, Egyptian Museum 89664.

2. A red ware flask, decorated with parallel horizontal incised and painted black and white lines. 24 cm. high × 16.2 cm. max. diam. (pl. LV.) Adams R.1. Leeds University.

3. A cream biscuit ware cup, decorated with a red painted mouth, 6.9 cm. high × 7.8 cm. max. diam. (pl. LV.) Adams W.30. Cairo, Egyptian Museum 89665. This cup was found inverted on the mouth of the flask, no. 2.

4. A glass pedestal cup, 9.6 cm. high × 9.3 cm. max. diam. (pl. LV.) Sheffield Museum 1966.295. This cup was found inverted on the mouth of the flask, no. 1. It was broken.

Grave 193.35

Superstructure: A stone-covered rubble mound, 5.3 m. diam. and 0.5 m. high.

Grave: Type I, 2.4 × 1.4 × 1.2 m. The orientation is NW–SE (35° W. of N.). The grave utilizes a vertical face of the bedrock for one wall.

Burial: The trunk and head of an infant were found in the south corner of the grave pit. However, the size of the grave indicates an original burial of an adult, no trace of which latter was found. There is no indication of the date of the infant burial.

Objects: None were found.

Grave 193.36

Superstructure: A stone-covered rubble tumulus, 4.9 m. diam. and 0.4 m. high.

Grave: Type I, 1.9 × 0.6 × 1 m. The orientation is NE–SW (57° E. of N.).

Burial: Some scattered bones of an adult.

Objects: None were found.

Grave 193.37

Superstructure: A stone-covered rubble tumulus, 5.5 m. diam. and 0.6 m. high.

Grave: Type IV, 1.87 × 1.3 × 0.95 m., with an orientation of E.–W. (87° W. of N.). At the west end is an entrance forecourt, 1.45 × 1.3 m., which is 0.5 m. above the grave floor and which is paved with mud-bricks. (pl. LVII.)

Burial: The body of a child, lying dorsally extended, head west. The skull was missing. This is perhaps a secondary Christian burial in an X-group grave.

Objects: None were found.

Grave 193.38

Superstructure: A stone-covered rubble tumulus, 8.8 m. diam. and 0.9 m. high.

Grave: Type VI, 2.3 × 0.35 × 0.5 m. The entrance shaft is 2.3 × 1.3 × 1.7 m. Orientation is ENE–WSW (66° E. of N.). (pl. LVI.)

Burial: The articulated legs and pelvic girdle (? *in situ*) of an adult female(?). Assuming these bones to be

E

undisturbed, the burial was placed in a crouched position on the right side with the head to the WSW. Other bones were scattered in the grave.

Objects: 1. A red ware jar with a matt cream slip. 21 cm. high×11.4 cm. max. diam. (pl. LVI.) Adams W.28. Reading Museum 83:67/2.

2. A buff ware, footed amphora with red painted 'splash' decoration on the shoulder. 29.1 cm. high×16.2 cm. max. diam. (pl. LVI.) Adams W.30. Durham GM 1964 551.

3. A red ware jar, decorated with parallel incised and black and white painted lines. 24.6 cm. high×15.6 cm. max. diam. (pl. LVI.) Adams R.1. Durham GM 1964 554.

4. A red ware footed cup, 12.1 cm. high×10.8 cm. max. diam. (pl. LVI.) Adams R.1. Royal Ontario Museum 963.15.5.

5. A red ware footed cup, 10.3 cm. high×11.7 cm. max. diam. (pl. LVI.) Adams R.1. Manchester Museum.

6. A red ware footed cup, decorated with incised horizontal lines and painted white vertical lines. 8.4 cm. high×9.6 cm. max. diam. (pl. LVI.) Adams R.1. Durham GM 1964 573.

7. A red ware bottle, decorated with incised horizontal parallel lines and white painted 'splash' and 'festoon' elements. 30.3 cm. high×19.2 cm. max. diam. (pls. LVI, LXXX.) Adams R.1. Manchester Museum.

8. A moulded red ware lamp with a frog on the top. The oval top is 8.7 cm. max. and the lamp is 3 cm. high. (pl. LVI.) Adams W.2. Ashmolean Museum 1962.940.

9. A cream biscuit ware cup, 8.7 cm. high×8.4 cm. max. diam. (pl. LVI.) Adams W.30. Location uncertain.

10. An assortment of shell disc, faience and white glass barrel, glass ball and red jasper drop pendant beads. No stringing order is preserved. (pl. LVII.) University College London 19550.

Grave 193.39

Superstructure: A stone-covered rubble mound, 6.1 m. diam. and 1.1 m. high.

Grave: Type I, 2.12×0.7×0.75 m., with an orientation of E.–W. (83° E. of N.). (pl. LVII.)

Burial: The articulated body of an adult female, lying crouched on the right side, head west, facing south.

Objects: 1. A cream biscuit ware cup, 7.5 cm. high×8.4 cm. max. diam. (pl. LVII.) Adams W.30. Cambridge Museum of Arch. and Eth. 63.200.

2. Half a bracelet of about thirty glass beads, 4 mm. diam., on the left wrist. University College London 19556.

Grave 193.40

Superstructure: A stone-covered rubble mound, 4 m. diam. and 0.2 m. high.

Grave: Type I, 1.5×0.35×0.5 m. The orientation is NNW–SSE (25° W. of N.).

Burial: The articulated head, torso, and pelvis of a small child, lying dorsally extended, hands on the pelvis, at the south end of the grave pit.

Objects: None were found.

Grave 193.41

Superstructure: A stone-covered rubble tumulus, 5.1 m. diam. and 0.4 m. high.

Grave: Type I, 1.45×0.45×0.7 m. The orientation is NW–SE (35° W. of N.).

Burial: The skull of an adult was found at the bottom of the pit.

Objects: None were found.

Grave 193.42

Superstructure: A stone-covered mound, 6 m. diam. and 0.8 m. high.

Grave: Type I, 1.75×1.25×1 m., orientated NE–SW (54° E. of N.).

Burial: None remained.

Objects: None were found.

Grave 193.43

Superstructure: A stone-covered rubble mound, 6 m. diam. and 1.2 m. high.

Grave: Type I, 2×0.5×0.62 m. The orientation is NW–SE (37° W. of N.). (pl. LVII.)

Burial: The disturbed remains of an adult male. Sufficient of the skeleton was articulated to enable the original burial position to be determined as crouched on the left side with the head to the NW.

Objects: None were found.

Grave 193.44

Superstructure: A stone-covered rubble tumulus, 4.8 m. diam. and 0.75 m. high.

Grave: Type II, 1.62×0.9×0.7 m. The brick vault in this instance stands 0.35 m. above the original surface of the ground. The orientation is NE–SW (52° E. of N.).

Burial: The scattered bones of an adult male, a few joints articulated and showing an originally crouched position.

Objects: Fragments of a red ware, two-handled pottery flask.

Remnants of a thin, yellowed cloth, which was probably originally a shroud covering the body.

Grave 193.45

Superstructure: A stone-covered rubble mound, 6 m. diam. and 0.2 m. high.

Grave: Type I, 2.15×1.15×0.8 m., orientated NE–SW (48° E. of N.).

Burial: The articulated body of an adult, lying dorsally extended, head SW, hands beside the pelvis. There is a second skull of an adult in the grave, the remains of an earlier burial.

Objects: A fragment, about 30 cm. square, of coarse, dark brown cloth matting with yellow stripes.

Grave 193.46

Superstructure: A stone-covered rubble tumulus, 3.5 m. diam. and 0.4 m. high.

Grave: Type IV, 2.3×0.72×1.25 m., with the entrance an additional 0.98 m. long. The orientation is E.–W. (82° W. of N.).

Burial: The articulated body of an adult, lying dorsally extended, head west, hands on the pelvis.

Objects: None were found.

Grave 193.47

Superstructure: A stone-covered rubble tumulus, 4.2 m. diam. and 0.35 m. high.

Grave: Type I, 2×0.75×0.65 m., orientated E.–W. (86° E. of N.).

Burial: The scattered bones of an adult.

Objects: None were found.

Grave 193.48

Superstructure: A stone-covered rubble mound, 4.8 m. diam. and 1.1 m. high.

Grave: Type I, 2×0.67×0.57 m. The orientation is E.–W. (78° W. of N.).

Burial: The scattered bones of an adult female and of a child.

Objects: None were found.

Grave 193.49

Superstructure: A stone-covered rubble mound, 5.5 m. diam. and 0.7 m. high.

Grave: Type I, 1.75×0.82×0.7 m., with an orientation of E.–W. (82° W. of N.). (pl. LVIII.)

Burial: The scattered bones of a young adult male.

Objects: 1. A red ware jar, decorated with black and white painted 'splash' elements and with horizontal parallel incised lines. 21 cm. high×16.8 cm. max. diam. (pl. LVIII.) Adams R.1. Birmingham Museum 138'63.

2. A red ware bowl with a matt cream slip, 4.5 cm. high×10.2 cm. max. diam. (pl. LVIII.) Adams W.2. Aberdeen Anthropological Museum 1109². The bowl contained several date stones.

Grave 193.50

Superstructure: A stone-covered rubble tumulus, 6.5 m. diam. and 0.8 m. high.

Grave: Type I, 1.95×0.87×0.72 m. The orientation is ENE–WSW (69° E. of N.). (pl. LVIII.)

Burial: The scattered bones of an adult.

Objects: 1. A buff ware cup with a black painted rim stripe, 7.5 cm. high×7.2 cm. max. diam. (pl. LVIII.) Adams W.2. Birmingham Museum 120'63.

2. A red ware cup, 9.3 cm. high×9.6 cm. max. diam. (pl. LVIII.) Adams R.1. Birmingham Museum 122'63.

Grave 193.51

Superstructure: A stone-covered rubble tumulus, 5.3 m. diam. and 0.6 m. high.

Grave: Type I, 2×0.75×0.62 m., orientated NW–SE (35° W. of N.).

Burial: The scattered bones of an adult male. Enough joints were left articulated for the original position to be determined as flexed.

Objects: Fragments of some blue cloth, probably the remains of a shroud.

Grave 193.52

Superstructure: A stone-covered rubble mound, 5 m. diam. and 0.8 m. high.

Grave: Type I, 2.25×0.75×0.6 m. The orientation is ENE–WSW (75° E. of N.).

Burial: The scattered bones of an adult.

Objects: None were found.

Grave 193.53

Superstructure: A stone-covered rubble tumulus, 3.2 m. diam. and 0.1 m. high.

Grave: Type I, 1.5×0.5×0.6 m., orientated ENE–WSW (72° E. of N.).

Burial: None remained.

Objects: None were found.

Grave 193.54

Superstructure: A rubble mound, 3.6 m. diam. and 0.3 m. high.

Grave: Type III, 1.5×0.55×0.8 m., the entrance adding another 0.75 m. to the length. The orientation is ENE–WSW (71° E. of N.). (pl. LVIII.)

Burial: The scattered bones of an adult.

Objects: None were found.

Grave 193.55

Superstructure: A stone-covered rubble tumulus, 5.8 m. diam. and 1.1 m. high.

Grave: Type I, 1.75×0.8×0.67 m., orientated ENE–WSW (66° E. of N.). (pl. LVIII.)

Burial: None remained.

Objects: 1. A red ware cup, 9.3 cm. high×9.6 cm. max. diam. (pl. LVIII.) Adams R.1. Royal Ontario Museum 963.15.6.
    2. A red ware flask, 26.1 cm. high×19.2 cm. max. diam. (pl. LVIII.) Adams R.1. Reading Museum 83:67/3.
    3. A red ware flask, 24.6 cm. high×16.8 cm. max. diam. (pl. LVIII.) Adams R.1. Rijksmuseum, Leiden F1963/8.2.

Grave 193.56

Superstructure: A stone-covered rubble mound, 5.5 m. diam. and 1 m. high.

Grave: Type I, 2×0.55×0.6 m. The orientation is E.–W. (85° W. of N.).

Burial: The articulated body of an adult, lying dorsally extended, head west, hands on pelvis.

Objects: None were found.

Grave 193.57

Superstructure: A stone-covered rubble tumulus, 6.3 m. diam. and 0.9 m. high.

Grave: Type I, 2.25×0.8×0.6 m., orientated NE–SW (47° E. of N.).

Burial: None remained.

Objects: None were found.

Grave 193.58

Superstructure: A stone-covered rubble tumulus, 4.5 m. diam. and 0.4 m. high.

Grave: Type I, 2×0.4×0.6 m. The orientation is N.–S. (7° W. of N.).

Burial: The scattered bones of an adult.

Objects: None were found.

Grave 193.59

Superstructure: A stone-covered rubble mound, 3.2 m. diam. and 0.5 m. high.

Grave: Type I, 1.37×0.5×0.25 m., with undisturbed fill. The orientation is NE–SW (55° E. of N.).

Burial: The articulated body of a child, lying dorsally extended, head west, hands beside pelvis.

Objects: None were found.

Grave 193.60

Superstructure: A stone-covered rubble mound, 5.5 m. diam. and 0.8 m. high.

Grave: Type VI, 1.7×0.48×0.5 m., the entrance shaft being 1.8×0.8×1.1 m. The orientation is ENE–WSW (76° E. of N.).

Burial: The articulated body of a male adult, lying in a flexed position on the left side, head west.

Objects: None were found.

Grave 193.61

Superstructure: A stone-covered rubble tumulus, 5 m. diam. and 0.75 m. high.

Grave: Type I, 2×0.82×0.5 m.

Burial: The scattered bones of two adult (?) males.

Objects: None were found.

Grave 193.62

Superstructure: A stone-covered rubble tumulus, 5.3 m. diam. and 0.6 m. high.

Grave: Type I, 1.8×0.4×0.5 m. The orientation is NNW–SSE (26° W. of N.).

Burial: The scattered bones of a young adult.

Objects: 1. A red ware cup, decorated with parallel horizontal incised and painted black and white lines. 8.1 cm. high×9 cm. max. diam. (pl. LIX.) Adams R.1. Reading Museum 83:67/4.

Grave 193.63

Superstructure: A stone-covered rubble tumulus, 3.3 m. diam. and 0.7 m. high.

Grave: Type I, 1.5×0.82×0.8 m., orientated NE–SW (58° E. of N.).

Burial: The scattered bones of an adult.

Objects: None were found.

Grave 193.64

Superstructure: A stone-covered rubble mound, 2.7 m. diam. and 0.5 m. high.

Grave: Type I, 0.77×0.5×0.25 m., orientated NE–SW (50° E. of N.).

Burial: None was recovered.

Objects: None were found.

Grave 193.65

Superstructure: A stone-covered rubble mound, 4 m. diam. and 0.7 m. high.

Grave: Type I, 2.3×0.6×0.6 m., orientated ENE–WSW (60° E. of N.). (pl. LIX.)

Burial: The articulated body of an adult female, lying dorsally extended, head SW, left hand on the pelvis.

Objects: 1. A cream biscuit ware cup with brown painted decoration. 9.3 cm. high×9 cm. max. diam. (pl. LIX, LXXX.) Adams W.30. Blackburn Museum.

   2. A bracelet of white faience beads, 3 mm. diam. (pl. LIX.) Found on the left wrist of the body. University College London 19555.

Grave 193.66

Superstructure: A stone-covered rubble mound, 3 m. diam. and 0.1 m. high.

Grave: Type I, 1×0.4×0.3 m. The orientation is ENE–WSW (72° E. of N.).

Burial: The scattered bones of a child.

Objects: 1. A small red ware bottle with a yellow slip and painted decoration in black and red. 9 cm. high×7.8 cm. max. diam. (pl. LIX.) Adams W.30. A small piece of thin rope, found tied around the neck, was presumably originally to retain a lid or stopper. Cairo, Egyptian Museum 89666.

   2. A group of faience disc beads and one cowrie shell bead. (pl. LIX.) University College London 19548.

Grave 193.67

Superstructure: A stone-covered rubble tumulus, 3.5 m. diam. and 0.3 m. high.

Grave: Type I, 1.6×0.35×0.4 m., orientated E.–W. (86° E. of N.).

Burial: None remained.

Objects: Fragments of a red ware jar.

Grave 193.68

Superstructure: A stone-covered rubble tumulus, 2.5 m. diam. and 0.1 m. high.

Grave: Type I, 0.65×0.4×0.2 m., orientated NW–SE (33° W. of N.).

Burial: The skull of an infant.

Objects: None were found.

Grave 193.69

Superstructure: A stone-covered rubble mound, 5 m. diam. and 1 m. high.

Grave: Type I, 1.37×0.5×0.3 m. A natural vertical rock face and shelf are utilized to form part of this grave. (pl. LIX.)

Burial: The scattered bones of an adult. The burial must originally have been flexed or crouched in such a small grave.

Objects: 1. A red ware cup with white painted decoration. 6.6 cm. high×9 cm. max. diam. (pl. LIX.) Adams R.1. Liverpool University E6330.

   2. A group of blue faience cylinder beads, average diam. 4 mm. (pl. LIX.)

Grave 193.70

Superstructure: A stone-covered rubble tumulus, 3 m. diam. and 0.25 m. high.

Grave: Type I, 0.7×0.25×0.2 m. The orientation is E.–W. (82° E. of N.).

Burial: None remained.

Objects: None were found.

Grave 193.71

Superstructure: A stone-covered rubble mound, 3.8 m. diam. and 0.5 m. high.

Grave: Type I, 1.57×0.6×0.5 m., orientated NE–SW (53° E. of N.).

Burial: The scattered bones of an adult female and of an infant.

Objects: None were found.

Grave 193.72

Superstructure: A stone-covered rubble tumulus, 7.7 m. diam. and 0.8 m. high.

Grave: Type I, 1.9×0.65×0.55 m. The orientation is NNW–SSE (26° W. of N.).

Burial: The scattered bones of two adults.

Objects: None were found.

Grave 193.73

Superstructure: A stone-covered rubble mound, 4.5 m. diam. and 0.35 m. high.

Grave: Type I, 1.6×0.45×0.35 m., orientated ENE–WSW (70° E. of N.).

Burial: The scattered bones of two infants.

Objects: None were found.

Grave 193.74

Superstructure: A stone-covered rubble mound, 5 m. diam. and 0.6 m. high.

Grave: Type I, 2.1×0.45×0.5 m., orientated ENE–WSW (65° E. of N.).

Burial: The articulated bones of the upper half of an adult, lying dorsally extended, head to WSW.

Objects: None were found.

Grave 193.75

Superstructure: A stone-covered rubble tumulus, 3 m. diam. and 0.2 m. high.

Grave: Type I, 1.25×0.5×0.35 m. The orientation is ENE–WSW (71° E. of N.).

Burial: Nothing remained.

Objects: None were found.

Grave 193.76

Superstructure: A stone-covered rubble tumulus, 6 m. diam. and 0.5 m. high.

Grave: Type I, 2×0.4×0.3 m., orientated E.–W. (81° E. of N.).

Burial: The scattered bones of an adult female.

Objects: None were found.

Grave 193.77

Superstructure: A stone-covered rubble mound, 6 m. diam. and 0.7 m. high.

Grave: Type I, 2.44×0.6×0.6 m. The orientation is ENE–WSW (67° E. of N.).

Burial: The scattered bones of an adult.

Objects: None were found.

Grave 193.78

Superstructure: A stone-covered rubble mound, 4 m. diam. and 0.1 m. high.

Grave: Type VI, cut into bedrock, 1.65×0.35×0.42 m. The entrance shaft is 1.65×0.72×1 m. and orientation is WNW–ESE (79° W. of N.).

Burial: The scattered bones of two adults.

Objects: None were found.

Grave 193.79

Superstructure: A stone-covered rubble tumulus, 3 m. diam. and 0.15 m. high.

Grave: Type I, 2×0.55×0.2 m. The orientation is ENE–WSW (74° E. of N.).

Burial: The articulated body of a child, lying dorsally extended, head WSW, hands beside the pelvis.

Objects: None were found.

Grave 193.80

Superstructure: A stone-covered rubble tumulus, 2 m. diam. and 0.5 m. high.

Grave: Type I, 1×0.4×0.3 m., orientated E.–W. (86° E. of N.).

Burial: None remained.

Objects: None were found.

Grave 193.81

Superstructure: A stone-covered rubble mound, 4.1 m. diam. and 0.65 m. high.

Grave: Type I, 2×0.75×0.65 m., orientated E.–W. (81° E. of N.).

Burial: None remained.

Objects: None were found.

Grave 193.82

Superstructure: A stone-covered rubble mound, 2.5 m. diam. and 0.15 m. high.

Grave: Type I, 1.6×0.9×0.7 m. The orientation is E.–W. (88° E. of N.).

Burial: The scattered bones of a young adult, apparently originally lying in a semi-contracted position.

Objects: None were found.

Grave 193.83

Superstructure: A stone-covered rubble mound, 5.5 m. diam. and 0.7 m. high.

Grave: Type III, 1.65×0.8×0.8 m., the entrance pit adding a further 0.7 m. to the length. The orientation is NE–SW (53° E. of N.). (pl. LIX.)

Burial: The articulated skeleton of an adult, lying dorsally extended with the head to the NE and hands beside the pelvis.

Objects: A brown ware jar with matt cream slip and black painted decoration. Adams W.30. Also a part of a red ware cup, Adams R.1.

Grave 193.84

Superstructure: A stone-covered rubble tumulus, 2.25 m. diam. and 0.15 m. high.

Grave: Type I, 1.1×0.4×0.3 m., orientated E.–W. (80° E. of N.).

Burial: Nothing remained.

Objects: None were found.

Grave 193.85

Superstructure: A stone-covered rubble mound, 6 m. diam. and 0.4 m. high.

Grave: Type III, 1.48×0.8×0.9 m., with an entrance adding a further 0.75 m. to the length. The orientation is ENE–WSW (74° E. of N.).

Burial: The articulated body of an adult, lying dorsally extended, head to the ENE, hands on the pelvis. Also in the fill were the scattered bones of another adult.

Objects: None were found.

Grave 193.86

Superstructure: A stone-covered rubble mound, 3.7 m. diam. and 0.65 m. high.

Grave: Type I, 1.8×0.8×0.6 m., orientated E.–W. (82° E. of N.).

Burial: The scattered bones of an adult were found.

Objects: None were found.

Grave 193.87

Superstructure: A stone-covered rubble tumulus, 4 m. diam. and 0.25 m. high.

Grave: Type I, 1×0.45×0.55 m. The orientation is NE–SW (53° E. of N.).

Burial: The skull of a child.

Objects: None were found.

Grave 193.88

Superstructure: A stone-covered rubble mound, 2.75 m. diam. and 0.35 m. high.

Grave: Type I, 2×0.65×0.57 m., orientated E.–W. (87° W. of N.).

Burial: The scattered bones of a child.

Objects: None were found.

Grave 193.89

Superstructure: A stone-covered rubble mound, 3.6 m. diam. and 0.2 m. high.

Grave: Type II, 1.75×0.7×0.6 m. The orientation is ENE–WSW (73° E. of N.).

Burial: None remained.

Objects: None were found.

Grave 193.90

Superstructure: A stone-covered rubble tumulus, 2.2 m. diam. and 0.35 m. high.

Grave: Type I, 1.2×0.4×0.35 m., orientated WNW–ESE (73° W. of N.).

Burial: The scattered bones of a child.

Objects: None were found.

Grave 193.91

Superstructure: A stone-covered rubble mound, 3.2 m. diam. and 0.3 m. high.

Grave: Type I, 1.35×0.4×0.55 m. The orientation is WNW–ESE (73° W. of N.).

Burial: Nothing remained.

Objects: None were found.

Grave 193.92

Superstructure: A stone-covered rubble tumulus, 3.5 m. diam. and 0.1 m. high.

Grave: Type I, 0.8×0.65×0.6 m., orientated ENE–WSW (76° E. of N.).

Burial: Nothing remained.

Objects: None were found.

Grave 193.93

Superstructure: A stone-covered rubble mound, 3.8 m. diam. and 0.5 m. high.

Grave: Type I, 2×0.85×0.8 m., with the orientation NW–SE (43° W. of N.).

Burial: The articulated body of an adult male, lying in a flexed position on the left side, head NW.

Objects: None were found.

Grave 193.94

Superstructure: A stone-covered rubble tumulus, 4 m. diam. and 0.5 m. high.

Grave: Type I, 1.52×0.8×1.1 m., orientated NNW–SSE (23° W. of N.). (pl. LIX.)

Burial: The scattered bones of a child.

Objects: 1. A brown ware amphora with a matt cream slip. 22.5 cm. high×12.6 cm. max. diam. (pl. LIX.) Adams W.28. Ashmolean Museum 1962.929.

2. A brown ware jar with a matt cream slip. 15.9 cm. high×15.6 cm. max. diam. (pl. LIX.) Adams W.30. Manchester Museum 20952.

Grave 193.95

Superstructure: A stone-covered rubble tumulus, 4 m. diam. and 0.4 m. high.

Grave: Type I, 1.5×0.62×0.65 m. The orientation is NNW–SSE (25° W. of N.).

Burial: None was found.

Objects: 1. A string of white faience disc beads, average diam. 4 mm. (pl. LIX.) Nicholson Museum 63.210.

Grave 193.96

Superstructure: An earth mound, 2.5 m. diam. and 0.5 m. high.

Grave: Type I, 1.1×0.6×0.6 m., orientated ENE–WSW (67° E. of N.).

Burial: None remained.

Objects: None were found.

Grave 193.97

Superstructure: An earth mound, 4 m. diam. and 0.5 m. high.

Grave: Type I, 2.25×0.97×1.25 m. The orientation is NW–SE (37° W. of N.).

Burial: The articulated body of an adult female, lying dorsally extended, head to the NW, hands on the pelvis.

Objects: None were found.

Grave 193.98

Superstructure: A stone-covered rubble tumulus, 6.5 m. diam. and 0.7 m. high.

Grave: Type I, 1.75×0.75×1 m., orientated N.–S. (7° E. of N.). (pl. LIX.)

Burial: The body of a small child, lying dorsally extended in a broken amphora.

Objects: None were found.

Grave 193.99

Superstructure: A stone-covered rubble tumulus, 6 m. diam. and 0.4 m. high.

Grave: Type I, 2.75×0.85×0.8 m., orientated ENE–WSW (72° E. of N.).

Burial: The articulated body of a child, lying semi-contracted on the back, head WSW, was found 0.25 m. above the floor of the grave. There were also found the scattered bones of an adult.

Objects: None were found.

Grave 193.100

Superstructure: A stone-covered rubble mound, 3.5 m. diam. and 0.1 m. high.

Grave: A rectangular chamber, 1.1×0.8×0.32 m. high, attained through a central entrance hole, 0.87×0.52×0.25 m. deep. The orientation is E.–W. (88° W. of N.).

Burial: The leg of a child.

Objects: None were found.

Grave 193.101

Superstructure: An earth tumulus, 5 m. diam. and 0.4 m. high.

Grave: Type I, 1.87×0.8×0.75 m., orientated ENE–WSW (78° E. of N.). (pl. LIX.)

Burial: None remained.

Objects: 1. A red ware cup, 9 cm. high×11.4 cm. max. diam. (pl. LIX.) Adams R.1. Rijksmuseum, Leiden F1963/8.3.

2. An iron javelin blade, 7.5 cm. long×2.7 cm. wide, with a tang of 2.7 cm. length. A slight twist of leather at the tang gives evidence of how the blade was bound on to its shaft. (pl. LIX, LXXXVI. 7.) University College London 19542.

Grave 193.102

Superstructure: An earth tumulus, 3.5 m. diam. and 0.4 m. high.

Grave: Type I, 1.7×0.6×0.5 m. The orientation is NNW–SSE (17° W. of N.).

Burial: None remained.

Objects: None were found.

Grave 193.103

Superstructure: An earth mound, 4 m. diam. and 0.4 m. high.

Grave: Type I, 1.65×0.67×0.73 m., orientated ENE–WSW (66° E. of N.).

Burial: Some scattered bones of an adult(?).

Objects: None were found.

Grave 193.104

Superstructure: A stone-covered rubble tumulus, 5 m. diam. and 0.5 m. high.

Grave: Type I, 1.75×0.63×0.87 m. The orientation is NE–SW (51° E. of N.). (pl. LX.)

Burial: Only the skull of an adult was found.

Objects: 1. A wooden archer's finger loose, 3.3 cm. long× 4.7 cm. max. diam. A fingernail and some skin were found adhering to the interior of the hole. (pl. LX.) Location uncertain.

2. A red ware jar, 31.5 cm. high×22.8 cm. max. diam. (pl. LX.) Adams R.1. Manchester Museum 20953.

3. Roughly shaped white stone pendant beads. (pl. LX.) University College London 19547.

Grave 193.105

Superstructure: No trace remained.

Grave: Type I, 1.9×0.67×0.87 m., orientated ENE–WSW (67° E. of N.).

Burial: The scattered bones of an adult female.

Objects: 1. Half a patterned woollen carpet, apparently deliberately cut in two. (pl. LXXXVIII. 1.) British Museum 66708. This piece has been studied by Mr Donald King of the Victoria and Albert Museum and his report is found below on p. 87.

Also found in this tomb were fragments of a blue cloth, which, together with the carpet, had wrapped the body.

Grave 193.106

Superstructure: No trace remained.

Grave: Type I, 2×0.75×0.65 m. The orientation is NE–SW (38° E. of N.).

Burial: The scattered bones of an adult male.

Objects: The fragmentary remains of a leather basket and of a red ware flask (Adams R.1).

Grave 193.107

Superstructure: An earth mound, 6.1 m. diam. and 0.75 m. high.

Grave: Type I, 2.15×1.02×1.23 m. The orientation is ENE–WSW (58° E. of N.).

Burial: The scattered bones of an adult male.

Objects: 1. A pair of leather sandals, 25 cm. long. (pl. LX.) Ashmolean Museum 1962.954a, b.

3. The remains of a leather arrow quiver. The top, decorated by tooling, together with the loop handle, is 20 cm. in length with an inside diam. of 4.4 cm. Part of the bag of the quiver has perished, but some 24 cm. still remains. (pl. LX.) Ashmolean Museum 1962.951.

Also found were the largely destroyed remains of a pair of unused sandals and the remains of a twisted gut bowstring.

Grave 193.108

Superstructure: A stone-covered rubble tumulus, 2.75 m. diam. and 0.08 m. high.

Grave: Type I, 1.7×0.75×0.5 m.

Burial: The articulated trunk and limbs of a small child, lying in a contracted position on the left side.

Objects: 1. A red ware cup, with black and white painted decoration, 8.1 cm. high×9.6 cm. max. diam. (pl. LX.) Adams R.1. Otago Museum E62.23.

Grave 193.109

Superstructure: A stone-covered rubble mound, 5 m. diam. and 0.15 m. high.

Grave: Type III, 1.75×0.75×0.45 m., the entrance ramp being an additional 0.8 m. long. The orientation is NNW–SSE (28° W. of N.).

Burial: The skull of an adult.

Objects: 1. A ribbed, red ware amphora, 38.7 cm. high× 19.8 cm. max. diam. (pl. LXI.) Adams R.1. Aberdeen Anthropological Museum 1109[2].

Grave 193.110

Superstructure: A stone-covered rubble tumulus, 4.5 m. diam. and 0.25 m. high.

Grave: Type I, 2.5×0.87×0.65 m., orientated ENE–WSW (69° E. of N.).

Burial: None remained.

Objects: None were found.

Grave 193.111

Superstructure: An earth tumulus, 5 m. diam. and 0.5 m. high.

Grave: Type I, 2×0.65×0.77 m.

Burial: The scattered bones of an adult.

Objects: 1. A cream biscuit ware cup with brown painted decoration, 7.5 cm. high×9 cm. max. diam. (pls. LX, LXXX.) Adams W.30. Otago Museum E62.25.

2. A group of white faience cylinder beads, average 4 mm. long. (pl. LX.) University College London 19546.

Grave 193.112

Superstructure: An earth mound, 4.5 m. diam. and 0.4 m. high.

Grave: Type I, 1.85×0.62×0.67 m. The orientation is NW–SE (42° W. of N.).

Burial: The scattered bones of an adult.

Objects: None were found.

Grave 193.113

Superstructure: A stone-covered rubble tumulus, 3.7 m. diam. and 0.1 m. high.

Grave: Type I, 1.1×0.6×0.55 m., orientated E.–W. (84° E. of N.).

Burial: None remained.

Objects: 1. A group of shell disc beads, average 2 mm. diam. (pl. LX.) University College London 19553.

Grave 193.114

Superstructure: An earth tumulus, 5 m. diam. and 0.5 m. high.

Grave: Type I, 1.87×0.57×0.5 m., orientated NNW–SSE (13° W. of N.).

Burial: The articulated skeleton of an adult male, lying dorsally extended, head NNW, the hands resting on the pelvis.

Objects: None were found.

Grave 193.115

Superstructure: A stone-covered rubble mound, 3.8 m. diam.

Grave: Type I, 2.9×0.9×0.5 m., orientated ENE–WSW (72° E. of N.).

Burial: Nothing remained.

Objects: None were found.

Grave 193.116

Superstructure: A stone-covered rubble mound 4 m. diam. and 0.5 m. high.

Grave: Type I, 1.55×0.75×0.62 m. The orientation is NE–SW (38° E. of N.).

Burial: The scattered bones of an adult.

Objects: Fragments of a coarse linen body wrapping.

Grave 193.117

Superstructure: An earth mound, 5 m. diam. and 0.5 m. high.

Grave: Type I, 2×0.78×0.7 m., orientated NE–SW (48° E. of N.).

Burial: None remained.

Objects: None were found.

Grave 193.118

Superstructure: A stone-covered rubble mound, 4 m. diam. and 0.5 m. high.

Grave: Type I, 1.7×0.85×0.63 m., orientated NE–SW (55° E. of N.).

Burial: The articulated body of an adult male, lying on the right side in a crouched position, head to the SW.

Objects: Some yellow(ed) cloth, which was wrapped around the body.

Grave 193.119

Superstructure: A stone-covered tumulus.

Grave: Type I, 2.4×0.45×0.35 m. The orientation is NNW–SSE (19° W. of N.).

Burial: None remained.

Objects: None were found.

Grave 193.120

Superstructure: A stone-covered rubble tumulus, 18 m. diam. and 2.25 m. high.

Grave: Type IV, 3×1.5×1.7 m., the entrance adding a further 2 m. to the length. The orientation is ENE–WSW (73° E. of N.).

Burial: The scattered bones of a young adult.

Objects: 1. Part of an iron strap, 1.2 cm. wide, with a series of bends in it which presumably originally fitted a wooden box or some such container. (pl. LXI.) Location uncertain.

Grave 193.121

Superstructure: A stone-covered rubble tumulus, 21.3 m. diam. and 4.5 m. high.

Grave: Type II, 2.7×1.5×1.65 m., orientated NNW–SSE (27° W. of N.).

Burial: Nothing remained.

Objects: 1. A pink ware, ribbed amphora with a matt cream slip, 56.4 cm. high×24.6 cm. max. diam. (pl. LXI.) Adams U.3. There are two dockets on the shoulder, one (a) in black ink, and one (b) in red ink, both reproduced here in copies kindly made by Dr G. T. Martin. Their interpretation is problematic. Two further red dockets, at the handles, are too faint to be copied with certainty.

(*a*)

(*b*)

Cambridge Museum of Arch. and Eth. 63.191.

2. A red ware jar, decorated with parallel horizontal painted black and white bands, 31.2 cm. high×21.6 cm. max. diam. (pl. LXI.) Adams R.1. Reading Museum 118:65/3.

3. A brown ware jar with a matt cream slip, 30.8 cm. high×19.2 cm. max. diam. (pl. LXI.) Adams W.30. Queen's University, Belfast QAD/7/133.

4. Fragments of a pink ware amphora similar to no. 1, above.

5. Fragments of another similar pink ware amphora.

6. Portions of a brown ware jar with matt cream slip. (pl. LXI.) Adams W.30.

7. Part of a brown ware jar with matt cream slip and brown painted decoration. (pl. LXI.) Adams W.30.

8. Part of a red ware jar with black and yellow painted horizontal bands. (pl. LXI.) Adams R.1.

9. A portion of a cream biscuit ware cup with a red painted mouth. (pl. LXI.) Adams W.30.

10. Fragments of a red ware amphora.

11. Fragmentary glass of at least two dishes.

12. An iron nail, 6.1 cm. long. (pl. LXI.) University College London 19552.

13. A bronze ring, 3.1 cm. outside diam. and 0.3 cm. thick. (pl. LXI.). Nicholson Museum 63.213.

Grave 193.122

Superstructure: A stone-covered rubble mound, 12.6 m. diam. and 1.55 m. high.

Grave: Type I, 3.05×1.7×1 m. The orientation is WNW–ESE (63° W. of N.). (pl. LXII.)

Burial: The scattered bones of an adult.

Objects: 1. A brown ware jar with a yellow slip and black painted mouth, 25.2 cm. high×19.8 cm. max. diam. (pl. LXIII.) Adams W.30. Cairo, Egyptian Museum 89667.

2. A red ware jar, decorated with horizontal parallel incised lines, 27.6 cm. high×16.8 cm. max. diam. (pl. LXIII.) Adams R.1. Otago Museum E62.10.

3. A red ware footed cup with white painted 'festoon' decoration, 12.6 cm. high×12 cm. max. diam. (pl. LXII.) Adams R.1. Otago Museum E62.16.

4. A red ware footed cup with black and white painted 'festoon' decoration, 9.6 cm. high×11.4 cm. max. diam. (pl. LXII.) Adams R.1. Nicholson Museum 63.181.

5. A red ware footed cup with black and white painted lozenge decoration, 11.4 cm. high×11.4 cm. max. diam. (pl. LXII.) Adams R.1. Aberdeen Anthropological Museum 1109².

6. A red ware footed cup with white painted lozenge and streak decoration, 13.2 cm. high×12.6 cm. max. diam. (pl. LXII.) Adams R.1. Ashmolean Museum 1962.921.

7. A brown ware footed cup with a matt cream slip and brown painted decoration, 9.6 cm. high×7.8 cm. max. diam. (pl. LXII.) Adams W.30. Aberdeen Anthropological Museum 1109².

8. A brown ware jar with a matt cream slip and a brown painted vine decoration, 25.5 cm. high×19.8 cm. max. diam. The mouth is missing from this jar. (pls. LXIII, LXXVII.) Adams W.30. Fitzwilliam Museum E.3.1962. This jar and the following one, no. 9, are identical.

9. A brown ware jar, exactly similar to no. 8 above. (pl. LXIII.) British Museum 66556.

10. A red ware spouted vessel, enclosed but with a perforated top, 14.1 cm. high×13.2 cm. max. diam. (pl. LXIII.) Adams R.1. Cairo, Egyptian Museum 89668.

11. A brown ware cup with a matt cream slip and brown and white painted decoration around the rim, 9 cm. high×8.4 cm. max. diam. (pl. LXII.) Adams W.30. Durham GM 1964 579.

12. A small pestle of igneous rock, 6.1 cm. high×4.9 cm. max. diam. (pl. LXII.) Birmingham Museum 144'63a.

13. A brown ware jar, 6.9 cm. high×5.4 cm. max. diam. (pl. LXII.) This vessel had been used as a lamp and when found was inverted into the mouth of no. 14, below. Cairo, Egyptian Museum 89669.

14. A brown ware jar 16.5 cm. high×11.4 cm. max. diam. (pl. LXII.) It was heavy when found, and presumably contained oil, used as fuel for the lamp, no. 13, which was also used as a stopper for this vessel. Cairo, Egyptian Museum 89669.

15. An ivory *kohl* tube, 2.9 cm. diam. and 8.2 cm. long, found together with an iron *kohl* stick, 12 cm. long, enclosed in a leather case or jacket, the top third of which is tooled in a fluted manner. (pl. LXII.) Royal Ontario Museum 963.15.26a, b, c.

16. An iron corner fitting (? from a bier or a box), 6.5 cm. long ×3cm. wide on each side. It was originally attached with three round-headed nails on each side. (pl. LXII.) University College London 19549.

17. Beads of faience and glass in various small shapes. (pl. LXII.) University College London 19554.

Grave 193.123

Superstructure: A stone-covered rubble tumulus, 5.7 m. diam. and 0.85 m. high.

Grave: Type I, 2.6×0.8×0.85 m., orientated N.–S. (10° W. of N.).

Burial: Nothing remained.

Objects: None were found.

Grave 193.124

Superstructure: A stone-covered rubble mound 5.4 m. diam. and 0.45 m. high.

Grave: Type I, 1.2×0.8×0.55 m., orientated NW–SE (37° W. of N.).

Burial: Only the skull of a child remained.

Objects: None were found.

Grave 193.125

Superstructure: A stone-covered rubble tumulus, 6 m. diam. and 0.9 m. high.

Grave: Type I, 1.85×0.85×0.6 m. The orientation is NE–SW (39° E. of N.).

Burial: The skull of a child.

Objects: None were found.

Grave 193.126

Superstructure: A stone-covered rubble mound, 6.3 m. diam. and 0.5 m. high.

Grave: Type I, 1.95×0.5×0.65 m., orientated N.–S. (11° W. of N.). (pl. LXIII.)

Burial: The articulated leg of an adult.

Objects: 1. A portion of a red ware jug with black and white painted decoration.

2. Part of a small, red ware, one-handled jug with a black slip.

3. A red ware cup, 9 cm. high×9.6 cm. max. diam. (pl. LXIII.) Adams R.1. Manchester Museum 20954.

4. A leather sandal, 25.4 cm. long. (pl. LXIII.) Ashmolean Museum 1962.952.

Grave 193.127

Superstructure: A stone-covered rubble tumulus, 6.9 m. diam. and 1.4 m. high.

Grave: Type I, 1.55×0.95×0.5 m., orientated NNW–SSE (17° W. of N.).

Burial: None remained.

Objects: None were found.

Grave 193.128

Superstructure: A stone-covered rubble mound, 3.3 m. diam. and 0.15 m. high.

Grave: Type I, 1.5×1×0.6 m., orientated NNW–SSE (28° W. of N.).

Burial: The skull of a child.

Objects: None were found.

Grave 193.129

Superstructure: A stone-covered rubble mound, 4 m. diam. and 0.3 m. high.

Grave: Type I, 0.9×0.35×0.35 m. The orientation is NW–SE (55° W. of N.).

Burial: None remained.

Objects: None were found.

Grave 193.130

Superstructure: A stone-covered rubble tumulus, 4.3 m. diam. and 0.15 m. high.

Grave: Type I, 2×0.9×0.8 m., orientated ENE–WSW (68° E. of N.).

Burial: Nothing remained.

Objects: None were found.

Grave 193.131

Superstructure: A stone-covered rubble tumulus, 4.25 m. diam. and 0.35 m. high.

Grave: Type I, 2×0.5×0.4 m., orientated ENE–WSW (59° E. of N.).

Burial: The scattered bones of an adult.

Objects: None were found.

Grave 193.132

Superstructure: A stone-covered rubble mound, 9.5 m. diam. and 1.25 m. high.

Grave: Type IV, 2.5×1.35×1.38 m., the entrance pit adding another 1 m. to the length. The orientation is E.–W. (80° W. of N.).

Burial: The articulated, headless body of a young adult male, lying dorsally extended, head west, the hands on the pelvis.

Objects: None were found.

Grave 193.133

Superstructure: A stone-covered rubble tumulus, 18 m. diam. and 3 m. high.

Grave: Type IV, 2.37×1.75×1.60 m., the entrance pit being an additional 0.72 m. long. The orientation is NNW–SSE (27° W. of N.).

Burial: The bones of an adult male were found to have been heaped together in the south corner of the tomb.

Objects: 1. An archer's finger loose of black and white porphyritic rock, 4.3 cm. long. (pl. LXV.) Durham GM 1964 565.

2. A red ware cup, 11.4 cm. high×11.4 cm. max. diam. (pl. LXIV.) Adams R.1. Liverpool University E6326.

3. A brown ware jar, with a matt cream slip and red painted 'splash' decoration, 24.6 cm. high×18.6 cm. max. diam. (pl. LXIV.) Adams W.30. Liverpool University E6324.

4. A cream biscuit ware cup with brown painted decoration, 9.3 cm. high×7.5 cm. max. diam. (pl. LXIV.) Adams W.30. Reading Museum 83:67/21.

5. A red ware cup with white painted 'festoon' decoration, 11.1 cm. high×12 cm. max. diam. (pl. LXV.) Adams R.1. Ashmolean Museum 1962.924. This cup is identical to no. 7, below.

6. A red ware cup, 8.7 cm. high×9 cm. max. diam. (pl. LXIV.) Adams R.1. Ashmolean Museum 1962.923.

7. A red ware cup with white painted 'festoon' decoration, 11.1 cm. high×12 cm. max. diam. (pl. LXV.) Adams R.1. Liverpool University E6319. This cup is identical to no. 5, above.

8. A cream biscuit ware cup with brown painted decoration, 8.7 cm. high×7.8 cm. max. diam. (pl. LXIV.) Adams W.30. Royal Ontario Museum 963.15.20.

9. A red ware amphora, 36 cm. high×18.6 cm. max. diam. (pl. LXIV.) Adams R.1. Manchester Museum 20956.

10. A brown ware amphora, with a matt cream slip and black painted vine decoration, 35.4 cm. high × 18 cm. max. diam. (pl. LXIV.) Adams W.30. British Museum 66544.

11. A cream biscuit ware spouted cup with black and red painted decoration, 8.7 cm. high × 12.3 cm. max. diam. (pl. LXV, LXXX.) Adams W.30. Cairo, Egyptian Museum 89720.

12. A red ware flask with white painted 'splash' decoration, 25.5 cm. high × 18 cm. max. diam. (pl. LXIV.) Adams R.1. Liverpool University E6317.

13. A brown ware flask with matt cream slip and red painted 'splash' decoration, 26.1 cm. high × 17.4 cm. max. diam. (pl. LXV.) Adams W.30. Aberdeen Anthropological Museum 1109².

14. A cream biscuit ware cup with a decoration of red and black painted parallel bands, 9 cm. high × 9.13 cm. max. diam. (pl. LXV.) Adams W.30. British Museum 66569.

15. A cream biscuit ware cup, 7.5 cm. high × 8.7 cm. max. diam. (pl. LXV.) Adams W.30. Aberdeen Anthropological Museum 1109².

16. A red ware flask with black and white painted 'splash' decoration, 24.6 cm. high × 20.7 cm. max. diam. (pl. LXIV.) Adams R.1. Ashmolean Museum 1962.928.

17. Nine iron nails, average 10.6 cm. long, which were originally possibly part of a bier. (pl. LXV.) University College London 19541.

18. A large red ware amphora, 90 cm. high × 39.6 cm. max. diam. (pl. LXIV.) Adams U.9. University College London 19596.

Also found, but unregistered, are a red ware flask with white painted decoration; two red ware cups similar to no. 2, above; a cream biscuit ware cup similar to no. 15, above; and an undetermined number of glass cups.

Grave 193.134

Superstructure: A stone-covered rubble mound, 8 m. diam. and 0.9 m. high.

Grave: Type IV, 2.05 × 1 × 1.45 m. The entrance pit is 0.82 m. long and the orientation is NE–SW (55° E. of N.).

Burial: The articulated body of an adult female, lying dorsally extended, head to the SW and the hands on the pelvis.

Objects: 1. A pink ware flask with black painted horizontal bands on the shoulder, 28.8 cm. high × 20.1 cm. max. diam. (pl. LXV.) Adams R.1. Ashmolean Museum 1962.927.

2. A red ware flask with a white painted 'splash' decoration, 26.7 cm. high × 20.4 cm. max. diam. (pl. LXV.) Adams R.1. Location uncertain.

3. A red ware flask with a white painted 'splash'

decoration, 26.1 cm. high × 18.6 cm. max. diam. (pl. LXV.) Adams R.1. Ashmolean Museum 1962.936.

4. A cream biscuit ware cup, decorated with painted red spots on the rim, 8.4 cm. high × 8.4 cm. max. diam. (pl. LXV.) Adams W.30. Otago Museum E62.24.

5. Part of a brown ware amphora with matt cream slip and a black painted vine motif, 33.7 cm. high × 15.6 cm. max. diam. (pl. LXV.) Adams W.30. Location uncertain.

Also found in the grave were fragments of three small glass bowls or goblets (restored as nos. 6 and 7 on pl. LXV).

Grave 193.135

Superstructure: A rubble mound.

Grave: Type II, 2.5 × 1.7 × 1.42 m., orientated ENE–WSW (70° E. of N.). (pl. LXVI.)

Burial: The articulated body of an adult male, lying dorsally extended, with the head to WSW and the hands on the pelvis. The skin of this inhumation was preserved and was a deep black colour and had a varnished appearance. Possibly the condition was the result of an attempt at preservation or mummification.

Objects: 1. An archer's finger loose, made of black and white porphyritic stone, 4 cm. long × 4.1 cm. max. diam. (pl. LXVI.) Location uncertain.

2. The decayed remains of probably a wooden bed. These include the rectangular corner and a socketed leg, which is reconstructed in the drawing on pl. LXVI.

Also found were the remains of cloth wrappings or garments around the body.

Grave 193.136

Superstructure: A stone-covered rubble mound, 8 m. diam. and 0.9 m. high.

Grave: Type IV, 2.35 × 1.4 × 1.2 m., with the entrance pit an additional 0.4 m. long. The orientation is NE–SW (35° E. of N.).

Burial: There were the scattered bones of an adult in the fill.

Objects: 1. A red ware cup, 9.3 cm. high × 9 cm. max. diam. (pl. LXVI.) Adams R.1. Aberdeen Anthropological Museum 1109².

2. A cream biscuit ware cup, decorated with red and black painted parallel bands, 9 cm. high × 9 cm. max. diam. (pl. LXVI.) Adams W.30. Nicholson Museum 63.203.

3. A red ware flask with black and white painted 'splash' decoration, 28.5 cm. high × 18.6 cm. max. diam. (pl. LXVI.) Adams R.1. Nicholson Museum 63.204.

4. A red ware amphora, 36 cm. high × 17.4 cm. max. diam. (pl. LXVII.) Adams R.1. Cairo, Egyptian Museum 89722.

Grave 193.137

Superstructure: A stone-covered rubble tumulus, 9 m. diam. and 0.9 m. high.

Grave: Type I, 2×0.6×0.87 m., orientated NW–SE (48° W. of N.).

Burial: Only the skull of an adult remained.

Objects: 1. A red ware cup, 8.4 cm. high×7.2 cm. max. diam. (pl. LXVII.) Adams R.1. Cambridge Museum of Arch. and Eth. 63.199.

2. A red ware flask, decorated with parallel horizontal painted bands in black and white, 31.8 cm. high×20.4 cm. max. diam. (pl. LXVII.) Adams R.1. University College London 19583.

3. A brown ware flask with a matt cream slip and red and black painted 'splash' decoration, 30 cm. high×19.2 cm. max. diam. (pl. LXVII.) Adams W.30. Cairo, Egyptian Museum 89721.

4. A brown ware flask with matt cream slip and red and black painted 'splash' decoration, 28.8 cm. high×18.6 cm. max. diam. (pl. LXVII.) Adams W.30. Liverpool University E6323.

Grave 193.138

Superstructure: A rubble mound, 13.5 m. diam. and 1.6 m. high.

Grave: Type II, 2.15×1.6×1.45 m., orientated NE–SW (36° E. of N.). The grave was eccentrically located under the NW part of the mound.

Burial: The disturbed body of an adult female(?). A few bones are still articulated to one another and indicate that the original burial position was dorsally extended with the head to the NE.

Objects: 1. A cream biscuit ware cup with brown painted decoration, 7.5 cm. high×7.8 cm. max. diam. (pls. LXVII, LXXX.) Adams W.30. Cairo, Egyptian Museum 89723.

2. A cream biscuit ware cup with brown painted decoration, 8.5 cm. high×8.7 cm. max. diam. (pls. LXVII, LXXX.) Adams W.30. Cairo, Egyptian Museum 89524.

3. A cream biscuit ware cup with brown painted decoration, 8.7 cm. high×8.4 cm. max. diam. (pl. LXVII.) Adams W.30. Liverpool University E6335.

4. A red ware flask decorated with a red and black painted 'splash' motif, 25.5 cm. high×18.6 cm. max. diam. (pl. LXVIII.) Adams R.1. Reading Museum 83:67/22.

5. A red ware flask with black painted 'splash' decoration, 31.5 cm. high×20.4 cm. max. diam. (pl. LXVIII.) Adams R.1. Queen's University, Belfast QAD/7/139.

6. A red ware flask with white painted 'splash' decoration, 31.5 cm. high×20.4 cm. max. diam. Adams R.1. Queen's University, Belfast QAD/7/131. This flask is identical to no. 5, above, except for the colour of the decoration.

7. A brown ware amphora, 52.5 cm. high×22.8 cm. max. diam. (pl. LXVII.) Adams U.2. Nicholson Museum 63.205.

(*a*) Fragments of a white biscuit ware cup with brown painted decoration, 8.2 cm. high×7.5 cm. max. diam. (pl. LXVII.) Adams W.30.

(*b*) Fragments of a white biscuit ware cup with brown painted decoration, 7.5 cm. high×8.1 cm. max. diam. (pl. LXVII.) Adams W.30.

Also found in the fill were the remains of a red blanket, the badly destroyed remains of a wooden bed, and a conical mud-jar seal, the sealing of which is unreadable.

Grave 193.139

Superstructure: A stone-covered rubble tumulus, 11 m. diam. and 1.45 m. high.

Grave: Type III, 2.12×1.25×1 m., the entrance being an additional 1.1 m. long. The orientation is ENE–WSW (70° E. of N.).

Burial: The articulated body of an adult female, lying dorsally extended, head west, hands on the pelvis.

Objects: 1. A red ware cup, 9.6 cm. high×8.7 cm. max. diam. (pl. LXVIII.) Adams R.1. Aberdeen Anthropological Museum 1109².

2. A cream biscuit ware cup with red painted decoration, 8.7 cm. high×9 cm. max. diam. (pl. LXVIII.) Adams W.30. Ashmolean Museum 1962.925.

3. A cream biscuit ware cup with black painted decoration, 8.5 cm. high×9.6 cm. max. diam. (pls. LXVIII, LXXX.) Adams W.30. Rijksmuseum, Leiden F1963/8.24.

4. A brown ware amphora with red and black painted decoration, 27.7 cm. high×18.6 cm. max. diam. (pls. LXVIII, LXXVIII.) Adams W.11. Leeds University.

5. A red ware flask with black and white painted 'splash' decoration, 24.9 cm. high×17.4 cm. max diam. (pl. LXVIII.) Adams R.1. British Museum 66550.

Also found in this grave were a red ware cup similar to no. 1 and a cream biscuit ware cup similar to no. 2.

Grave 193.140

Superstructure: A stone-covered rubble mound, 7.5 m. diam. and 1.25 m. high.

Grave: Type I, 2.5×0.95×1 m., orientated WNW–ESE (69° W. of N.).

Burial: The articulated body of a youth (? female), lying dorsally extended, head WNW, hands on the pelvis.

Objects: 1. A red ware flask with a painted black rim stripe, 22.8 cm. high×16.2 cm. max. diam. (pl. LXVIII.) Adams R.1. Royal Ontario Museum 963.15.21.

2. A brown ware flask with a matt cream slip and black painted decoration, 23.4 cm. high × 15.3 cm. max. diam. (pl. LXVIII.) Adams W.30. British Museum 66553.

3. A cream biscuit ware cup with red painted decoration, 8.1 cm. high × 8.4 cm. max. diam. (pl. LXVIII.) Adams W.30. Reading Museum 118:65/4.

4. A cream biscuit ware cup with red painted decoration, 9.3 cm. high × 9 cm. max. diam. (pls. LXVIII, LXXX.) Adams W.30. British Museum 66571.

5. A bronze bangle bracelet with a scalloped outer face, 5 cm. diam. and 0.2 cm. thick. (pl. LXVIII.) Nicholson Museum 63.212.

6. A string of blue and green glass drop pendants and white and blue glass ball beads; together with a second string of dark blue glass composite beads. (pl. LXVIII.) Nicholson Museum 63.240.

7. Four crescentic silver ear-rings, 1.2 cm. average diam. (pl. LXVIII.) Nicholson Museum 63.220, 63.221, 63.222, 63.223.

Grave 193.141

Superstructure: A rubble mound, 10 m. diam. and 1.5 m. high.

Grave: Type IV, 2.6 × 1.5 × 1.05 m., the entrance adding 1.05 m. to the length. The orientation is WNW–ESE (63° W. of N.).

Burial: The scattered bones of two adults.

Objects: 1. Two large white stone beads. (pl. LXIX.) Location uncertain.

Grave 193.142

Superstructure: A rubble mound, 7 m. diam. and 1.5 m. high.

Grave: Type III, 2 × 1.25 × 0.88 m. The entrance ramp is 1.75 m. long and the orientation is NW–SE (41° W. of N.).

Burial: None remaining.

Objects: None were found.

Grave 193.143

Superstructure: A rubble mound, 14 m. diam. and 3 m. high.

Grave: Type II, 2.75 × 1.25 × 1.5 m., orientated WNW–ESE (67° W. of N.).

Burial: The decapitated, but otherwise articulated body of an adult male, lying dorsally extended, head to the WNW, hands on the pelvis.

Objects: None were found.

Grave 193.144

Superstructure: A rubble mound, 18 m. diam. and 3 m. high.

Grave: Type III, 2.3 × 1.45 × 1.25 m., the entrance being an additional 0.55 m. long. The orientation is NW–SE (52° W. of N.).

Burial: The articulated body of an adult male, lying dorsally extended, head to the NW, hands on the pelvis.

Objects: None were found.

Grave 193.145

Superstructure: A rubble tumulus 25 m. diam. and 5 m. high.

Grave: Type IV, 1.75 × 1.2 × 1.24 m. The entrance is 0.55 m. long and the orientation is WNW–ESE (66° W. of N.).

Burial: The scattered bones of an adult male.

Objects: 1. A red ware jar, 26.1 cm. high × 22.8 cm. max. diam. (pl. LXIX.) Adams R.1. Liverpool University E6338.

2. A red ware cup, with painted black and white 'splash' decoration, 12.6 cm. high × 12 cm. max. diam. (pl. LXIX.) Adams R.1. Cambridge Museum of Arch. and Eth. 63.198.

3. A red ware ribbed cup, 8.4 cm. high × 9.3 cm. max. diam. (pl. LXIX.) Adams R.1. Aberdeen Anthropological Museum 1109^2.

4. A red ware cup, 9.6 cm. high × 8.7 cm. max. diam. (pl. LXIX.) Adams R.1. Reading Museum 83:67/23.

5. A red ware cup, 9.4 cm. high × 9.6 cm. max. diam. (pl. LXIX.) Adams R.1. Otago Museum E62.20. This cup and no. 6 are identical.

6. A red ware cup, 9.4 cm. high × 9.6 cm. max. diam. (pl. LXIX.) Adams R.1. Manchester Museum 20184. This cup and no. 5 are identical.

Also found in this grave, a number of fragments of glass vessels.

Grave 193.146

Superstructure: A rubble mound, 9 m. diam. and 1.5 m. high.

Grave: Type IV, 1.75 × 1.02 × 1.23 m., the entrance adding 0.75 m. to the length. The orientation is ENE–WSW (73° E. of N.).

Burial: Nothing remained.

Objects: None were found.

Grave 193.147

Superstructure: A rubble mound, 13 m. diam. and 2 m. high.

Grave: Type I, 2.62 × 1.45 × 1.60 m., orientated ENE–WSW (71° E. of N.).

Burial: The scattered bones of an adult.

Objects: 1. A red ware flask with a matt cream slip and

black painted decoration, 16.2 cm. high × 12.6 cm. max. diam. (pl. LXIX.) Adams W.30. Cairo, Egyptian Museum 89725.

2. A red ware flask with a matt cream slip and black painted horizontal bands, 27 cm. high × 18 cm. max. diam. (pl. LXIX.) Adams W.30. Otago Museum E62.14.

3. A red ware flask with black painted mouth, 24 cm. high × 18 cm. max. diam. (pl. LXIX.) Adams R.1. Cambridge Museum of Arch. and Eth. 63.193.

4. A red ware cup, 9 cm. high × 9.6 cm. max. diam. (pl. LXIX.) Adams R.1. Cambridge Museum of Arch. and Eth. 63.194.

5. A bronze bell, 5.2 cm. high × 4.4 cm. max. diam., with the remains of an iron clapper. (pl. LXIX.) University College London 19539.

Grave 193.148

Superstructure: A rubble mound, 13 m. diam. and 1.75 m. high.

Grave: Type IV, 2.65 × 1.78 × 1.45 m. The entrance adds 0.7 m. to the length and the orientation is E.–W. (85° E. of N.).

Burial: Nothing remained.

Objects: 1. A red ware flask with black and white painted 'splash' decoration, 29.1 cm. high × 18 cm. max. diam. (pl. LXIX.) Adams R.1. Leeds University.

2. Fragments of a large, brown ware amphora. (pl. LXIX.) Adams U.3. Rijksmuseum, Leiden F1963/8.27.

3. Part of a small, brown ware flask with incised decoration on the shoulder. (pl. LXIX.) Adams R.31.

Also found were fragments of four brown ware flasks, all with matt cream slip and black and red painted decoration. All Adams W.30. All similar in form to no. 1, above.

Grave 193.149

Superstructure: A rubble tumulus, 10 m. diam. and 1.7 m. high.

Grave: Type IV, 2.1 × 1.43 × 1.1 m. The entrance is 0.72 m. long and the grave is orientated NW–SE (47° W. of N.).

Burial: The articulated body of an adult male, lying dorsally extended, head to the NW and wrapped in a reed matting.

Objects: None were found.

Grave 193.150

Superstructure: A rubble mound, 17 m. diam. and 2.7 m. high.

Grave: Type IV, 2.35 × 1.5 × 1.25 m., with the entrance 0.52 m. long. The orientation is WNW–ESE (58° W. of N.).

Burial: The scattered bones of an adult female.

Objects: None were found.

Grave 193.151

Superstructure: A rubble mound, 10 m. diam. and 1.2 m. high.

Grave: Type IV, 2.3 × 1.35 × 1.55 m. The entrance is 1.32 m. long and the orientation WNW–ESE (76° W. of N.).

Burial: The scattered bones of an adult male.

Objects: 1. A red ware cup with white painted decoration, 12.9 cm. high × 10.8 cm. max. diam. (pl. LXX.) Adams R.1. Fitzwilliam Museum E.2.1962. This cup and nos. 2 and 3, below, are identical.

2. A red ware cup with white painted decoration, 12.9 cm. high × 10.8 cm. max. diam. (pl. LXX.) Adams R.1. Otago Museum E62.17.

3. A red ware cup with white painted decoration, 12.9 cm. high × 10.8 cm. max. diam. (pl. LXX.) Adams R.1. Nicholson Museum 63.206.

4. A red ware cup, 9.9 cm. high × 9 cm. max. diam. (pl. LXX.) Adams R.1. Leeds University.

5. A cream biscuit ware cup with brown painted decoration, 8.4 cm. high × 9 cm. max. diam. (pls. LXX, LXXX.) Adams W.30. Rijksmuseum, Leiden F1963/8:25.

6. A polished, red ware flask, 26.7 cm. high × 18 cm. max. diam. (pl. LXX.) Adams R.1. Manchester Museum 20957.

7. A brown ware flask with a matt cream slip and black painted decoration, 26.7 cm. high × 16.8 cm. max. diam. (pls. LXX, LXXIX.) Adams W.30. British Museum 66552.

8. A brown ware flask with a matt cream slip and black painted decoration, 26.8 cm. high × 16.8 cm. max. diam. (pl. LXX.) Adams W.30. Cambridge Museum of Arch. and Eth. 63.197.

9. A brown ware flask with a matt cream slip decorated with a brown painted vine motif, 27.9 cm. high × 17.7 cm. max. diam. (pl. LXX.) Adams W.30. British Museum 66547.

10. A red ware amphora, 67.2 cm. high × 17.3 cm. max. diam. (pl. LXX.) Adams U.2. Cairo, Egyptian Museum 89726.

Also recovered from this tomb are a conical mud sealing, with a rectangular impression, part of which is legible and reads TMNH (pl. LXX); part of a red ware cup similar to no. 4; part of another brown ware flask with a matt cream slip and black painted decoration; part of a red ware flask with black and white painted decoration similar to that on no. 9; and one large iron nail.

Grave 193.152

Superstructure: A rubble mound, 6 m. diam. and 0.6 m. high.

Grave: Type III, 1.87×0.73×0.8 m., with the entrance 0.95 m. long. The orientation is NW–SE (50° W. of N.).

Burial: The articulated body of an adult female, lying dorsally extended, head to the NW, the hands on the pelvis.

Objects: 1. There were the remains of a small necklace of blue glass composite beads. (pl. LXXI.) Location uncertain.

There was also a small iron fitting.

Grave 193.153

Superstructure: A rubble mound, 5 m. diam. and 0.35 m. high.

Grave: Type IV, 1.4×0.95×0.85 m. The entrance adds 0.75 m. to the length and the grave is orientated WNW–ESE (73° W. of N.).

Burial: There were the disturbed remains of a small child. Part of the spine, the pelvis, and the legs and head are articulated and indicate the burial originally lay dorsally extended, head WNW.

Objects: None were found.

Grave 193.154

Superstructure: A rubble mound, 6 m. diam. and 0.8 m. high.

Grave: Type I, 2.95×0.75×1 m., orientated WNW–ESE (76° W. of N.).

Burial: Nothing remained.

Objects: 1. A biscuit ware cup with chocolate brown painted decoration, 9 cm. high×8.8 cm. max. diam. (pl. LXXI.) Adams W.30. University College London 19581. This and the following piece are identical.

2. A biscuit ware cup with chocolate brown painted decoration, 9 cm. high×8.8 cm. max. diam. (pls. LXXI, LXXX.) Adams W.30. Reading Museum 83:67/24.

3. A brown ware flask with a matt cream slip, 25.8 cm. high×17.4 cm. max. diam. (pl. LXXI.) Adams W.30. Leeds University.

4. A brown ware flask with matt cream slip and black painted rim, 26.7 cm. high×16.8 cm. max. diam. (pl. LXXI.) Adams W.30. Manchester Museum 20958.

5. A red ware flask, 27.6 cm. high×16.2 cm. max. diam. (pl. LXXI.) Adams R.1. Manchester Museum 20966.

Grave 193.155

Superstructure: A rubble mound, 5 m. diam. and 0.35 m. high.

Grave: Type III, 1.65×0.6×0.81 m., the entrance being 0.45 m. long and the orientation E.–W. (84° W. of N.).

Burial: Nothing remained.

Objects: There were only a few fragments of a wooden object, a box(?).

Grave 193.156

Superstructure: A stone-covered rubble tumulus, 10 m. diam. and 1.5 m. high.

Grave: Type I, 3.25×1.27×1.6 m., orientated NNE–SSW (14° E. of N.).

Burial: The articulated lower trunk, pelvis, and legs of an adult male, lying dorsally extended, with the head to the SSW.

Objects: 1. A red ware spouted flask with a matt cream slip, decorated with a black painted vine motif, 32.4 cm. high×19.5 cm. max. diam. (pls. LXXI, LXXVII.) Adams W.30. Cairo, Egyptian Museum 89726 bis.

2. A ribbed red ware amphora with a matt cream slip, 27.7 cm. high×18.6 cm. max. diam. (pl. LXXI.) Adams W.28. Otago Museum E62.12.

3. A red ware flask with white painted decoration, 25.6 cm. high×21 cm. max. diam. (pls. LXXI, LXXVII.) Adams R.1. Blackburn Museum.

4. A red ware flask, 30 cm. high×21.3 cm. max. diam. (pl. LXXII.) Adams R.1. Cambridge Museum of Arch. and Eth. 63.196.

5. A red ware cup, 7.8 cm. high×8.7 cm. max. diam. (pl. LXXI.) Adams R.1. Cambridge Museum of Arch. and Eth. 63.195.

6. A small, red ware bottle with painted decoration in red and black, 8.4 cm. high×7.8 cm. max. diam. (pl. LXXI.) Adams R.1. Cairo, Egyptian Museum 89727.

7. A small, red ware bottle, 10.8 cm. high×9.3 cm. max. diam. (pl. LXXI.) Adams U.2. Blackburn Museum.

8. A red ware bottle, 16.5 cm. high×12 cm. max. diam. (pl. LXXI.) Adams R.1. Otago Museum E62.13.

Grave 193.157

Superstructure: A rubble mound, 15 m. diam. and 2 m. high.

Grave: Type IV, 2.33×1.37×1.67 m. The entrance adds 0.75 m. to the length and the orientation is NNW–SSE (29° W. of N.).

Burial: The scattered bones of an adult female(?).

Objects: None were found.

Grave 193.158

Superstructure: A stone-covered rubble tumulus, 10 m. diam. and 1.6 m. high.

Grave: Type IV, 2.12×1.52×1.55 m., with the entrance 1.35 m. long and the orientation NW–SE (44° W. of N.).

Burial: There were the scattered bones of an adult male.

Objects: 1. A red ware cup, 12 cm. high × 11.4 cm. max. diam. (pl. LXXII.) Adams R.1. Manchester Museum 20967.

2. A red ware cup, decorated with black painted spots, 11.1 cm. high × 13.2 cm. max. diam. (pl. LXXII.) Adams R.1. Leeds University.

3. A cream biscuit ware cup, 9 cm. high × 9 cm. max. diam. (pl. LXXII.) Adams W.29 or W.30. Reading Museum 83:67/25.

4. A red ware cup, identical to no. 2 above, decorated with black painted spots, 11.1 cm. high × 13.2 cm. max. diam. (pl. LXXII.) Adams R.1. Queen's University, Belfast QAD/7/123.

5. A red ware flask with black and white painted decoration, 29.4 cm. high × 21.6 cm. max. diam. (pl. LXXII.) Adams R.1. Otago Museum E62.8.

6. A red ware flask with black and white painted decoration, 27.9 cm. high × 22.2 cm. max. diam. (pl. LXXII.) Adams R.1. Birmingham Museum 140'63.

7. A red ware flask with white and black painted decoration, 29.4 cm. high × 18.9 cm. max. diam. (pl. LXXII.) Adams R.1. Cairo, Egyptian Museum 89728.

8. A small red ware amphora, 39.6 cm. high × 20.4 cm. max. diam. (pl. LXXII.) Adams R.1. Manchester Museum 20968.

Also found in the fill of this grave were the following: part of a red ware flask similar to no. 5, above; part of a small brown ware amphora with a white slip and black painted vine decoration (Adams W.30); the remains of a badly decayed pair of leather sandals; an iron brace or fitting from a box; and fragments of a glass vessel.

Grave 193.159

Superstructure: A rubble tumulus, 9 m. diam. and 1.3 m. high.

Grave: Type IV, 1.55 × 1.04 × 1.55 m. The entrance adds 1.12 m. to the length and the orientation is ENE–WSW (59° E. of N.). (pl. LXXIII.)

Burial: There were a few scattered bones in the fill.

Objects: 1. A cream biscuit ware cup with brown painted decoration, 8.4 cm. high × 8.7 cm. max. diam. (pl. LXXIII.) Adams W.30. Royal Ontario Museum 963.15.22.

2. A red ware cup with black and white painted 'splash' decoration, 11.7 cm. high × 11.7 cm. max. diam. (pl. LXXIII.) Adams R.1. Rijksmuseum, Leiden F1963/8.26.

3. A red ware cup, 8.7 cm. high × 10.2 cm. max. diam. (pl. LXXIII.) Adams R.1. Queen's University, Belfast QAD/7/125.

4. A red ware flask with black and white painted 'splash' decoration, 31.2 cm. high × 19.5 cm. max. diam. (pl. LXXIII.) Adams R.1. Location uncertain.

5. A pair of bronze ear-rings, 2 cm. diam. and 0.4 cm. thick. (pl. LXXIV.) Nicholson Museum 63.216, 63.217. There were also the remains of a glass vessel.

Grave 193.160

Superstructure: A stone-covered rubble tumulus, 9 m. diam. and 0.8 m. high.

Grave: Type IV, 1.9 × 1.15 × 1.47 m. The entrance is 1.35 m. long and the orientation is WNW–ESE (73° W. of N.).

Burial: The scattered bones of an adult (?) female.

Objects: The fragmentary remains of two khaki-coloured blankets, one with red stripes, the other with brown stripes.

Grave 193.161

Superstructure: A rubble mound, 6 m. diam. and 0.5 m. high.

Grave: Type II, 2.6 × 0.85 × 0.9 m., orientated NNW–SSE (18° W. of N.). The bottom 0.28 m. of the grave is dug into bedrock.

Burial: The scattered bones of an adult (?) female.

Objects: None were found.

Grave 193.162

Superstructure: A rubble mound, 14 m. diam. and 4 m. high. There is a rectangular brick grave, which was built on to the mound. It was found empty.

Grave: Type IV, 2.9 × 1.6 × 1.55 m., the entrance being 1.95 m. long. The orientation is NW–SE (44° W. of N.).

Burial: There were the disturbed remains of an adult male.

Objects: 1. A red ware cup, with black and white painted 'festoon' decoration, 10.2 cm. high × 12 cm. max. diam. (pl. LXXV.) Adams R.1. Otago Museum E62.28.

2. A red ware cup, with black and white painted 'festoon' decoration, 8 cm. high × 10 cm. max. diam. (pl. LXXV.) Adams R.1. Queen's University, Belfast QAD/7/124.

3. A red ware cup, with black and white painted 'festoon' decoration, 10.2 cm. high × 12.6 cm. max. diam. (pl. LXXV.) Adams R.1. Blackburn Museum.

4. A red ware cup identical to no. 3, above. (pl. LXXV.) Adams R.1. Leeds University.

5. A red ware cup, 11.7 cm. high × 11.4 cm. max. diam. (pl. LXXV.) Adams R.1. Ashmolean Museum 1962.922.

6. A cream biscuit ware cup with orange and brown painted decoration, 8.7 cm. high × 8.4 cm. max. diam. (pl. LXXIV.) Adams W.30. University College London 19582.

7. A red ware flask with black and white painted

decoration, 25 cm. high × 17 cm. max. diam. (pl. LXXIV.) Adams R.1. Queen's University, Belfast QAD/7/132.

8. A red ware flask with black and white painted decoration, 27.6 cm. high × 19.2 cm. max. diam. (pl. LXXV, LXXX.) Adams R.1. Cairo, Egyptian Museum 89729.

9. A red ware flask with black and white painted decoration, 27 cm. high × 19.8 cm. max. diam. (pl. LXXIII.) Adams R.1. Leeds University.

10. A red ware jar, 36.9 cm. high × 26.4 cm. max. diam. (pl. LXXIII.) Adams R.1. Royal Ontario Museum 963.15.23.

11. A brown ware amphora, 57.9 cm. high × 17.4 cm. max. diam. (pl. LXXIV.) The interior is coated with a resinous substance, which also has spilled around the outside of the rim. On the shoulder is a two-line inscription in black ink in Greek, recorded in facsimile on pl. LXXIV.

Adams U.18. Cambridge Museum of Arch. and Eth. 63.192.

12. A brown ware amphora with a matt cream slip decorated with a black painted vine motif, 35.7 cm. high × 21.6 cm. max. diam. (pl. LXXIV.) Adams W.30. Cairo, Egyptian Museum 89730.

13. A brown ware ribbed amphora, 61.2 cm. high × 19.8 cm. max. diam. Adams U.2. There is a conical mud sealing intact on the mouth of this vessel and the impression, which is picked out in red, occurs three times. (pl. LXXIV.) British Museum 66554.

14. A variety of glass, faience, bone, and stone beads. (pl. LXXIV.) Location uncertain.

Also found in the fill of this tomb was part of a cream biscuit ware cup identical to no. 6, above; and part of a brown ware amphora similar to no. 11, above, with ✕ marked on the shoulder in black ink.

THE MEROÏTIC TEXTS FROM THE
QAṢR IBRÎM CEMETERIES

N. B. MILLET

THE Meroïtic texts from the Qaṣr Ibrîm cemetery, although disappointingly few in number, include two which are surely among the most important of those which have come to light in the recent Nubian campaign. These two funerary stelae, found together and much alike in appearance, style, and content, offer more points of attack for the would-be decipherer than most such funerary monuments, and consequently can be made to provide a high number of new hypotheses regarding the meaning of words, grammatical structures, and other aspects of the interpretation of Meroïtic. For the decipherment, *sensu stricto*, of Meroïtic was of course accomplished by Griffith in the first two decades of this century; the task that remains is one of interpretation, for lack of a better word, of their contents, and it is the firm belief of the writer that this calls for willingness on the part of the investigator to evolve hypotheses freely, to be prepared to guess if it seems useful so to do, and in general to extract as much material for consideration as possible from the surviving evidence. It may be objected that such a free approach to the subject will necessarily breed error; let us hope that it be so, for demonstrated error represents an increase in knowledge, while excessive caution can be a distinct liability in the early development of a field of study.

In the following pages the two large stelae,

Ibrîm 1 and 2, are dealt with first, and the smaller pieces and fragments treated at the end.[1]

TEXT no. 1: Excavation number 192B.8.1: Cairo, *Journal d'entrée* 89699; sandstone stela with fourteen lines of Meroïtic linear script between rules. Height 50 cm., width 45 cm., thickness approximately 9 cm. Expedition photograph number 230. Fig. 1, pl. LXXXIX. 2.

Transcription

1. *woš : wetñyiñqeli : šori :*
2. *wetrri qo : tmeye qowi : yiq*
3. *rekye : terikeli terikelowi k*
4. *ditrye tedẖeli tedẖelowi*
5. *oẖoñteleb[a] yetmdelowi ẖrp*
6. *ẖñ kešoye[b] yetmdelowi pe*
7. *rite : adblis sqtikȩ[c] ye*
8. *tmdelowi : ttñlẖ : pelmošlis*
9. *pqebete : yetmdelowi : kiš*
10. *ri : mkesmeñ aẖid : kid : kišris*
11. *qelile : nbrlis I belebeltore I b*
12. *ẖe yedlis I teketin 9 : yed : tlt*
13. *[d]16 kelw : yikidbitelowi a*
14. *to mẖe bšẖekes : at mẖe bšẖrkes*

Notes on transcription

a. Perhaps *šošoñteleb*, but see below, in the commentary to this word.
b. Perhaps *keẖoye*.
c. The final letter may well be an *l*.
d. Although the sign for 'ten' begins somewhat to the left of the normal starting-point, there seems no trace of another numeral preceding it.

REM Heyler, Leclant, et al., *Répertoire d'épigraphie méroïtique* (Paris and Strasbourg, 1968–).
NG Inscriptions from Nag Gamûs cited in M. Almagro, *La necrópolis meroítica de Nag Gamus* (Madrid, 1965).
Tañy. The Stela of Tañyidamani: cf. Hintze in *Kush* 8 (1960), 125 ff.
AW Inscriptions from Arminna West published in Trigger, B. G.: *Meroitic Funerary Inscriptions from Arminna West* (New Haven, Conn., 1970).

---

[1] The following abbreviations are used in the text and notes:

MI F. Ll. Griffith, *Meroitic Inscriptions* I and II (London, 1911–12).

Kar, Sh F. Ll. Griffith, *Karanog: the Meroitic Inscriptions of Shablul and Karanog* (Philadelphia, 1911).

GA Inscriptions from Gebel Adda cited in Millet, *Meroitic Nubia* (University Microfilms, Ann Arbor, Michigan).

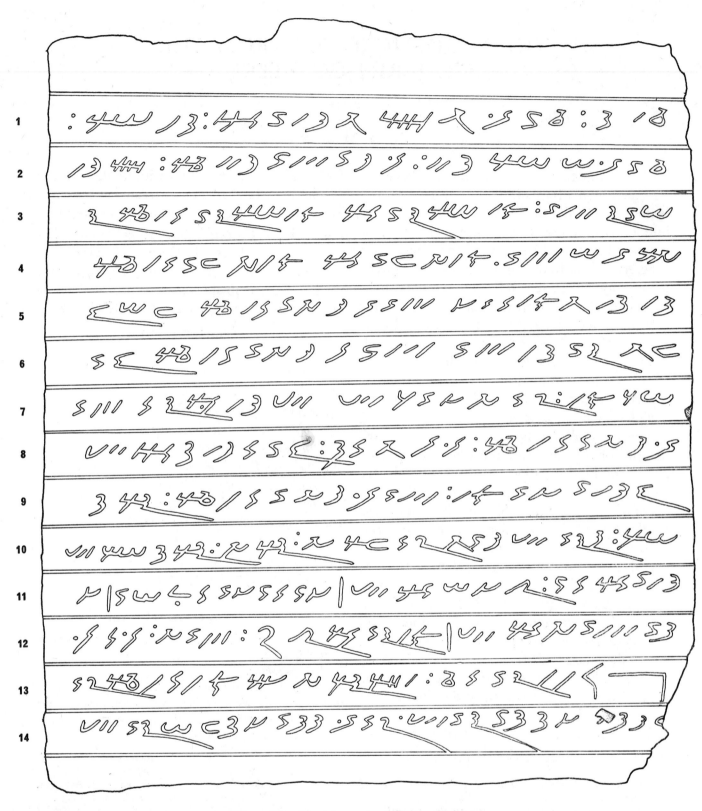

FIG. 1. Meroïtic stela no. 1. 192B.8.1. Scale 2:5

Commentary

In the following commentary the text is divided into its component clauses (*stiches*), identified by the letters *a*, *b*, *c*, etc.

a. woš : wetñyiñqeli : šori : ⸢²wetrri (:)

The text begins with the extended form of the invocation to Wosha and Ashore, the Meroïtic forms of Isis and Osiris. This formula has been most recently treated by K.-H. Priese in *Meroitiskii sbornik I*, Moscow, in press. See also Prof. Almagro's useful summary of the facts in *La necrópolis meroítica de Nag Gamus*, 231. Priese's analysis is thorough in the extreme, but the meaning of the terms *we-tñyi-ñqe-l* and *we-trr* remains obscure, save in that they are surely epithets of the two funerary deities, and are in the vocative.

b. qo : tmeye qo-wi :

c. yiq⸢³rekye : terike-li (:) *terike-lo-wi* (:)

d. k⸢ditrye (:) *tedhe-li* (:) *tedhe-lo-wi* (:)

These three clauses name the deceased and give his or her parentage: 'the noble Tameye, truly begotten of Iqarekaye, truly born of Kaditaraye.'[1] There is no indication here or elsewhere in the text as to the sex of the deceased. Tamoye is a woman's name in *Kar.* 81 and 86 and in *Far.* 27, but the names may not be related.

e. ⸢hohoñte-leb (:) *yetmde-lo-wi* (:)

This and the following clauses enumerate the persons who stood in the much-discussed *yetmde*-relationship to the deceased. For reasons which will appear in print elsewhere the present writer is inclined to take this to mean 'kin to' in the broadest sense, much as did Griffith in his pioneering study of the funerary texts.[2] Clause *e* would thus be rendered 'kin to the *hohoñte*-persons'. This title is unknown elsewhere in the body of Meroïtic texts, but is presumably that rendered in demotic Egyptian as *hhnʒte* in a graffito at Philae, dated to AD 48.[3] The *hhnʒte* there appears in company with the strategus, the *ššimete*, and the *ʾmeme* (?), and is presumably concerned either with the Meroïtic administration of the Dodecaschoenus or with the Isis temple establishment. For Egyptian *h* representing Meroïtic *h* an instance can be given in the demotic form *phrse* of the place-name *phrs*, Faras, which appears in an unpublished text from Adda.

f. hrp⸢⁶hñ (:) *kešoye* (:) *yetmde-lo-wi* (:)

'Kin to the city-governor Keshoye.' The high title of *hrphñ*, when qualified, is connected with towns, and some such meaning as suggested here must be involved. In this case the reader was presumably expected to know of what town a person of this particular family would be governor. It may have been Ibrîm itself, of course, but the only places actually known to have had *hrphñ*'s are Faras[4] and Atiye[4] (Sedeinga), and a town Shaqalaki[5] of unknown location and importance.

g. pe⸢rite : adb-li-s (:) *sqtike* (:) *ye⸢⁸tmde-lo-wi* :

Here the pattern seems to be the familiar

$$((T + (N + \text{definite article} + \text{gen.})) + P) + (V + lo + wi)$$

where Saqatike represents a personal name: thus, 'kin to the agent of the *adb*, Saqatike'. The agent of the *adb* is presumably a subordinate of the well-known 'general of the *adb*'. Much ink has been spilt, with little justification, over the word *adb*;[6] we have no real clue to its meaning save that of its use in contrast or in complement to *ato*, 'river, water', in the title *pelmoš ato-li-s*, 'general of the River'. Saqatike (or Saqatikala?) is a rather odd name, and may not be Meroïtic at all.

h. ttñ-lh : pelmoš-li-s (:) *⸢pqebete : yetmde-lo-wi* :

A clause in the same pattern as *g*, meaning 'kin to the chief *ttñ* of the general, Paqebete'. The title *ttñ* is well known now, although the exact meaning is of course unclear; persons with this title are known in connection not only with the generals, but with the princes of Akiñ and with the king. A 'chief *ttñ*', such as we have here, is attested in *AW* 5 as being in the service of the prince.

This clause terminates the portion of the text devoted to the family relationships of the deceased. He (or she) is thus related to a city-governor, an 'agent of the *adb*', and a 'chief *ttñ* of the general', as well as to more than one person bearing the very rare title of *hohoñte*. The fact that this title is cited first and in the plural suggests that it was a more or less hereditary office or function in the deceased person's family, while the other titles, each held by one relative, may well have been appointive. Whoever the dead Tameye may have been, there can be no doubt that some of his or her relatives held offices which must have put them in something like the senior group of local officials in Lower Nubia, outranked only by the great nobles of the two chief clans of the princely viceroys of Akiñ and the 'generals of the River', whose agents and deputies they were. This is of some importance when assessing the historical value of the following section of the text.

The succeeding clauses *i* and *j* are of an entirely different order, as is plain from the numerals involved in the last. A very similar set of phrases, involving the same verb-stem *kid*, occurs in the text next to be studied here (Ib. 2),

---

[1] For a summary of opinion on the meaning of the repeated filiation words, see B. G. Trigger, *Meroitic Funerary Inscriptions from Arminna West* (New Haven, 1970), 22.

[2] For another opinion, that of F. Hintze, see *Bulletin d'information méroïtique* 14 (1974), 33.

[3] Ph. 55 in Griffith, *Demotic Graffiti of the Dodecaschoenus* (Oxford, 1937).

[4] For references see *REM* word index.

[5] *GA* 20 and 21.

[6] A summary of the opinions with reference to the word *adb* will be found in Trigger, op. cit. 25 (contributed by A. Heyler).

and another badly damaged parallel, still unpublished, was found at Adda by the writer. There can be hardly any doubt that we have in all these cases statements of the gifts brought to the burial, or provided for the tomb, by certain persons eminent enough to make their contributions a matter of pride to the family of the deceased, and consequently worthy of mention on the tomb-stela. The gifts mentioned in the present text are numerous, and were apparently all donated by a single person. It may be pointed out that the careless attitude of the scribe or stone-cutter towards the use of the word-divider, so obvious in the preceding portions of the text, is now replaced by greater care.

    i. kiš⁺ⁱ⁰ri : mkesmeñ (:) *aḥid : kid : kišri-s* (:)

The division suggested here into two statements is of course highly tentative, in view of our lack of knowledge of Meroïtic grammar, and the point at which the division is to be made is debatable. The writer has taken the line that the clause *i* above states the fact of the donation and the name of the donor, while the succeeding clause describes the gift, leaving the subject unexpressed. Thus it is suggested that clause *i* is of the following pattern:

    kišri : mkesmeñ : aḥid : kid : kišri-s

    (T+P)+V+(N+(T+gen.))

representing, at another level, subject+verb+object. That the verb need not occupy the final position in the Meroïtic sentence is made quite clear by the similar phrases in Ib. 2, shortly to be described. *kid* is of course the verb-stem in the Ib. 2 clause *o*, but here shows a more elementary form and is followed by what appears to be a noun in the genitive. This noun is the same as the first word in the sentence, where one would expect the subject to stand, but seems unlikely to be a personal name, in view of its second appearance. The most likely solution is to regard *kišri mkesmeñ* as title followed by name, in the usual Meroïtic fashion we have seen above. *aḥid*, or something like it, is met with as a verb (? *aḥidebḥ*) in several places in the Akinidad Stela, where the subject-matter seems to be the number of prisoners, cattle, or like booty given to the temple. This interpretation of *aḥid* as a verb of sending, giving, or the like receives some support from the unpublished Adda tomb-stela *GA* 13+16, where we read in part]*mesrekelis* [1] *beltore : 1* [?]*e 10 keñ : 1 tlt 50 my : tk : teketi*[*n*] *.....s : 10 kelw : aḥide*[

The word *kelw*, as pointed out by Dr Priese,[1] is an enclitic which serves to indicate that a preceding series of nouns (here presumably the funerary gifts) are coordinate; in English we would best render it by the conjunction 'and', as 'X, Y, and Z'. In fact, in the Adda text it gives us notice of the end of the list of gifts representing the grammatical object, and the following word, *aḥide*, must be expected to be most probably the verb of donation. Thus the most probable rendering of clause *i* in Ib. 1 would be:

'The *kišri* Makesameñ sent/gave a present of *kišri*.'
I can only suppose that 'a present of *kišri*' means a present of objects worthy of a *kišri*-person, or of types associated with the functions of a *kišri*-person.

    The following clause *j* seems to enumerate the gifts themselves.

    j. ¹¹|*qelile : nbr-li-s 1* (:) *belebeltore 1* (:)
    *b*¹²|*he* (:) *yed-li-s 1* (:) *teketin 9* (:)
    yed : tlt ¹³*16* (:) *kelw : yikid-bite-lo-wi* (:)

Taking *yikid* as the verb of donation, we would appear to be in a position to interpret the clause more or less as follows:

'(He) presented a *qelile* of the *nbr*, 1; a *belebeltore*, 1; a *bḥe* of the *yed*, 1; *teketin*'s 9; and *tlt*-measures (??) of *yed*, 16.'

The suggestion that *yed : tlt : * is to be rendered as 'measures (of a substance called) *yed*' is here made on the basis of the structure, the earlier qualificatory expressions having the genitive structure N+(N+*li-s*), while in *yed : tlt : * we can discern only N+N, presumably either an adjectival or an appositional construction. Now *tlt* also occurs in the Adda text mentioned above, in:

    . . .e 10 keñ : 1 tlt 50 my, etc.

Here is found the qualifying *keñ* of the famous and much analysed text *MI* 101 of the Meroïtic Chamber at Philae, where it is again used in such a way as to indicate that it is not itself one of the series of gifts, but an attribute of certain of such, which are said to be of 'a *keñ*' or of 'two *keñ*'. The Adda fragment would then mention 'ten ....s (of) one *keñ*', and the following *tlt* 50 suggest rather noun plus number than adjective plus number, which would yield little in the way of sense.

Of the other gifts mentioned, we can compare the *belebeltore* that Tameye received with the *beltore* listed for the anonymous person at Adda. The *teketin* appears also in the Adda text, the number after it missing. The first of the gifts of Makesameñ, described as 'a *qelile* of the *nbr*' suggests itself as a possible Egyptian loan-word, either ϭⲗⲓⲗ 'burnt offering' or ⲕⲗⲏⲗ 'neck-chain'. Of the two, the writer is inclined to the latter, partly because a burnt offering seems to be an unlikely sort of gift to be dispatched or even commissioned from a distance, and partly because the word *nbr* itself cannot help but suggest the modern Nubian word for gold, ᴷ*nobrē*, ᴰ*naubrē*, which may for all we know be a borrowing from Meroïtic. This is, of course, the merest speculation, and one subject to the serious objection that it would hardly seem intelligent for a deceased Meroïte to boast publicly on his tombstone of the intrinsic value of his burial equipment.

    The verb, as we are certainly entitled to take it to be, would appear to be composed of the stem *kid* with a prothetic vowel /*i-*/, followed by the element -*bite*, on

---

[1] Priese, K.-H., in *Wissenschaftliche Zeitschrift der Humboldt-Universität zu Berlin. Gesellschafts- und sprachwissenschaftliche Reihe*, xx, 3 (1971), 275–85.

which the writer has remarked extensively elsewhere.[1] More can be said with regard to this combination when Ib. 2 is discussed below.

*k. a*¹⁺*to* (:) *mḫe* (:) *b-š-ḫe-ke-s* :
l. at (:) *mḫe* (:) *b-š-ḫr-ke-s* (:)

The text ends with the familiar formulae A and B. The first element, normally *p-* or *pi-*, here takes the form *b-*, as occasionally at Karanog and Adda.

Sufficient can be made out of this interesting and important text to justify a skeletal sort of 'translation', which will at least serve the purpose of making clear to the reader the writer's view of the structure of the text and its clauses. Most of the words remain untranslatable or at least of very dubious meaning, and the writer has been sparing of query-marks in view of the tentative nature of the entire rendering.

O Isis *wetñyiñqel*! O Osiris *wetrr*!
It is (?) the noble Tameye, the noble one,
truly begotten of Iqarekaye,
truly born of Kaditaraye.
He/she was kin to the *hoḥoñte*-persons;
he/she was kin to the city-governor Keshoye;
he/she was kin to the agent of the *adb*, Saqatike;
he/she was kin to the chief *ttñ* of the general, Paqebete.
The *kišri* Makesamen sent (?) a present of *kišri*: he presented

> a *qelile* of the *nbr*, 1;
> a *belebeltore*, 1;
> a *bḫe* of the *yed*, 1;
> *teketin*'s, 9;
> and *yed*, *tlt*-measures (??) 16.

??Much water may he/she drink, much bread (?) may he/she eat!

TEXT no. 2: Excavation number 192B.8.2: Cairo, *Journal d'entrée* 89700; sandstone stela with nineteen lines of Meroïtic linear script between rules. Height 65 cm., width 38 cm., thickness approximately 9 cm. Expedition photograph number 203. Fig. 2, pl. LXXXIX. 3.

Transcription

1. *woš : wedi : tñyiñ* [*qeli* :] *šori : wediñ* . .ᵃ
2. *yi : qo : ptsnoye*ᵇ *qowi : pḫomeḥimeye : te*
3. *rikelowi : tyešinoḥoye : tdḫelowi : ant*
4. *ḫšḫsliteb : stelowi : ššor : mkesmlitowi*

5. . . . *ạšoreḷḫ : ḫšḫslitowi : qo pḫomeye q*[*o*
6. *wi : p*]*tsnoye : terikelowi : myeqey*[*e*]
7. *tdḫelowi : msqoros ktkelitowi : ant*
8. *ḫšḫslis : 5 ni : yetmdelowi : te*
9. *ter : ḫšḫslitowi : amolḫ : ḫšḫs*
10. [*l*]*is : beliye : yetmdelo : kroro*
11. [*l*]*i : yikidke : mete : areqis 1 as* [*ị*]
12. *pestoli : yikidke : klmes 1 a*
13. [*ṣ*]*1 mlekye : qoleb : yikidbite*
14. [*lo* :] *mlo mrs ḫšḫslite*[*bk*]*wi : a*
15. [*to*] *: bšiḥebḫes : at mḫe : b*
16. [*šiḫ*]*rbḫes : atepoqedot*[*l*
17. *ḫe* :] *bšitkbḫes : woši : šore*
18. [*yi*] *: diklḫ : šyireqetelis : awšo*
19. [. .] . *teli tereqebḥeli : yetekelowi*

Notes on transcription

a. Only the tail of the final preserved letter is clear; therefore *a*, *p*, and *k* are also possible.
b. Or *ptsnye*; I am inclined to think that the scribe or stonecutter has omitted one of the two short strokes at the beginning of the *y*, since the long stroke ought surely to stand for the vowel *o*. The edge of the *p* is visible but not certain.

Commentary

Text no. 2 is the funerary stela of a man and his son. The text is less well preserved than that of Ib. 1, the beginnings of several lines having lost one or more letters due to damage along the right edge of the carved surface. The script is reasonably good, with little real confusion between the letters *m*, *ḫ*, and *š*; the use of the word divider (:), although not entirely consistent, is better observed than in the previously discussed text.

a. woš : wedi : tñyiñ[*qel-i* :] *šori : wediñ*..ᵖ*y-i* :
We have here what seems to be a new variant of the 'extended invocation', references to the treatment of which have been given above. In the case of the epithet of Isis an element *wedi*, marked off from what follows by the word divider, takes the place of the usual *we-* or *qe-*. The restoration of the second element is, of course, uncertain in view of what follows, but is supported by the traces. In the case of the epithet of Osiris, the element *wedi* is again present, but what follows cannot be reconciled with the usual *trr-i*.

b. qo : ptsnoye-qo-wi :
c. pḫomeḥimeye : teͨrike-lo-wi :
d. tyešinoḥoye : tdḫe-lo-wi :

---

[1] *Meroïtic Nubia* (unpublished Ph.D. dissertation, University Microfilms, Ann Arbor, Michigan, 1968), 241 ff.; Millet, *Meroitica* I (1973), 307 ff.

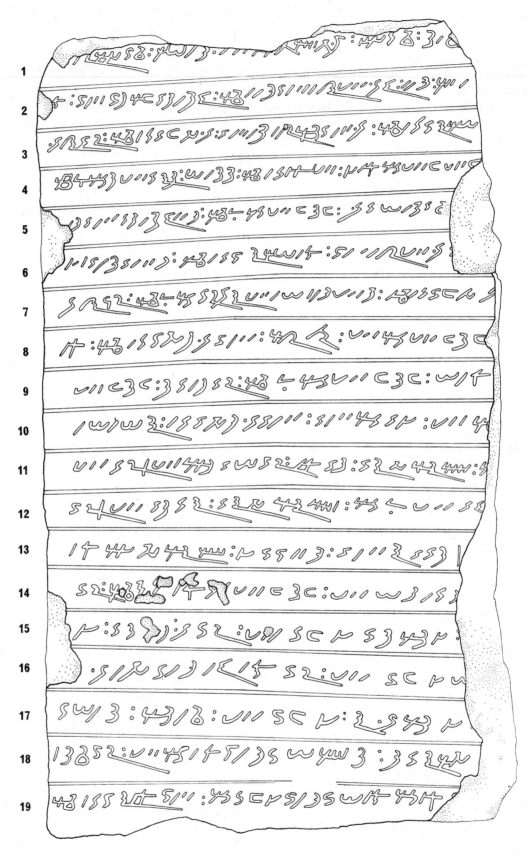

FIG. 2. Meroïtic stela no. 2. 192B.8.2. Scale 1:3

The name and parentage of the senior of the two dead persons are given in the usual format. The whole group bears Egyptian names, whose rendering in the Meroïtic is of some interest. The dead man himself is called Patasnoye, a name also known from Arminna (*AW* 1a), and most likely Egyptian. A guess would be that it is Egyptian **Pꜣ-(n)-tꜣ-šnwyt*, Coptic ⲡⲁⲧⲉϣⲏⲛ, 'the gardener', but the quality of the final vowel in the Meroïtic form is troublesome. The father's name, which is here as in Ib. 1 given precedence over that of the mother, is the Egyptian *Pꜣ-ꜥhm-ḫm*, 'Pakhom the younger'. The Meroïtic rendering *ḫime* for what appears in Coptic as ϣⲏⲙ, ϧⲏⲙ is interesting, but hardly unexpected. More instructive is the mother's name, which surely conceals what would appear in Coptic as ⲧⲁⲏⲥⲉ ⲛⲟϭ 'Taêse the elder', the second *o* of the second element being perhaps due to vowel harmony operating on an original *e*. The name *tyeši* is at any rate well-attested in Meroïtic, and the second element can hardly be other than as suggested. It is interesting to see Meroïtic *ḫ* used for the Egyptian palatal.

e. ant †ḫ-sḫs-li-s-leb : ste-lo-wi :

The deceased Patasnoye is here apparently called *ste* of the priests of the *ḫ-sḫs*, or *ḫ-šḫs*, as the word appears elsewhere in the text. The term *ste*, which appears in *MI* 97 and possibly elsewhere, would seem to be either another of the numerous kinship terms in use in Meroïtic or a more general term meaning 'favourite' or the like. Patasnoye's son, who is commemorated in our text immediately after, is said to be 'related (*ꜣyetmde*) to five priests of the *ḫ-šḫs*'. Now the term *yetmde* is itself of uncertain meaning; if it implies blood relationship of a broad kind, as the writer has taken it to, then the most likely explanation of *ste* is that it also implies a blood relationship, probably of a closer nature, to the same group. The meaning 'nephew' comes to mind, since 'brother' in Meroïtic is probably expressed by the word *wi(l)*, but this is of course purely hypothetical, and 'paternal uncle' is another possibility.

The following two *stiches* seem to be in the form title+ noun in the genitive+-*lo-wi*, and express the offices held by the deceased Patasnoye.

f. ššor : mkesm-li-s-lo-wi
    'He was *ššor*-officer of the *mkesm*.'

g. ⌐. .ašore-lḫ : ḫ-šḫs-li-s-lo-wi
    'He was . . . . . . of great Osiris, the *ḫ-šḫs*.' In view of the normal distribution of the known title *ššor* and of the expression *ant ḫshsliteb* just cited, the second word in each of these two stiches is most likely to be taken as a divine name, or perhaps rather epithet, in view of the presence of the article -*li*. *mkesm* may represent *mk* 'god' plus *sm* 'wife, consort' and be a parallel to the title *qore-sm* 'king's consort', or the more doubtful *ḫrphe-smlo-l* 'ruler's wife?' of Tañy. 138 and 150. 'Wife of (the) god' might conceivably at least be an epithet of the Isis of Philae or of Bigga, as the

better attested *p-tros*, whatever its meaning, must surely be. Alternatively *mkesm-li* may be for *mkesm(eñ)li*, and refer to the personage named in Ibrîm 1 (see p. 79 below). In the case of *ḫsḫs/ḫšḫs*, the form with *š* is to be preferred, since it occurs five times throughout the text as opposed to the single instance of the variant in *s*. Since *šḫs* does seem to occur as a morpheme[1] and since *ḫ-* as a prefix is known from a series of titles, the division *ḫ-šḫs-li*, representing probably N+Adj.+-*li*, seems least improbable. The pattern calls to mind the initial words of the funerary formulae C and D, respectively *ḫ-mlo-l* and *ḫ-lḫ-l*, where the second element in each case is an adjective of more or less ascertainable meaning. An element *ḫ-* also seems to occur in the well-known official titles *ḫrpḫñ, ḫlbiñ, ḫbḫeñ*, and one is tempted to see in it a generic word for 'magistrate, official' or the like. Hypothetically the meaning of the first words of the funerary formulae might then be 'the good magistrate' and 'the great magistrate', presumably in reference to Osiris as god and judge of the dead, with the *ḫ-šḫs* of the present text representing another variation on the same theme. In one of the funerary inscriptions from Nag Gamûs (*NG* 2) the deceased is said to be

ms : woš-s : ḫlḫi-li-s-lo-wi

or '*ms* of Isis and of the *ḫlḫi*', where we may possibly have a variant of the same divine epithet, if such it be, found in Formula D. Here of course the context permits a reference to Osiris, although other gods are not ruled out. Three or so signs missing from the beginning of line 5 presumably provided a priestly title before the phrase which seems to identify the god *ḫ-šḫs* with 'Osiris, the great'.

h. qo pḫomeye q[o⌐wi :
i. p]tsnoye : terike-lo-wi
j. myeqey[e] ꜣtdḫe-lo-wi

Following the titles of the father, we now have named the second of the two persons whom the stela commemorates: 'the noble Pakhomeye, begotten of Patasnoye, born of Mayeqeye.' The men's names are, of course, Egyptian, augmented by the frequent Late Meroïtic ending -*ye*. The mother, the wife of Patasnoye, has a name which is probably Meroïtic, although unattested elsewhere in this form. The son's titles and distinctions follow in the usual way.

k. msqoros [:] ktke-li-s-lo-wi :

Since this expression takes pride of place in the series of four distinctions listed, one is perhaps to assume that Pakhomeye felt his office of '*msqoros* of the Candace' to be his chief honour. Nothing is known about the function, if any, of a *ms-qoros*; the structure suggests it once meant '*ms* of the king', but a man called '*msqoros* of the king' was buried in an undistinguished tomb, G241, in the Karanog cemetery.[2] The chief interest of the title is, of course, that the mention of the Candace enables us to assume that the Meroïtic state structure was still in being in Pakhomeye's time, and was recognised in Lower Nubia.

---

[1] Tañy. 146.   [2] *Kar.* 91.

*l. ant*⁸₁ *ḫ-šḫs-li-s* : *5 -ni* : *yetmde-lo-wi* :
'He was related to five prophets of the *ḫ-šḫs*.' For the
particle *-ni* see the appendix to this article. I take this and
similar expressions to mean that a number, in this case five,
of the brothers and/or uncles of the deceased had in turn
held the office named.

*m. te*ᵒ*ter* : *ḫ-šḫs-li-s-lo-wi* :
'He was the *teter* (officer or priest) of the *ḫ-šḫs*.' *teter*'s
are known of other deities, notably Amanappa.

n. amo-lḫ : *ḫ-šḫs*¹⁰*-li-s* : *beliye* : *yetmde-lo* :
'He was related to the chief *amo* of the *ḫ-šḫs*, Beliye.' This
title seems unattested elsewhere, unless the *ame-yos* (*AW*
3a) is a variant thereof.

Up to this point the text has conformed closely to the
standard Late Meroïtic funerary memorial of Lower
Nubian type. There follows next a section closely parallel
to that of ll. 9–13 in Ib. 1, which seems here also to be most
probably a description of gifts made to the burial equipment or towards the funeral expenses. The operative
word is here, as in Ib. 1, the verb *kid*. The final element
-lo is not present after the first two appearances of the
verb, and a lacuna has removed the end of the last complex,
but it seems necessary to restore a *-lo* at the latter point, at
the broken beginning of line 14; it is unlikely, I think, that
there was room for the plural *-lebkwi*, even if we knew
enough about Meroïtic syntax to assume its appropriateness
after what seems to be a series of parallel predicates each
having its own separate singular subject. The section can
thus, it is suggested, be treated as a single *stiche*.

*o. kroro-*¹¹₁*[l]i* : *yikid-ke* : *mete* : *areqi-s 1 as* [*1*]
     subject + verb +   object
¹²*pesto-li* : *yikid-ke* : *klmes 1 a*¹³₁*[s] 1*
     subject + verb +   object
mlekye : *qo-leb* : *yikid-bite-*¹⁴₁*[lo:]*
     subject+object+   verb + *-lo*

The general burden seems to be:
'The *kroro*-officer presented? a small? *areqi*, 1 (lit. 'a
small one of *areqi*'?), (and) an *as*, 1; the prince presented?
a *klmes*, 1, (and) an *as*, 1; Malekaye presented? the *qo*'s.'

The nature of the gifts enumerated can only be guessed
at. The only person actually named, Malekaye, presents
'the *qo*'s', or 'the noble ones, noble things'. The word *qo*
has, of course, been the subject of much discussion;[1] all
that can be said with certainty is that it is (perhaps among
other things) an adjective of honorific meaning, which
survived in Nubian as late as the eleventh century. In
1911 Griffith suggested that the word, when used as a
substantive, might mean 'images, statues' or the like,[2]
and Monrneet de Villard so translated it much later.
Both suggestions were made on inadequate evidence, but
there is no reason that a word meaning 'noble' or the like

could not be used in such a way, just as its Egyptian
counterpart, *šps*, is used in Ptolemaic times. The reference
in the present text would presumably be to the *ba*-statues
so characteristic of Meroïtic tombs of the better class;
since there are two deceased persons commemorated,
Patasnoye and his son Pakhomeye, the plural 'images'
would be appropriate. One assumes that the funeral gifts
here enumerated were those presented at the funeral of the
last surviving of the two men named, when a single stone
was carved to commemorate both.

Of the other gifts, the object known as *klmes* is mentioned in two ostraca, while the noun *as* appears in a
funerary text from Arminna:[3]

as [:] *anis 14 ni* . . .

With regard to the donors, the *kroro* and the *pesto*-
prince, both here unnamed, are well known from Lower
Nubian texts. They are presumably mentioned only to
show the high regard that Patasnoye and Pakhomeye
enjoyed with the ruling aristocracy, and their names were
not regarded as germane. The reverse is true, or at least
apparently so, with the personage described as Malekaye;
he or she deserves some further discussion, for which see
p. 79 below.

The following group of *stiches* consists of funerary
formulae of a more or less familiar type.

p. mlo mr-s ḫšḫs-li-s-le[*bk*]*wi*

This is an interesting variant on a familiar theme; in
most examples of this formula the words *mlo mrs* are followed
by a place-name ending in the locative *-te*, while here it
ends in the divine name with the genitive ending. The
meaning of the formula itself is far from clear, but if we
take it here to mean 'good of favour/esteem/reputation of
the (god) Khashakhas', we will probably not be far off the
mark.

q. a ¹⁵*[to]* : *b-ši-ḫe-bḫe-s* :
r. at mḫe : *b-*¹⁶*[ši-ḫ]* *r-bḫe-s* :
s. atepoqe dot[*-l*¹⁷*ḫe*] *b-ši-tk-bḫe-s* :
The three funerary formulae which Griffith designated A,
B, and J, are here rendered with certain apparently dialectic
variants, initial *b-* taking place of the more usual *p-*, and
k being once replaced by *q* in the last of the three.

Appended to this group of funerary formulae, which
in one form or another is the common and anticipated
conclusion for a Meroïtic memorial text, is *stiche t*, the
final invocation 'Oh, Isis, oh, Osiris!', not uncommonly
found in this position in Late Meroïtic tomb stelae. Then
comes an unexpected addition in the form of a *stiche*
ending in the verb *yeteke*(*-lo*).

t. ¹⁸*dik-lḫ* : *šyireqete-li-s* : *awšo*¹⁹ . . . *te-li tereqe-bḫe-li* :
yeteke-lo-wi.
As in most segments of Meroïtic of an unfamiliar type, it is
impossible to say for certain even where the morpheme-

[1] See Hintze in *Kush* 8 (1960), 148.
[2] In Garstang, *Meroë, City of the Ethiopians* (Oxford,
1911), 69.
[3] *AW* 3a, l. 18.

boundaries are, and the division used above is a guess. Up to this point the scribe and the engraver of the stone have been unusually thorough and consistent (in so far as we can tell) in their use of the word-divider sign, and there is no warrant to assume that they have deviated here, even though .*teliterteqebheli* seems long and unwieldy even for Meroïtic. In attempting the analysis of this stiche the only starting points are the word-dividers, the article -*li*, and the final verb *yeteke*. This last word occurs in *MI* 89 in an interesting and possibly useful context, printed here with its probable componential analysis beneath:

plšn qbñ-s-li   penn 5-ni yeteke-lo
(N+(N+*s*)+*li*)+(N+♯)+V+*lo*

Now *plšn* is unlikely to be anything but the common Egyptian title *mr-šn*, Greek *lesonis*, 'temple administrator', attested so often in the Demotic graffiti from the Dodecaschoenus. In the phrase before us 'the *lesonis* of *qbñ*' would be the annually appointed administrator of the affairs of a god or place named *qbñ*; no such god is known, but the word may possibly represent the place-name Qûbân, the modern name for ancient Contra-pselchis, opposite Pselchis, the present-day Dakka. Indeed, Qaban may well have been the Meroïtic name for Dakka itself, for all we know. The word *penn*, here followed by the numeral 5 and the particle -*ni* (see the Excursus below), occurs later in the same text followed by the numeral 34(?), and also in an unpublished graffito on the hill of Mashankid, opposite Ballâna, which the writer saw in 1964, where a well-cut text of several lines begins with the phrase *penn 34* (?) . . . It also appears twice in the great Kalâbsha text, *MI* 94, followed by the word *tlte*. In view of all of this the writer is inclined to take *penn* as a better candidate for the meaning 'year' than was the *dime* suggested by Griffith on the basis of *MI* 69, 70, and 74.[1] The phrase 'five years(?)' which emerges suggests that the deceased of *MI* 89, Wayekiye, is boasting of having served for five years as *lesonis* of the temple of Qûbân, or possibly of Dakka, where this same post was certainly held by his son Harentyotef. The grammatical structure of the *stiche* would then be:

(Subject)+Object+Adverbial+Verb

'(He) performed-the-office-of?? the *lesonis* of Qaban (for) five years??'

In the interests of explicitness it should be pointed out that several other grammatical analyses are possible here. While few students of Meroïtic would quarrel with the componential analysis given above, many would be quick to point out, for instance, that the segment identified here as an 'adverbial' (in the broadest sense) is not marked as such in any way, and that *penn 5-ni* is more likely to function as object. The analysis put forward here, itself hypothetical, depends in turn on another hypothesis, namely, that *penn* is the

word for 'year'. Thus the investigator finds himself moving on increasingly unsure ground towards a very tentative conclusion, namely that the verb *yeteke*, here and elsewhere, may mean something like 'to perform' an office. It goes without saying that each succeeding rung of this ladder of hypothesis is that much less secure than the one beneath it.

If such be the general meaning of *yeteke*, one would expect *stiche t* of Ibrîm 2 under discussion to represent a grammatical structure such as

Subject (person)+Object (title of office)+Verb
or
Subject (person)+Object (title of office)+Adverbial+Verb.

I suggest that the words *dik-lh šyireqete-li-s awšo* . . . may represent a title and name comprising the subject, a person named 'the great *dik* of the *šyireqete* Awasho(ye?)'; a word *dik* occurs as an adverb in several texts, but not to my knowledge as a noun construable as a title. The following *lh* is, however, suggestive. The following .*teliterteqebhe-li* appears parallel in function to the *plšn qbñ-s-li* of *MI* 89, but is not a known title of office. Its length and possibly composite nature may conceal a nominal clause, perhaps descriptive of one who has 'performed' funerary rites on behalf of a person or has defrayed the expenses of the erecting of the stela itself. In such a case the included element -*bhe*- might be the plural dative complex suggested by Griffith,[2] referring to the two persons commemorated; 'the great *dik* of the *šyireqete*, Awasho(ye?), performed-the-office-of the one (-*li*) who *tereqe*'s the .*te* for them'.

It seems again useful to append a 'pseudo-translation' of the whole of the text of Ibrîm 2 to make clear in the reader's mind what the writer sees as the flow of the text.

O Isis *weditñyiñqel*! O Osiris *wediñ* . . .!
It is (?) the noble Patasnoye, the noble one,
begotten of Pakhomekhimeye, born of Tayeshinokhoye.
He was nephew (?) to the prophets of the *Ḥ-šḥs*;
he was *ššor*-officer of the *mkesm*;
he was . . . of great Osiris, the *Ḥ-šḥs*;
it is (?) the noble Pakhomeye, the noble one,
begotten of Patasnoye
born of Mayeqeye.
He was *ms-qoros* of the Candace;
he was kin to 5 prophets of the *Ḥ-šḥs*;
he was *teter* of the *Ḥ-šḥs*;
he was kin to the great *amo* of the *Ḥ-šḥs*, Beliye.
The *kroro*-officer presented a small *areqi*, 1,
    and an *as*,   1;
the prince presented a *klmes*,   1,
    and an *as*,   1;

---

[1] *JEA* 3 (1916), 29 ff.

[2] *JEA* 4 (1917), 25 ff.

and Malekaye presented the images.
They were good of favour (?) of the *Ḥ-šḫs.*
?? Water may they drink, much bread (?) may they eat!
(Formula J)
O Isis! O Osiris!
The great *dik* of the *šyireqete,* Awashoye, acted as the one who ......s the *.te* for them.

TEXT no. 3: Excavation number 192A.0.1: British Museum 66585; damaged sandstone offering-table of the decorated type, the spout, adjoining side, and another corner broken off and missing. Preserved dimensions: height 36 cm; width 32 cm; thickness 11 cm. Expedition photo. number 211. Plate LXXXVIII. 2.

Transcription

1. [   ]
2. [   ]
3. [   ]*wi* : *ḥmik* . . *e*
4. *tedḥelowi* : *wkeno*
5. *ke* : *terikelowi ato mḫ*
6. [·   ]
7. [   ]

Commentary

The standard funerary prayers, mentioning a person whose name is lost but whose mother was apparently named *ḥmik..e..,* and whose father's name ended in the element *-noke.*

TEXT no. 4: Excavation number 192A.0.3: University College London 19560. Plate LXXXVIII. 4. Sandstone fragment representing the corner of an offering table, bearing a few signs on one

preserved portion of raised frame, while the other preserved section is blank:

]*deqo.*[

Commentary

The signs remaining may represent part of the deceased's name, written without accompanying formulae.

TEXT no. 5: Excavation number 192C.1.2: British Museum no. 66584; sandstone offering table of 'basin' type. Height 25 cm; width 33 cm; thickness 11.5 cm. Plate LXXXVIII. 5.

Transcription

1. *woši šore*
2. *yi qo a-*
3. *dodoye qo*
4. *wi ato mḫe pšiḫe*
5. *kete at mḫe pši*
6. *kete*
7. [*blank*]

Commentary

No word-separators appear in this text, which commemorates one *adodoye.* The last word of Formula B is blundered.

Excursus on the element *-ni*

Rather than burden the commentary with a lengthy discussion of one point in Meroïtic grammar, it has been thought better to treat the final element *-ni* separately. This particle, as it seems best to term it, occurs after number signs in a small number of texts apart from Ib. 2; all of them can be conveniently tabulated together with the structural elements, in so far as they can be ascertained, in parallel columns.

		Object	Complement?	Adverbial ??	'Verb/noun'+ (Predicate)	
1.	Ib. 2	*ant ḫ-sḫs-li-s 5-ni*			*yetmde-*	*lo-wi*
2.	REM 1057	*sbe 3-ni*			*bqo-*	*lo*
3.	REM 1057	*nob br-1ḫ l-ni*	*dt-wes-li*		*yikḫe-*	*lo*
4.	MI 89	*plšn qbñ-s-li*		*penn 5-ni*	*yeteke-*	*lo*
5.	MI 89			*penn 34-ñ-kw*	*ḫ-tke-*	*lo*
6.	AW 3a	*as anis 14-ni*			*doke-*	*lo*
7.	Sh. 8	*apote-lḫ 3-ni*			*ste-*	*lo*
8.	Kar. 47	*kdi akw 5-nw*			*ḫtekkešdešte-l mtes-*	*lo*

The variations in the form of the particle are interesting. If we leave out of consideration the element *-kw* in ex. 5, which is most likely explained (from its occurrence in MI 101) as a coordinating conjunction of some kind, we have the forms:

-ni
-n
-nw

The parallelism with the fuller forms of the definite article *-l* treated by Heyler[1] is striking:

---

[1] *Comptes rendus du Groupe linguistique d'études chamito-sémitiques,* t. XI, fac. 2 (1966–7), 105–34.

-ni   -li
-n (= /-ne/?)   -le
-nw   -lw

In each example it is to be noted (a) that the noun preceding the complex Numeral+-ni is in the singular, and (b)
that the definite article -li is absent. The function of the
particle -ni seems clear if we compare ex. 1 from our
Ibrîm text with a common type of *stiche* from other funerary
texts:

Ib. 2   ant ḫ-šḫs-li-s 5-ni yetmde-lo-wi
        'He was related to five prophets of the Ḫ-šḫs.'
Kar. 21 ant mnp-s-leb   yetmde-lo-wi
        'He was related to the prophets of Amanappa.'

The parallelism here seems to rule out the necessity of
considering other functions for -ni, such as an ordinal
function; it would seem to have been simply a numerator
for indefinite nouns, rather like the class numerators in
Chinese. Its frequent absence after numeral signs elsewhere in the corpus suggests either that it was facultative,
like so many other elements in Meroïtic, or that it was
regarded as part of the number-word represented by the
numeral, and its presence deduced and read by the ancient
reader from the context. As pointed out in an earlier paper,[1]
the corresponding pattern with enumerated definite nouns
seems to have been either:

Noun+-li+number
ex. di-lḫ-l tbo   (MI 123)
'the two great ladies'

              or

Noun+-leb+number
ex. ašori pilqe-te-leb tbo (MI 101)
'the two (forms of) Osiris-in-the-Abaton'

Perhaps the choice between singular or plural forms of the
article depended on the particular nuance it was desirable
to convey. In any case, the fact that the number-word in
these two examples is written out and does not show an
ending in -ni makes it impossible on the evidence to regard
the element as a numerator usable for both indefinite and
definite numerands.

A note on some personages mentioned in the texts

kišri : mkesmeñ : The word *kišri* does not resemble any
other known Meroïtic title, and although it might be
divided into something like *ki-šri*, the resulting elements
do not look particularly familiar. If it was pronounced (as I
suppose it was) approximately /kišari/, it is conceivable
that we have here a Meroïtic rendering of the Latin
caesar, καῖσαρ in Greek, and represented in Egyptian at
this time as g(y)srs or k(y)srs. Meroïtic š as an equivalent of
Egyptian s is well established, and the final s of the Egyptian

form might well have been dropped by the Meroïtes,
since it constitutes the Meroïtic genitive; alternatively
they may have adopted the word directly from Greek. The
following personal name *mkesmeñ* could quite well be a
Meroïtic rendering of such a name as Maximinus or
Maximianus; in view of the weakness of the vowel *e*
in Meroïtic, and its frequent use in the transcription of
Egyptian words to separate consonants which in the original
form clusters, it would be the obvious device for dealing
with the foreign /-ks-/. The pronunciation would presumably have been on the order of /maksamen/. Of the
several imperial Roman figures which might be represented
the most likely candidate would probably be Maximin
Daia (Galerius Valerius Maximinus), appointed Caesar
for the Orient and Egypt in the year 305; of the rulers
named Maximin or Maximian, he was the only one to
have had a particular connection with Egypt. The idea put
forward here meets with two specific objections besides
the obvious one of over-boldness in terms of our present
ignorance of Meroïtic material. The first is phonetic; the
penultimate vowel in Maximinus, in both Greek and Latin,
is long, and to suppose that it would be represented by
Meroïtic *e*, the weakest member of the Meroïtic vowel
system, would require the assumption that the vowel
quantity had been considerably distorted from the original.
The second objection is that there is no particular reason to
assume that Tameye was so important a person as to
justify the sending of funeral gifts by a Caesar of the
Tetrarchy. It is of course perfectly possible that Tameye
was a very influential person indeed, since even Wayekiye I
does not give himself any titles in his epitaph (MI 89),
and it would seem that Tameye's family ranked high in the
service of the generals; he or she may have been more
elevated than we are led to think by the lack of a high
title in the text of the stela. It may well have been of some
concern to a Roman Caesar of the crumbling Tetrarchy to
secure his Egyptian frontiers by diplomatic means before
entering, as Maximin Daia did, the bloody contest for
supremacy in the Empire. If all this be admitted as a
possible interpretation, it would be necessary to see in the
phrase *kid : kišri-s* : the designation of the funeral gift
as something worthy or typical of a Caesar, or as in some
sense an official present.

mlekye : A personage bearing this name or title appears
several times in the texts from Lower Nubia. The form of
the word, with its -ye ending, suggests a personal name,
a conclusion supported by some contexts, but one not
compatible with all of the evidence. The problem is com-
pounded by the well-known difficulty in dating most of
our documents, since it is hard to say whether we are
dealing with more than one person or not. A review of the
evidence would seem to be in order.

[1] Millet, *Actes du premier congrès international de linguistique sémitique et chamito-sémitique, Paris 1969* (The Hague/Paris, 1973), 392–7.

Apart from the occurrence in Ib. 2, where Malekaye appears as a donor along with such exalted persons as an unnamed viceroy and a *kroro*, the word is found in several other texts:

GA 39 (unpublished): The deceased, a woman named Shakhiye, is said to be *ššor atbo-s mlekye yetmde-lo-wi* 'related to the *ššor* of two (?) Malekaye'. Here the pattern is, or appears to be, the familiar one of title followed by name. The title is a new one, and the translation of *atbo* as a form of the known word for 'two' is questionable. Six of the other named relatives are entitled *mleke-yos*, an apparent expansion of the known title *mleke* by the element *yos*, and one wonders if the name *mlekye* is not simply formed from it, as *apoteye* from the title *apote* (*Kar.* 21).

AW 3a: This commemorated two persons of uncertain sex, who are described as related to a governor of Faras and other worthies, among them a *mlekye*:

> *mlekye   mrde   pesto-li-s-li   mrde   pelmoš-li-s-li   kelw*
> *ḥrpḫe-bḫe-li yetmde-leb-k-wi*

It is unclear how many persons are actually mentioned in this passage, but I am inclined to take everything that follows after *mlekye* and preceeds the word of relationship as epithets of *mlekye*, and understand 'they were related to *mlekye*, the *mrde* of the prince and *mrde* of the general as well (*kelw*), the *ḥrpḫe-bḫe*'. The word *mrde* is unknown elsewhere but suggests a relationship to *mr* in the often encountered phrase *mlo mr-s*. Perhaps some such gloss as 'favoured' might not be far off. What the last phrase in the *stiche* means is even more obscure. *bḫe* has variously been identified as a plural dative pronoun 'to, for them', and (by the writer) as in some cases a plural subject marker for verbs. Thus either 'the one who governs for them' or 'the one (to whom) they (i.e. the prince and general) give commands' might be suggested. Whatever the meaning of the *stiche* may be, it is difficult to garner any impression from it other than that the personage designated as *mlekye* is being represented as of considerable importance *vis-à-vis* the provincial administration of Lower Nubia.

AW 4: This badly damaged stela does not preserve any indication of the name or parentage of the deceased, but a very long *stiche*, beginning in line 8 with the title *apote* and ending with the word *yetmdelo* in line 13, is apparently one of a series of *stiches* expressing relationship to various envoys, to the chief envoys, and to a general named Pawarite. The *stiche* in question is complex in structure, apparently containing many clauses, which can perhaps be best set out as follows:

> *apote adoye*
>   (*apote qe* ⚏ *yeteyitke,*
>   *aprs 707 yerote qori [tk] tbrke,*

> *dpre awto-s-li tbrke,*
> *aprs awto-s ato-li aḥe-l tbrke,*
> *dmrke awto-s-li tbrke,*
> *mlekye ḳelmeši-te-li tmñ yiroḫe-te-l) yetmde-lo*

I am suggesting that the *stiche* is a very much extended *yetmde*-clause of the usual type, stating the relationship of the deceased to the envoy Adoye, whose name is then qualified with the series of statements that follows, describing qualities or activities. The verb(?) *tbrke* is prominent; a single final definite article *-l* closes the series of statements. The last clause, containing the word *mlekye*, contains, as it happens, words whose meaning can be guessed at, although the grammatical scheme is unclear. *kelmeši* has the look of a place-name, being followed by the locative particle *-te*, and *tmñ* is definitely a place, one of the several in the Karanog area associated so strongly with the family of the princes; the verb is the word *yiroḫe* which I have conjectured to mean 'send'.[1] The structure might be analysed as follows:

	mlekye	*kelmeši-te-li*	*tmñ*	*yiroḫe-te-l*
		Noun+-*li*	Noun	Verb+*l*
(Subject)		Object	Indirect	Verb
			Object?	

The meaning might then be 'the one who sent *mlekye*-who-was-in-Kelameši (to) Tamañ'. What the implications of such an understanding of the text might be can only be guessed. One wonders whether the name Kelameši (or Kalemeši) might not be the Meroïtic name of Kalâbsha, whose modern name is presumably an analogized Arabic version of the older Talmis (Eg. *talmise).

MI 132: In this stela in Moscow the deceased, Wayeteye, is the son of the general Atankitanideye known from a Philae graffito and from the stela TWA 198.[2] He is said himself to be '*ḫlbiñ* of the *adb*', and there follows another descriptive *stiche*:

> *mlekye ḫlbiñ yitki-te-lo*

The structure here is ambiguous, but perhaps the most likely interpretation is 'he was *ḫlbiñ*-officer in Yitaki (Tôshka?) of *mlekye*', that is, a local deputy of the mysterious magnate.

There is also a reference to *mlekye* in the unpublished stela of Abaratoye from Tumâs, and we are thus faced with the very real problem of whether all the references to the *mlekye* are indeed to the same individual. If the two Ibrîm texts are more or less contemporary, and the similarity of their style and content suggest this strongly to the mind of the writer—and if the identification of the *kišri mkesmeñ* with Maximin Daia be allowed—there is a considerable

---

[1] *Ägypten und Kusch* (Schriften zur Geschichte und Kultur des alten Orients 13, Berlin, 1977), 318.

[2] Ph. 411; for TWA 198 see Trigger, in *Postilla* (New Haven, Conn.), no. 72 (20 Dec. 1962), 1 ff.

span of years between the *mlekye* mentioned in the Tumâs text (Abaratoye can hardly have lived much beyond the year 260), and the one referred to as living about 300. It seems to me that we must take *mlekye* as a title rather than as a name, despite its appearance, or perhaps as a name used as a title in later times, like the name Caesar.

The personage so designated does seem in any case to have had strong connections with both the princes of Akiñ and the generals, and perhaps even to have acted for them. Whether or not the '*ššor* of both' Malekaye of *GA* 39 was the original one of the series must, of course, remain only the subject of speculation.

G

THE COPTIC TEXTS

by

E. S. Meltzer

THE Coptic texts from the cemeteries at Qaṣr Ibrîm comprise six funerary stelae and three ostraca. One of the latter is extremely puzzling and may not be in Coptic (see below); otherwise, the texts are in Saʿidic. All of these texts were surface finds and thus have no archaeological context.

The writer tenders his thanks to Professor H. S. Smith, who made the facsimile copies of the six stelae, to Mr A. J. Mills for entrusting him with this material, to Mr T. G. H. James of the British Museum for photographs of the ostraca, and to Professors R. J. Williams and J. M. Plumley for many valuable suggestions which have been incorporated into the text (some pivotal ones being given special mention).

I THE STELAE

1. 193 Surface. Durham GM 1964 561. Plates LXXV, XCI. 5. Sandstone, 20.9 cm. wide × 26.5 cm. high. A rectangular border of straight lines encloses the text; the upper right corner is broken off.

Translation

⸓God is One, the Hel⸓per, the Immortal.⸓ He has gone to ⸓ rest, namely the B⸓lessed *Ta⸓rouepoxx⸓8⸓a* on day ten ⸓ of Epēp in ⸓10⸓ peace, Amen.

Notes

Ll. 1–4 For the 'God is One . . .' formula, see E. Petersen, *ΕΙΣ ΘΕΟΣ. Epigraphische, formgeschichtliche und religionsgeschichtliche Untersuchung* (Forschungen zur Religion und Literatur des Alten und Neuen Testaments, N.F., H. 24 Göttingen, 1926); and M. Cramer, *Archäologische und epigraphische Klassifikation koptischer Denkmäler des Metropolitan Museum of Art, New York und des Museum of Fine Arts, Boston, Mass.* (Wiesbaden, 1957), 3, 33. The opening words εἷς θεός (ὁ βοηθός) in Greek are also common on Coptic tombstones (e.g., Cramer nos. 2, 5, 6, 14, 24–6); Cramer no. 55 gives ογα πε πноγτε πбонеос and thereafter diverges from our examples.

Ll. 6–8 ϣϣ seems certain at the end of l. 7 and o seems probable on the basis of the photograph. The name of the deceased (male) seems to be ταρογεποϣϣа, which Professor Plumley suggests might be a Nubian name. The rubbing corroborates the ϣϣ but for the preceding abraded letter shows what looks like an angular trace at the bottom: ▨ (??).

2. 193.33.2 Surface. Durham GM 1964 560. Plates LXXVI, XCI. 1. Sandstone, 21 cm. wide (intact) × 20.8 cm. high.

A rectangular border of straight lines encloses the text; a large portion of the right side is broken off (see below).

Translation

⸓Go[d] is One, [the Helpe]⸓r, the Immortal: . . . ⸓saying / that (?): You have (?) died . . . ⸓ in the wor[ld] . . . [She di(?)]⸓ed, namely the Bl[essed (f.)] ⸓Lady (??) . . . [on day]⸓ 19 of Mesore [in pea]⸓ce, Am[en].

Notes

Nearly the entire right half of this stela is broken off; the lines probably averaged 16–17 letters across. This bears on the restorations suggested.

The restoration [τε πбонео], eight letters, is obvious.

L. 2. There seems to be a small oblique divider following πατμογ; I cannot as of yet fill in the lacuna on this line.

L. 3. If not the end of a word, ϫε probably introduces a quotation, most likely biblical. Professor Williams suggests that since the deceased is a woman, αρμογ might be a faulty writing of αρεμογ 'you have died' (2 f.s.), the beginning of the quotation or address.

L. 4. The restoration [αcϫω]κεбоλ 'she died' (lit. 'came to an end, fulfilled herself') seems most likely, giving the pronoun resumed by π̄σι in the next line.

L. 5. Is there room for one more letter after м[ακαρια]?

L. 6. The name of the deceased is troublesome. Does it start at the beginning of the line? Prof. Plumley suggests that κερ might be an abbreviation for Greek κυρία 'Lady'; he also notes that the two letters after the second ε might be cμ̄ or πμ̄ rather than τμ̄, and that the last fully preserved letter looks more like ⳳ than ⲁ. Are we dealing with another Nubian name?

L. 6. Restore [ϩⲛⲥⲟⲩ] at the end of the line, introducing the date.

L. 7. Restore [ϩⲛⲟⲩⲉⲓ] at the end of the line. It is likely that ⲉⲓ belongs at the end of this line rather than the beginning of the next, as despite the break the beginning of the next line seems to be blank; moreover, the number of letters would fit.

L. 8. On the basis of the photograph, read ϩ rather than ⲑ.

3. 193 Surface. Plates LXXVI, XCI. 4. Red Sandstone, 17.8 cm. wide × 22.5 cm. high.

Along the upper border are three crosses; between the first and second is the abbreviation ⲓ̄ⲥ̄ 'Jesus', between the second and third ⲭ̄ⲥ̄ 'Christ'. There are straight lines along the three remaining borders.

Translation

¹ For the remembrance of ² the Blessed (f.) Hel³lene (on) the day ⁴ in which she has gone to rest, ⁵ the seventeenth day ⁶ of Pharmuthi. ⁷ O Lord Jesus, may you ⁸ set her soul at rest ⁹ in the bosom of Abr¹⁰aham and Isaac and ¹¹ Jacob, in peace, ¹² Amen. Pharmuthi 15.

Notes

L. 1. Cf. the formula ⲡ(ⲉ)ϩⲟⲟⲩ ⲙ̄ⲡⲣ̄ⲙ̄ⲙⲉⲉⲩⲉ 'the day of remembrance . . .', Cramer, op. cit., p. 31–3.

L. 5. Note the erroneous feminine suffix ⲥ̄ resuming ⲡⲉϩⲟⲟⲩ under the influence of the feminine suffixes pertaining to the deceased.

Ll. 5–6. The date ⲡⲉⲥⲟⲩⲙ̄ⲛ̄ⲧⲏ is certainly to be taken as 'day 17' (Crum, 440) rather than 'tenth day' (cf. Crum, 187).

L. 11. Note ⲛ for ϩⲛ and the spelling ⲏⲣⲏⲛⲏ for ⲉⲓⲣⲏⲛⲏ.

L. 12. The discrepancy between this date and that given in ll. 5–6 suggests that it was added as a correction. Also note the spelling of Pharmuthi with ⲡ in l. 6, and with ⲫ in the abbreviation.

4. 193.33.3 Surface. British Museum 66582. Plates LXXV, XCI. 2. Sandstone, 15.9 cm. wide × 38.8 cm. high.

This stela is quite weathered, with a horizontal crack about 24 cm. down and pieces broken off at the bottom. There is an ornate cross in the bottom section below the text.

Translation

¹ . . . ² by the [providence(?)] ³ of God ⁴ Almigh⁵ty, he has g[one] ⁶ to rest, nam[ely the] ⁷ Blessed (m.)⁸ Andreas⁹ [day(?)] . . . ¹⁰ . . . the Lord¹¹ God, Jesus Christ,¹² may He set at rest¹³ [him (?)] in the bosom of A¹⁴braham and [Isa]ac and ¹⁵Jacob. [Ame]n,¹⁶ so be it.

Notes

L. 1. The traces are too meager to be intelligible.

L. 2. Restoring Greek πρόνοια.

Ll. 9–10. ⲥⲟⲩ is a more likely restoration than ϩⲟⲟⲩ; the date should follow. The passage between ⲥⲟⲩ and ⲡⲭ̄ⲥ remains obscure.

Ll. 12–13. Professor Plumley suggests that the passage be taken as 'May he (be at) rest'; but this verb is clearly used transitively in stela 3 above, and possibly 5 below. The use of -ⲱ in ⲁⲛⲁⲡⲁⲩⲱ is unusual; in Saʿidic one expects -ⲉ, -ⲉⲓ, or -ⲓ.

L. 13. Restoring Greek κόλπος as a synonym of ⲕⲟⲩⲛ︥.

L. 14. Note the abbreviation ⳉ 'and', as well as the spelling ⲁⲃⲣⲁⲁⲙ (rather than ⲁⲃⲣⲁϩⲁⲙ as in 3 above), in which the last ⲁ is conflated with the ⲙ.

L. 16. On the basis of the photograph, no ⲉ should be read at the beginning of this line.

5. 192 Surface. Plates LXXVI, XCI. 3. Sandstone, 26.9 cm. wide × 34.1 cm. high.

This stela has a raised border, the top and bottom plain, the sides carved in imitation of a pair of columns. The surface of the stela is carved with uniform register lines; at the bottom the lines of the text no longer correspond to these, the last line being on the border itself. A cross, much worn, precedes the text on the top line.

Translation

¹According to the des²tiny which God³ gave to Adam⁴ (Saying): Adam, you are⁵ clay, to clay (*from next line*) you shall return again,⁶ she has gone to⁷ rest, namely the Blessed (f.) R(?) . . . ⁸*mata*, (on) the 23rd of the month of Thoth, 9th indiction. ⁹–¹⁰ God will (set at) rest her soul. ¹¹ Amen.

Notes

L. 1. Note the use, here and in l. 4, of ⳋ for ⲟⲩ.

L. 5. The phrase ⲉⲡⲕⲁϩ in the next line has been translated here because of the use of the Second Future.

L. 7. Note the ⳝ added above the line for an abbreviated

writing of ⲛ̄ϭⲓ. The last two letters on the line are uncertain. Professor Plumley regards the former as ⲥ rather than ⲣ, and wonders whether the last might not be ⲁ, yielding a name ⲥⲁⲙⲁⲧⲁ. However, it does not resemble the other examples of ⲁ in this text; it looks more like the type of filler which appears after ⲟⲁⲙⲏⲛ, but a filler in the middle of a name seems to make no sense.

L. 8. Indiction is elsewhere abbreviated ⲓⲛ̄ⲁ rather than ⲓⲛ, but there seems no other possibility. If the reading ⲑ is correct it is the ninth Indiction; if ⲉ, the fifth.

Ll. 9–10. On the basis of the photograph, the last letter in line 9 should be ⲉ rather than ⲥ. Here the lapicide has obviously become very cramped; the most likely interpretation of the text seems to be that l. 9 belongs *after* ⲡⲛⲟⲩⲧⲉ; when inserted there it yields the sentence ⲡⲛⲟⲩⲧⲉ ⲛⲁⲁⲛⲁⲡⲁⲩⲉ ⲛ̄ⲧⲉⲥⲯⲩⲭⲏ 'God will (give) rest (to) her soul.' (Thus we would take the second letter in l. 9 as ⲁ rather than ⲁ.) We have seen the transitive use of ⲁⲛⲁⲡⲁⲩⲉ in 3 above, and probably in 4. Professor Plumley wonders whether the passage could not be taken without transposition of lines and read ⲁⲥⲁⲛⲁⲡⲁⲩⲉ ⲡⲛⲟⲩⲧⲉ ⲛ̄ⲧⲉⲥⲯⲩⲭⲏ 'She has gone to rest, (O) God of her soul', noting that the First Future would be unusual in such an expression. However, comparing the tracing with the photograph, the reading ⲛⲁ- seems indicated. The photograph also shows what seem to be two oblique hatches over the ⲛ.

6. 193 Surface. Durham GM 1964 559. Plate XCI. 6. No scale given with photograph.

This is a fragment, rather worn. A horizontal line is carved below the first partial line of text preserved.

Translation

¹ . . . ² . . . the day ³–⁴ in which she has gone to rest, the day ⁵ ⌜eight⌝ of Pa⟨o⟩pe . . .

Notes

Ll. 3–4. We would expect ⲛ̄ⲧⲁⲥⲙ̄ⲧⲟⲛ ⲙ̄ⲙⲟⲥ ⲛ̄ⲟ̄ⲏⲧϥ̄. There is no room for ⲙ̄ⲙⲟⲥ which has clearly been omitted. The letter after ⲧ on l. 4, which at first glance looks like ⲏ, is ⲉϥ with a scratch in the stone; compare the ⲏs in l. 1 and ⲟ̄ⲏⲧ of l. 4. L. 4 ends with ⲡⲉⲥⲟⲩ 'the day (date)'.

L. 5. The date is expected here; Professor Williams suggests [ⲯⲁ]ⲥ⌜ⲟⲩⲛ⌝[ⲛ] ⲡⲁ⟨ⲟ⟩ⲡ⌜ⲉ⌝.

II THE OSTRACA

1. 192B Surface. British Museum 66573. Plate XCII. 1. Pottery ostracon, height 14.0 cm., width 14.6 cm.

Six lines across the upper part of the sherd, and traces of a seventh at the upper right edge.

Comments

This ostracon is extremely puzzling; the language of the text has not been identified with certainty. The writer is particularly grateful to Professor Plumley for his helpful comments, which have been utilized in the following discussion.

ⲁⲡⲟⲥⲧⲟⲗⲟⲥ 'apostle' (in the fourth full line) and ⲁ⌜ⲡ⌝ⲁ ⲗⲟⲅⲅⲓⲛⲟⲥ ⲉⲡⲓⲥⲕⲟⲡⲟⲥ 'Father (?) Longinus, Bishop' (the last line) are immediately apparent; however, a consecutive reading in Coptic has not been achieved. The writer wondered at first whether the text might be in Old (or Mediaeval) Nubian; the letter ϫ̅, which does not seem to be Coptic, occurs at least five times, and there are two possible examples of an ending -ⲗ̄: ⲁⲡⲟⲥⲧⲟⲗⲟⲥⲥⲗ̄ (but why the double ⲥ?) and . . . ⲱⲕⲗ̄. But this identification presents problems. Which of the Nubian letters is ϫ̅, the *w* (usually ⳟ or ⳡ) or the *ñ* (ⳝ)? The three other Nubian letters absent from Coptic do not occur, and ⲟ̄, which is rare in Nubian, appears at least four times in our text. The absence of other Nubian morphology is also notable; however, Coptic morphology seems no more readily identifiable. On the basis of the last line, perhaps Coptic is more likely, as the distinctively Nubian terminology is not employed. The writer's impression is that this text is epistolary in nature.

The writer hopes that further research and comparison will make it possible to unravel this intriguing text, and looks forward to suggestions and observations which may advance its interpretation.

2. 192B Surface. British Museum 66574. Plate XCII. 2. Pottery ostracon, height 8.3 cm., width 13.6 cm.

Seven lines, with traces of two others on the top and bottom edges respectively; the writing becomes very faint about half-way across. Only the complete lines are numbered in the following discussion.

Translation

. . . ¹ . . . now(?) . . . ² him(?), he shall not . . . ³ . . . he does not give it(?)/them(?) . . . ⁵ for he said . . . ⁶ (that) . . . ⁷ . . .

Notes

L. 1. The line begins ⲟⲩⲧⲉⲛⲟ⌜ⲩ⌝.
L. 3. The line begins ϥⲛⲛⲉϥⲧⲣ. Is the next letter ⲓ, or is that the first stroke of another letter?

L. 4. Is the first letter on the edge ⲛ? The third letter does not look like ⲉϥ; could it be ⲟ̦?

L. 5. ⲁϥϫⲟⲟⲥⲧⲁⲣ is clear.

L. 6. The group following ϫⲉ looks like ⲛⲁⲛ̄ⲟ̦ⲟ; the ⲟ̦ looks more like that letter than ⲣ. Could the ⲁ possibly be a small, blotched writing of ϯ? If so, the writer would venture the rather daring reading ⲛϯⲛ̄ⲟ̦ⲟ[ⲧ] 'I do not trust/believe', restoring the qualitative of ⲛⲁⲟ̦ⲧⲉ (Crum, 246); a quotation is very likely after ϫⲉ (unless of course it is the end of a previous word).

3. 192B Surface. British Museum 66575. Plate XCII. 3. Pottery ostracon, height 12.0 cm., width 11.4 cm.

The writing is extremely faint. Several letters can be detected on three lines on the narrow left edge (where the text apparently begins) and faint traces are visible elsewhere, but a reading has not been achieved.

APPENDIX OF TECHNICAL REPORTS

A. Plant remains from the mortar 192.2.10 from Qaṣr Ibrîm

by

W. M. STEELE *and* A. H. BUNTING

The material submitted consisted of soil containing two kinds of grains, which at first sight appear to be sorghum and pearl millet, together with what appear to be pieces of the pericarps of the larger grains, other plant debris including wood, and what are possibly pieces of pedicels or inflorescence branches. Except for the grains, there are no other unequivocally identifiable grass spikelet parts. Neither the grains, nor the plant detritus, are carbonized; but the grains do appear to be mineralized, and as a photograph (pl. XCIII. 5) shows, this change has occurred within the tissues as well as at the surface. Were they under water for this to happen?

Grain size

17 'sorghum' grains
Length	mean 4.4 mm.	range 3.9–5.0 mm.
Greatest breadth	mean 3.6 mm.	range 3.2–3.9 mm.

10 'millet' grains
Length	mean 2.6 mm.	range 2.4–2.9 mm.
Greatest breadth	mean 1.8 mm.	range 1.5–2.1 mm.

Grain morphology

The small grains are rounded at the apex and pointed at the base (pl. XCIII. 1) and look like pearl millet (*Pennisetum typhoides*).

The large grains (pl. XCIII. 2) are more or less ovoid, and biconvex with their greatest diameter about ⅓ their length from the apex. They resemble grains of sorghum in general appearance. Several bear what may be the stump of a pedicel and the remains of styles. However, no pedicelled spikelets[1] were present in the material, though most samples of sorghum grain contain at least a few. None of the grains have the flattened surface found in many modern sorghums. This may be because they became swollen in water, but otherwise it may be that they are the fruits of a biconvex sorghum like the durras, which are grown in Egypt and the Sudan. However, in the durras the pedicelled spikelets are more than usually persistent, so

that the absence of pedicelled spikelets in this material tends to discount this suggestion.

The surface of one grain appears to bear a glume (or the cast of a glume) with nerves (the middle grain on the R side of pl. XCIII. 2). Many of the grains have lost some or all of their pericarp. A constant feature of broken pieces of pericarp from the base of grains is a raised disc on the inner concave surface above where the stalk was attached (pl. XCIII. 3 and 4). In fresh material, after the endosperm has been removed with HCl, a deeply pigmented ring is visible in the same position inside both white or brown pericarps. It seems possible that this tissue is harder or more resistant to decay, so that in ancient material it appears as a slightly raised disc.

Grain anatomy

A comparison of photographs of sections through modern sorghum (pl. XCIII. 6) and Qaṣr Ibrîm grains (pl. XCIII. 5) also suggests that the archaeological material includes both pericarp and endosperm. The walls of endosperm cells appear to have been mineralized, or at least greatly thickened.

Identity of the material

The grains certainly appear to be the seeds of a grass because (i) one of the grains bore what looks like a piece of a glume and (ii) the outer layer of the grain is much too thick to be the testa of a seed, which taken along with the other evidence suggests that it is the pericarp of a caryopsis such as a grass fruit.

Favouring the view that the large grains are sorghum are:

a. The shape and appearance of the grains.

b. Over-all dimensions. For *S. bicolor* var. *durra* Doggett gives 4–6 mm. × 2.5–6 mm. Compare 3.9–5.0 mm. × 3.2–3.9 mm. in this material.

c. Characteristic raised disc inside pericarp, similar in size and position to the pigmented layer in a modern grain.

d. No other grass, wild or cultivated, with grains of

---

[1] In sorghum and grasses related to it, the spikelets are of two kinds, sessile and pedicelled, borne in pairs consisting of one of each kind. The sessile spikelets contain both male and female parts, so that grains form in them;

the adjacent pedicelled spikelets are male or sterile. Though the pedicelled spikelets tend to be shed as the ear matures, at least a few remain attached up to harvest time.

this size and shape is known to us from the Northern Sudan.

Against this view is the absence of any pedicelled spikelets (above). Perhaps the Qaṣr Ibrîm sample had been very carefully winnowed before it was put in the mortar.

From the point of view of crop evolution, the presence of millet and sorghum together in Nubia in the first millennium AD is not surprising. However, we are not able to explain how the cells of the endosperm became thickened, perhaps mineralized, without assuming that the grain was in water. If it was, why did it not decompose? If it was not, how did the cells become thickened?

The grains represented in pl. XCIII. 5 and 6 were embedded in 'Epon' resin for sectioning.

B. Report on the woollen pile rug from tomb 193.105 at Qaṣr Ibrîm

by

DONALD KING

Dimensions

The rug is preserved in its complete length of 6ft. 3¼ in./ 191 cm. (including the web ends of 2¼ in./6 cm., but excluding the warp fringe of 4 in./10 cm., at each end). The preserved width is probably rather more than half the original width which, to judge from the distribution of the pattern, was probably about 4ft. 3 in./129 cm. or possibly about 5 ft./152 cm. (including side webs of about ¾ in./2 cm.).

Technique

The warp is composed of S-plied salmon pink woollen threads, 13 per inch. The main weft is composed of triple picks of Z-spun salmon pink woollen thread, 6 picks per inch. After every second pick is a row of Senna loops[1] which have been cut, forming a flat-lying cut pile. These loops are composed of pairs of Z-spun woollen threads in various colours: undyed, yellow, pink, red, light blue, blue, light green, green, and dark brown. There are 19–20 loops per sq. in. At each end of the rug, before the warp fringe, is a plait formed of a pair of Z-spun yellow woollen threads. A pair of Z-spun dark green woollen threads form an additional fringe all round the pile area.

Pattern (Pl. LXXXVIII. 1)

The main surviving feature is a longitudinal border showing a row of five triangular-headed arches, each resting on a pair of columns with stepped bases and bell-shaped capitals. Beneath each arch is a tree; these trees are of two different types, arranged alternately. Between each pair of arches is a tree of a third type. The central panel of the rug is red, with a rectangular frame of running waves in blue. On either side of this are smaller square panels, of two different kinds. One type contains chevrons of many colours, the other is subdivided into four small squares each containing a cross or rosette. The pattern of the short

end borders is uncertain. The border with various trees, and the main field subdivided into squares and rectangles are reminiscent of the surviving Persian garden-carpets of the seventeenth–eighteenth centuries, and it is quite possible that the rug was intended to evoke the idea of a garden. This concept was familiar at an early date, witness the great garden-carpet called 'the spring of Khosrō' captured by the Arabs at Ctesiphon in 637.

Origin and Date

Examples of the comparatively rare Senna loop technique have been found at Dura, Auja el-Hafir, Antinoë, and Bahnasa. It was probably in use in various parts of the Near East, at least from the third to the eighth century. A fragmentary rug from Antinoë, in the Metropolitan Museum, New York, though more finely woven than the Qaṣr Ibrîm rug, seems to have been almost identical with it in materials, colours and technical details. It was dated about 400 AD by Dimand,[2] sixth century by Riefstahl.[3] A small fragment from Bahnasa in the Victoria and Albert Museum is also in the Senna loop technique but differs from the Qaṣr Ibrîm rug in materials, colours and most other respects, and gives the impression of being considerably later in date; there is fairly good reason to assign it to the middle of the eighth century. The colours of the Qaṣr Ibrîm rug, and the use of rainbow effects indicate a relationship with the weft loop cloths showing late classical and early Christian subjects, which have been found in considerable numbers in Egypt. They are usually assigned to the fourth–fifth centuries but may well run on into the sixth and seventh. The comparative evidence suggests that the Qaṣr Ibrîm rug was made in the Near East, possibly in Egypt, probably in the fifth–sixth century, though a fourth or seventh century dating cannot be absolutely excluded.

[1] Louisa Bellinger, *Textile Analysis: Pile Techniques in Egypt and the Near East*, 1955 (Textile Museum, Washington, Workshop Notes, Paper No. 12).

[2] In *Metropolitan Museum Studies*, 4 (1933), 151–62.
[3] In *Mitteil. des Deutschen Archäol. Instituts, Röm. Abt.*, 48 (1933), 126–52.

C. The chemical analyses of some glasses from Qaṣr Ibrîm

by

ROBERT H. BRILL

Four specimens of glass were submitted to the Corning Museum of Glass for chemical analysis by T. G. H. James on behalf of the Egypt Exploration Society. The glasses were excavated at the site of Qaṣr Ibrîm in Nubia, and are thought to date from the fourth to sixth centuries AD. The specimens consist of fragments of very thin-walled blown glass vessels ranging in colour from pale green through amber. The glass itself is bubbly in all cases, and the fragments show no signs of weathering.

We have carried out quantitative atomic absorption analyses for the major components and semi-quantitative emission spectrographic analyses for certain minor and trace elements. The results are compiled in the attached table.

The glasses are of the expected soda–lime–silica variety ($Na_2O:CaO:SiO_2$) as are the vast majority of glasses predating the medieval period. The soda and lime values, however, are somewhat lower than in the majority of early glasses, and this, along with the general low level of impurities and minor elements, makes the silica contents somewhat higher than are normally found.

The glasses are of the low potash–low magnesia type (low K_2O–low MgO).[1] This indicates that the soda used for melting the glass was probably natron, rather than soda derived from plant ashes. The glasses contain manganese (MnO) and no antimony (Sb_2O_5). Manganese was commonly used as a decolorizer to offset the greenish colour due to iron impurities. These facts are consistent with a date of manufacture later than about 350 AD and point to an origin in Egypt, possibly along the Syro-Palestinian coast, or in Italy, as contrasted to more easterly origins such as are associated, for example, with Sassanian glasses. The similarity in minor and trace element concentrations suggests that the four glasses are very likely to have been made in the same factory, but it is difficult to say just where this factory was located. The glasses could be products of a local Nubian industry, or they may have been imported from one of the regions mentioned above. The extreme fragility of the vessels argues somewhat against long-distance transport, but not conclusively so.

One possible place of manufacture is the third- to fourth-century Egyptian factory at Karanis.[2] We have analysed a few samples from Karanis, but because these analyses were carried out before our analytical techniques were fully developed, we are hesitant to include the results here. Superficially, their compositions are very close to those of the Qaṣr Ibrîm glasses. In the near future our analyses of Karanis glasses will be expanded, and it should become possible to say whether or not the Qaṣr Ibrîm glasses could be products of the Karanis factory. Even so, however, Dr Sidney M. Goldstein, Associate Curator of Ancient Glass at The Corning Museum of Glass, has observed that the Qaṣr Ibrîm glasses do not resemble the usual Karanis types. There are differences in the ways the bases are made and very thin-walled vessels are not characteristic of known Karanis glasses.

As a matter of further interest, we have compared the compositions of the Qaṣr Ibrîm glass with those of glasses excavated at Sedeinga.[3] The latter date from the third century AD. The differences among the compositions are typical of the chemical variation found among glasses made in different places or in different periods. For example, the Sedeinga glasses contain examples of both the low potash–low magnesia type and the high potash–high magnesia type. Some contain manganese and others antimony. But in no instance does the combination of these compositional features match the compositions of the Qaṣr Ibrîm glasses. It can be concluded that the glass made in Nubia or traded either up the Nile or across trans-desert routes, consisted of the wares of different factories working in different technological traditions and/or with different raw materials.

SAMPLE DESCRIPTIONS

Glasses from Qaṣr Ibrîm

These glasses were excavated at Qaṣr Ibrîm. They date from the fourth to fifth centuries AD according to Mr T. G. H. James, who originally provided the samples, on the basis of information provided by the excavators.

[1] R. H. Brill, 'The Scientific Investigation of Ancient Glasses', *Proceedings VIIIth International Congress on Glass, London*, The Society of Glass Technology, 1968, 47–68.

[2] D. B. Harden, *Roman Glass from Karanis*, University of Michigan Studies, Humanistic Series, vol. XLI, 1936, University of Michigan Press.

[3] R. H. Brill, 'Scientific Examinations of Some Glasses from Sedeinga' (in press).

352 Foot of thin-walled vessel with flat, wide body. Greenish aqua, bubbly, some very large blisters. No weathering.

353 Fragment of conical thin-walled vessel with small coiled foot. Body is of pale amber glass and foot of turbid green glass, bubbly. No weathering.[1]

354 Fragment of footed, thin-walled beaker(?). Pale greenish glass, bubbly, inclusions in foot, and several blisters. No weathering.

355 Rim fragment of large thin-walled vessel with flaring rim. Very pale greenish glass, bubbly. No weathering.

[1] This piece comes from grave 192A.7. None of the other three could be identified in the excavation records.

GLASSES FROM QAṢR IBRĪM

		Beaker Aqua 352	Beaker Amber 353	Beaker Aqua 354	Vessel Aqua 355
SiO_2	d	$\simeq 76$	$\simeq 73$	$\simeq 70$	$\simeq 72$
Na_2O	a	12.9	11.7	15.9	15.7
CaO	a	5.33	5.26	6.32	4.88
K_2O	a	0.60	0.74	0.65	0.58
MgO	a	0.44	0.73	0.53	0.40
Al_2O_3	a	2.07	2.37	2.36	2.10
Fe_2O_3	a	0.71	2.30	0.89	0.86
TiO_2		0.15	0.42	0.18	0.17
Sb_2O_5		nf	nf	nf	nf
MnO	a	0.58	2.37	1.51	1.09
CuO		0.000X	0.00X	0.00X	0.00X
CoO		nf	nf	nf	nf
SnO_2		0.00X	0.00X	0.00X	0.00X
Ag_2O		nf	nf	nf	nf
PbO		0.00X	0.00X	0.02	0.00X
BaO		0.01	0.05	0.02	0.03
SrO		0.10	0.18	0.18	0.13
Li_2O		nf	nf	nf	nf
Rb_2O		—	—	—	—
B_2O_3		0.03	0.03	0.03	0.03
V_2O_5		nf	0.01	nf	nf
Cr_2O_3		nf	nf	nf	nf
NiO		nf	nf	nf	nf
ZnO		nf	nf	nf	nf
ZrO_2		nf	0.03	nf	nf
Bi_2O_3		nf	nf	nf	nf
P_2O_5	c	—	0.95	1.03	1.79

Notes:
a by atomic absorption.
c by colorimetry.
d SiO_2 estimated by difference.
All other values by emission spectrography.
Date of report, 19 February, 1976.

CONCORDANCE OF EXCAVATION NUMBERS
AND MUSEUM ACCESSION NUMBERS

EGYPTIAN MUSEUM,
  CAIRO

192.2.6: 89670
192.2.11: 89671
192.2.12: 89672
192.2.13: 89673
192.2.24: 89674
192.2.41: 89675
192.2.57: 89676
192.2.61: 89677
192.11.8: 89678
192.14.4: 89679
192.15.2: 89680
192.20.2: 89681
192.21.1: 89682
192.23.5: 89683
192.23.15: 89684
192.23.17: 89685
192.23.37: 89686
192.23.39: 89687
192.24.3: 89688
192.24.5: 89689
192.25.3: 89690
192.25.5: 89691
192.27.1: 89692
192.28.1: 89693
192.29.2: 89694
192.29.3: 89695
192.51.2: 89706
192.51.3: 89707
192.59.1: 89709
192.73.1: 89710
192.93.1: 89711
192.97.1: 89714
192.98.1: 89712
192.105.1: 89713
192.111.1: 89715
192.112.1: 89716
192.113.1: 89717
192.120.1: 89718
192.129.1: 89719
192A.3.4: 89696
192A.24.1: 89701
192B.8.1: 89699
192B.8.2: 89700
192B.9.1: 89697
192B.10.4: 89698
192D.2.3: 89702
192D.2.4: 89703
192D.2.5: 89704
193.30.3: 89663
193.34.1: 89664
193.34.3: 89665

193.66.1: 89666
193.122.1: 89667
193.122.10: 89668
193.122.13: 89669
193.122.14: 89669
193.133.11: 89720
193.136.4: 89722
193.137.3: 89721
193.138.1: 89723
193.138.2: 89524
193.147.1: 89725
193.151.10: 89726
193.156.1: 89726 *bis*
193.156.6: 89727
193.158.7: 89728
193.162.8: 89729
193.162.12: 89730

THE BRITISH
  MUSEUM, LONDON

192.2.35: 66548
192.2.36: 66577
192.2.58: 66545
192.5.2: 66542
192.11.10: 66560
192.13.7: 66539
192.15.1: 66568
192.23.3: 66561
192.23.10: 66566
192.23.20: 66563
192.23.21: 66546
192.23.31: 66578
192.23.32: 66576
192.23.52: 66557
192.28.6: 66559
192.38.2: 66543
192.74.2: 66567
192.78.2: 66564
192.80.1: 66555
192.96.1: 66562
192.117.2: 66565
192.119.2: 66570
192.133.2: 66540
192A.0.2: 66580
192A.3.2: 66558
192B.0.4: 66573
192B.0.5: 66574
192B.0.6: 66575
192C.0.5: 66583
192C.1.2: 66584
193.30.7: 66541
193.33.3: 66582
193.105.1: 66708

193.122.9: 66556
193.133.10: 66544
193.133.14: 66569
193.139.5: 66550
193.140.2: 66553
193.140.4: 66571
193.151.7: 66552
193.151.9: 66547
193.162.13: 66554

UNIVERSITY COL-
  LEGE LONDON,
  THE PETRIE
  MUSEUM

192.2.10: 19559
192.2.20: 19537
192.2.25: 19531
192.2.26: 19530
192.2.29: 19534
192.2.30: 19535
192.2.32: 19565
192.2.53: 19569
192.5.1: 19561
192.7.1: 19568
192.13.11: 19540
192.17.3: 19562
192.20.1: 19567
192.21.5: 19564
192.21.10: 19563
192.23.11: 19566
192.23.12: 19559
192.23.18: 19595
192.23.28: 19532
192.23.29: 19533
192.23.34: 19522
192.23.35: 19521
192.23.36: 19519
192.23.50: 19597
192.24.2: 19574
192.29.4: 19573
192.29.6: 19520
192.29.7: 19524
192.71.3: 19571
192.79.1: 19572
192.82.1: 19570
192.111.3: 19579
192.116.3: 19578
192A.0.3: 19560
192A.3.3: 19575
192A.4.2: 19576
192A.4.7: 19558
192A.7.1: 19527
192A.7.5: 19528

192A.7.6: 19529
192A.25.1: 19526
192B.9.8: 19551
192D.2.7: 19544
193.32.2: 19538
193.38.10: 19550
193.39.2: 19556
193.65.2: 19555
193.66.2: 19548
193.101.2: 19542
193.104.3: 19547
193.111.2: 19546
193.113.1: 19553
193.121.12: 19552
193.122.16: 19549
193.122.17: 19554
193.133.17: 19541
193.133.18: 19596
193.137.2: 19583
193.154.1: 19581
193.162.6: 19582

ASHMOLEAN
  MUSEUM, OXFORD

192.1.3: 1962.938
192.2.16: 1962.945
192.2.22: 1962.946
      1962.947a–e
      1962.948
192.2.50: 1962.944
192.6.5: 1962.920
192.11.5: 1962.916
192.11.6: 1962.917
192.12.2: 1962.931
192.17.1: 1962.915
192.17.5: 1962.914
192.18.4: 1962.934
192.21.6: 1962.926
192.23.1: 1962.939
192.26.4: 1962.932
192.28.7: 1962.919
192.30.1: 1962.953
192.41.6: 1962.956 a, b
192.51.1: 1962.937
192.71.1: 1962.930
192.117.1: 1962.933
192A.1.1: 1962.949
192A.1.2: 1962.918
192A.24.3: 1962.955a, b
192B.0.1: 1962.941
192B.0.2: 1962.942
192B.0.3: 1962.943
192B.8.3: 1962.950

193.38.8: 1962.940
193.94.1: 1962.929
193.107.1: 1962.954 a, b
193.107.3: 1962.951
193.122.6: 1962.921
193.126.4: 1962.952
193.133.5: 1962.924
193.133.6: 1962.923
193.133.16: 1962.928
193.134.1: 1962.927
193.134.3: 1962.936
193.139.2: 1962.925
193.162.5: 1962.922

ANTHROPOLOGICAL
MUSEUM, MARI-
SCHAL COLLEGE,
ABERDEEN

192.2.40: 1109^2
192.2.43: 1109^2
192.2.62: 1109^2
192.12.1: 1109^2
192.12.3: 1109^2
192.23.4: 1109^2
192.23.23: 1109^2
192.25.1: 1109^2
192.25.4: 1109^2
192.26.5: 1109^2
192.94.1: 1109^2
192.98.2: 1109^2
192.133.1: 1109^2
192A.7.3: 1109^2
192D.3.1: 1109^2
193.30.14: 1109^2
193.49.2: 1109^2
193.109.1: 1109^2
193.122.5: 1109^2
193.122.7: 1109^2
193.133.13: 1109^2
193.133.15: 1109^2
193.136.1: 1109^2
193.139.1: 1109^2
193.145.3: 1109^2

BIRMINGHAM CITY
MUSEUM AND
ART GALLERY

192.2.10: 142'63
192.2.38: 133'63
192.2.64: 130'63
192.18.2: 127'63
192.23.12: 142'63
192.23.33: 141'63
192.23.47: n.n.
192.26.1: 129'63
192.29.5: 119'63
192.34.1: 134'63
192.34.3: 135'63
192.34.4: 118'63
192.34.5: 128'63

192.36.4: 137'63
192.41.4: 139'63
192.45.1: 117'63
192.46.3: 131'63
192.49.1: 126'63
192.49.2: 124'63
192.73.2: 132'63
192B.9.2: 125'63
192B.9.5: 116'63
192C.2.2: 121'63
192C.4.2: 136'63
193.49.1: 138'63
193.50.1: 120'63
193.50.2: 122'63
193.122.12: 144'63a
193.158.6: 140'63

BLACKBURN
MUSEUM AND ART
GALLERY
(No accession numbers
assigned.)
192.2.46
192.14.3
192.46.2
192.67.7
192.69.1
192.116.2
193.65.1
193.156.3
193.156.7
193.162.3

FITZWILLIAM
MUSEUM, CAM-
BRIDGE

192.2.19: E.1.1962
192.2.63: E.6.1962
192.14.6: E.7.1962
192.36.3: E.5.1962
192A.6.3: E.4.1962
193.122.8: E.3.1962
193.151.1: E.2.1962

MUSEUM OF AR-
CHAEOLOGY AND
ETHNOLOGY,
CAMBRIDGE

192.2.51: 63.180
192.15.3: 63.178
192.18.3: 63.181
192.23.19: 63.183
192.29.1: 63.179
192.34.6: 63.182
192.119.4: 63.185
192A.4.3: 63.186
192A.4.4: 63.187
192A.7.4: 63.188
192A.17.3: 63.189

192C.0.2: 63.190
193.39.1: 63.200
193.121.1: 63.191
193.137.1: 63.199
193.145.2: 63.198
193.147.3: 63.193
193.147.4: 63.194
193.151.8: 63.197
193.156.4: 63.196
193.156.5: 63.195
193.162.11: 63.192

GULBENKIAN
MUSEUM OF
ORIENTAL ART
AND ARCHAEO-
LOGY, DURHAM

192.2.31: GM 1964 581
192.11.7: GM 1964 570
192.13.2: GM 1964 568
192.13.3: GM 1964 567
192.13.5: GM 1964 549
192.14.7: GM 1964 580
192.23.48: GM 1964 562
192.23.49: GM 1964 564
192.28.2: GM 1964 550
192.45.2: GM 1964 576
192.51.5: GM 1964 577
192.53.1: GM 1964 578
192.67.1: GM 1964 569
192.111.2: GM 1964 548
192.121.1: GM 1964 571
192A.4.5: GM 1964 558
192A.5.1: GM 1964 552
192A.6.1: GM 1964 555
192A.6.2: GM 1964 574
192A.9.1: GM 1964 557
192A.11.2: GM 1964 575
192A.16.2: GM 1964 572
192B.9.3: GM 1964 556
193.surface:
        GM 1964 559
193.surface:
        GM 1964 561
193.30.1: GM 1964 566
193.30.13: GM 1964 553
193.33.surface:
        GM 1964 560
193.38.2: GM 1964 551
193.38.3: GM 1964 554
193.38.6: GM 1964 573
193.122.11:
        GM 1964 579
193.126.1: GM 1964 563
193.133.1: GM 1964 565

LEEDS UNIVERSITY
(No accession numbers
assigned.)
192.2.55

192.5.3
192.11.11
192.13.1
192.13.9
192.17.2
192.23.7
192.23.9
192.41.1
192.46.1
192.52.1
192.83.1
192A.24.2
192D.2.1
193.34.2
193.139.4
193.148.1
193.151.4
193.154.3
193.158.2
193.162.4
193.162.9

LIVERPOOL CITY
MUSEUM

192.2.9: 1962.333.1
192.2.23: 1962.333.3
192.2.49: 1962.333.2

LIVERPOOL UNI-
VERSITY, SCHOOL
OF ARCHAEOLOGY
AND ORIENTAL
STUDIES

192.2.48: E1500
192.6.1: E6312
192.6.3: E6328
192.8.1: E6327
192.11.2: E6334
192.11.9: E6316
192.13.6: E6315
192.14.1: E6336
192.23.2: E6325
192.23.8: E6332
192.23.43: E6320
192.36.1: E6322
192.54.1: E6314
192.64.1: E6329
192.64.3: E6309
192.67.4: E6318
192.82.2: E6310
192.121.2: E6333
192.123.2: E6331
192.133.3: E6321
192A.4.1: E6313
192A.12.2: E6311
193.30.11: E6337
193.69.1: E6330
193.133.2: E6326
193.133.3: E6324

193.133.7: E6319
193.133.12: E6317
193.137.4: E6323
193.138.3: E6335
193.145.1: E6338

MANCHESTER
MUSEUM
(Not all objects assigned
museum numbers.)
192.2.45:
192.34.2:
192.81.1:
192A.12.1: 20955
192A.16.1: 20185
North Group.
    3.1: 20186
193.38.5
193.38.7
193.94.2
193.104.2: 20953
193.126.3: 20954
193.133.9: 20956
193.145.6: 20184
193.151.6: 20957
193.154.4: 20958
193.154.5: 20966
193.158.1: 20967
193.158.8: 20968

READING MUSEUM
AND ART
GALLERY
192.2.37: 83:67/6
192.6.2: 83:67/5
192.17.4: 83:67/7
192.23.14: 83:67/8
192.23.44: 118:65/1
192.26.2: 83:67/9
192.26.3: 83:67/10
192.58.1: 83:67/14
192.59.2: 83:67/15
192.60.1: 83:67/16
192.67.5: 83:67/18
192.78.1: 83:67/19
192.94.2: 83:67/20
192.110.1: 118:65/2
North Group.
    5.2: 83:67/17
192B.10.3: 83:67/11
192D.1.1: 83:67/12
192D.2.2: 83:67/13
193.30.18: 83:67/1
193.38.1: 83:67/2
193.55.2: 83:67/3
193.62.1: 83:67/4
193.121.2: 118:65/3
193.133.4: 83:67/21
193.138.4: 83:67/22

193.140.3: 118:65/4
193.145.4: 83:67/23
193.154.2: 83:67/24
193.158.3: 83:67/25

SHEFFIELD
MUSEUM
192.2.56: 1966.293
192.23.45: 1966.297
193.34.4: 1966.295

DEPARTMENT OF
ARCHAEOLOGY,
THE QUEEN'S
UNIVERSITY,
BELFAST
192.2.17: QAD/7/130
192.2.42: QAD/7/115
192.14.2: QAD/7/122
192.21.7: QAD/7/134
192.21.9: QAD/7/121
192.21.11: QAD/7/136
192.23.24: QAD/7/129
192.23.27: QAD/7/119
192.23.30: QAD/7/116
192.27.2: QAD/7/138
192.28.4: QAD/7/117
192.28.5: QAD/7/117
192.57.2: QAD/7/135
192.67.6: QAD/7/118
192.67.8: QAD/7/118
192.76.2: QAD/7/137
192A.18.1: QAD/7/126
192C.2.1: QAD/7/127
193.30.10: QAD/7/128
193.121.3: QAD/7/133
193.138.5: QAD/7/139
193.138.6: QAD/7/131
193.158.4: QAD/7/123
193.159.3: QAD/7/125
193.162.2: QAD/7/124
193.162.7: QAD/7/132

NICHOLSON
MUSEUM, SYDNEY,
AUSTRALIA
192.1.1: 63.182
192.2.8: 63.209
192.2.14: 63.208
192.2.34: 63.183
192.2.54: 63.207
192.2.65: 63.218
192.4.2: 63.219
192.13.4: 63.224
192.15.4: 63.185
192.15.5: 63.214
192.20.3: 63.211
192.21.3: 63.186

192.21.4: 63.187
192.23.13: 63.188
192.23.16: 63.189
192.23.25: 63.190
192.28.3: 63.191
192.41.3: 63.192
192.51.4: 63.196
192.56.1: 63.197
192.77.1: 63.199
192.77.2: 63.200
192.80.3: 63.201
192.119.3: 63.202
192A.19.1: 63.184
North Group.
    5.1: 63.198
192B.9.4: 63.193
192B.10.2: 63.194
192D.2.6: 63.195
193.30.2: 63.179
193.30.6: 63.180
193.95.1: 63.210
193.121.13: 63.213
193.122.4: 63.181
193.136.2: 63.203
193.136.3: 63.204
193.138.7: 63.205
193.140.5: 63.212
193.140.6: 63.240
193.140.7: 63.220
    63.221
    63.222
    63.223
193.151.3: 63.206
193.159.5: 63.216
    63.217

OTAGO MUSEUM,
DUNEDIN, NEW
ZEALAND
192.2.7: E62.29
192.2.15: E62.31
192.2.44: E62.30
192.3.1: E62.27
192.11.1: E62.5
192.17.7: E62.15
192.23.6: E62.2
192.23.26: E62.19
192.67.3: E62.4
192.78.3: E62.21
192.116.1: E62.6
192A.7.2: E62.18
192A.11.1: E62.22
192B.10.1: E62.9
193.30.8: E62.11
193.30.12: E62.7
193.30.17: E62.26
193.108.1: E62.23
193.111.1: E62.25
193.122.2: E62.10

193.122.3: E62.16
193.134.4: E62.24
193.145.5: E62.20
193.147.2: E62.14
193.151.2: E62.17
193.156.2: E62.12
193.156.8: E62.13
193.158.5: E62.8
193.162.1: E62.28

ROYAL ONTARIO
MUSEUM,
TORONTO, CANADA
192.1.6: 963.15.24
192.2.28: 963.15.27 a, b
192.2.47: 963.15.7
192.2.52: 963.15.25
192.13.10: 963.15.8
192.17.6: 963.15.9
192.21.8: 963.15.10
192.23.22: 963.15.11
192.23.42: 963.15.12
192.23.51: 963.15.15
192.24.1: 963.15.13
192.25.2: 963.15.14
192.38.1: 963.15.16
192.73.4: 963.15.17
192.80.2: 963.15.18
192.119.1: 963.15.19
193.30.4: 963.15.2
193.30.5: 963.15.3
193.30.9: 963.15.4
193.31.1: 963.15.1
193.38.4: 963.15.5
193.55.1: 963.15.6
193.122.15:
    963.15.26 a, b, c
193.133.8: 963.15.20
193.140.1: 963.15.21
193.159.1: 963.15.22
193.162.10: 963.15.23

RIJKSMUSEUM VAN
OUDHEDEN,
LEIDEN, THE
NETHERLANDS
192.2.39: F1963/8.28
192.2.60: F1963/8.5
192.4.1: F1963/8.30
192.6.4: F1963/8.4
192.11.4: F1963/8.6
192.13.8: F1963/8.7
192.18.1: F1963/8.8
192.23.41: F1963/8.29
192.24.4: F1963/8.9
192.57.1: F1963/8.13
192.64.2: F1963/8.14
192.67.2: F1963/8.15

192.71.2: F1963/8.16
192.72.1: F1963/8.17
192.73.3: F1963/8.18
192.74.1: F1963/8.19
192.76.1: F1963/8.20
192.85.1: F1963/8.21

192.111.4: F1963/8.22
192.112.2: F1963/8.23
192C.0.1: F1963/8.11
192C.0.3: F1963/8.12
192C.4.1: F1963/8.10
193.30.15: F1963/8.1

193.55.3: F1963/8.2
193.101.1: F1963/8.3
193.139.3: F1963/8.24
193.148.2: F1963/8.27
193.151.5: F1963/8.25
193.159.2: F1963/8.26

CORNING MUSEUM
OF GLASS, CORN-
ING, NY, USA
192A.7.b: 353

PLATE II

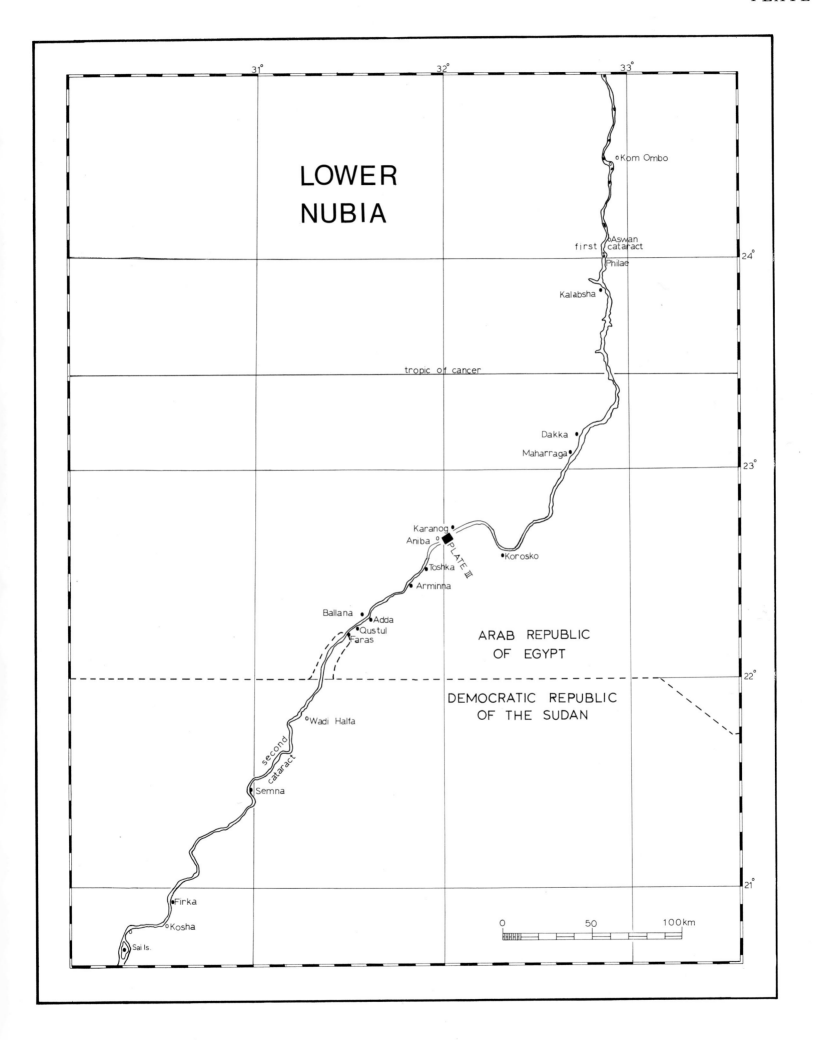

LOWER
NUBIA

ºKom Ombo

ºAswan
first cataract
Philae

Kalabsha •

tropic of cancer

Dakka •
Maharraga •

Karanog •
Aniba º
PLATE III
ºKorosko

• Toshka

• Arminna

Ballana •
• Adda
ºQustul
Faras •

ARAB REPUBLIC
OF EGYPT

DEMOCRATIC REPUBLIC
OF THE SUDAN

ºWadi Halfa

second cataract

Semna •

Firka •
ºKosha
Sai Is.

0   50   100 km

PLATE III

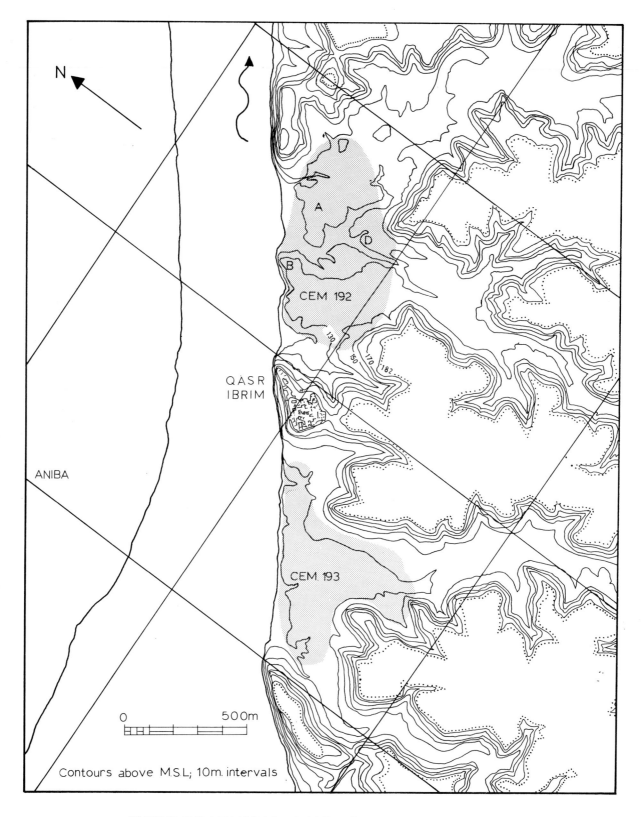

TOPOGRAPHICAL MAP OF CONCESSION

PLATE IV

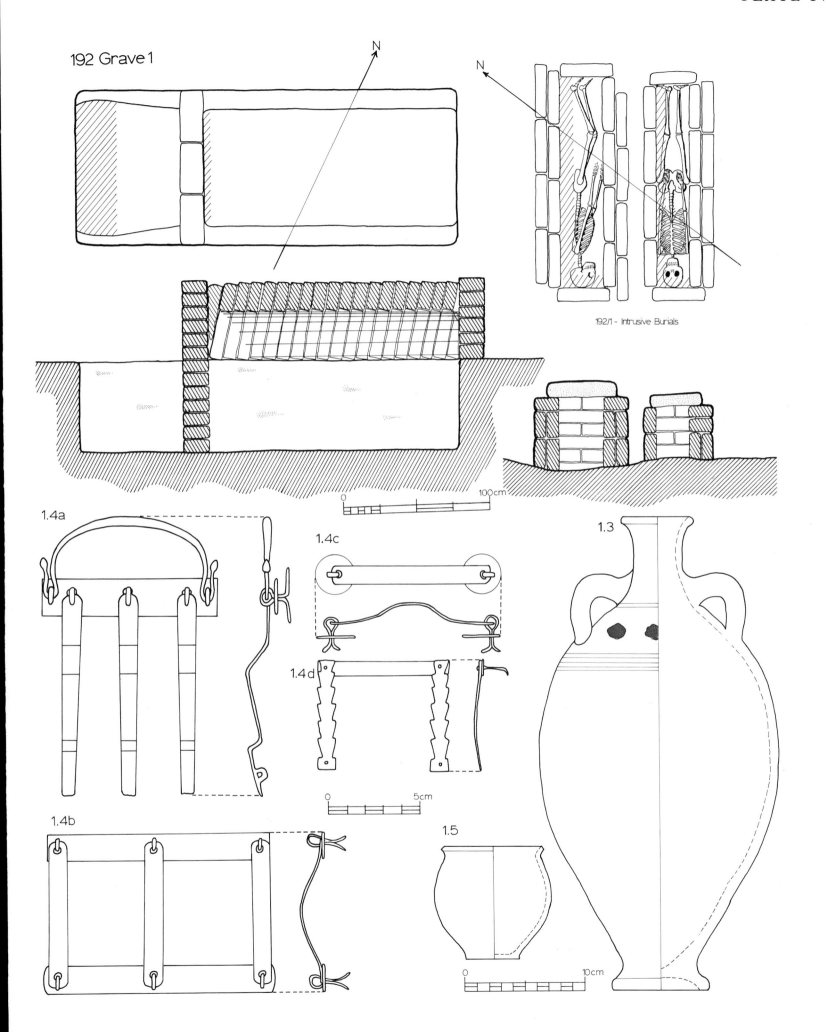

192 Grave 1

192/1 - Intrusive Burials

1.4a

1.4c

1.4d

1.3

1.4b

1.5

0   100cm

0   5cm

0   10cm

PLATE V

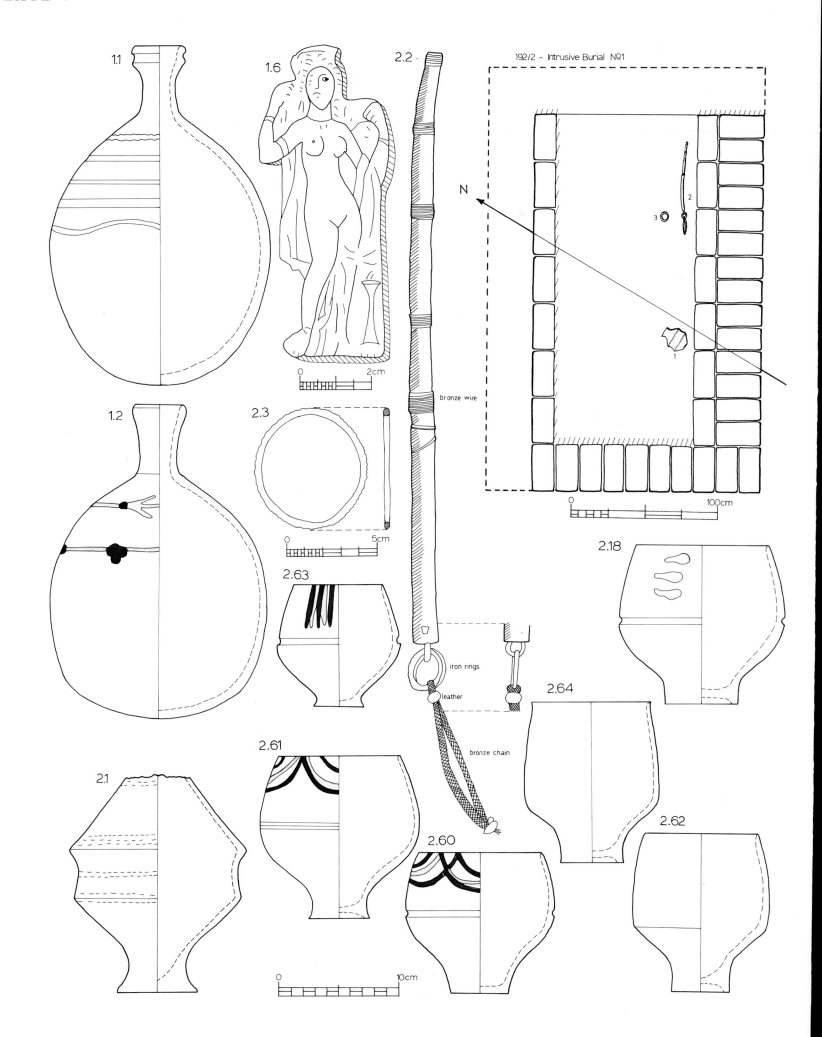

1.1

1.6

2.2

1921/2 – Intrusive Burial Nº1

N

bronze wire

1.2

2.3

0   2cm

0   5cm

2.18

2.63

iron rings

leather

bronze chain

2.64

2.61

2.60

2.62

2.1

0   100cm

0   10cm

PLATE VI

192 Grave 2

2.15

top

2.11

2.12

bottom

0   100cm

0   5cm

N

PLATE VII

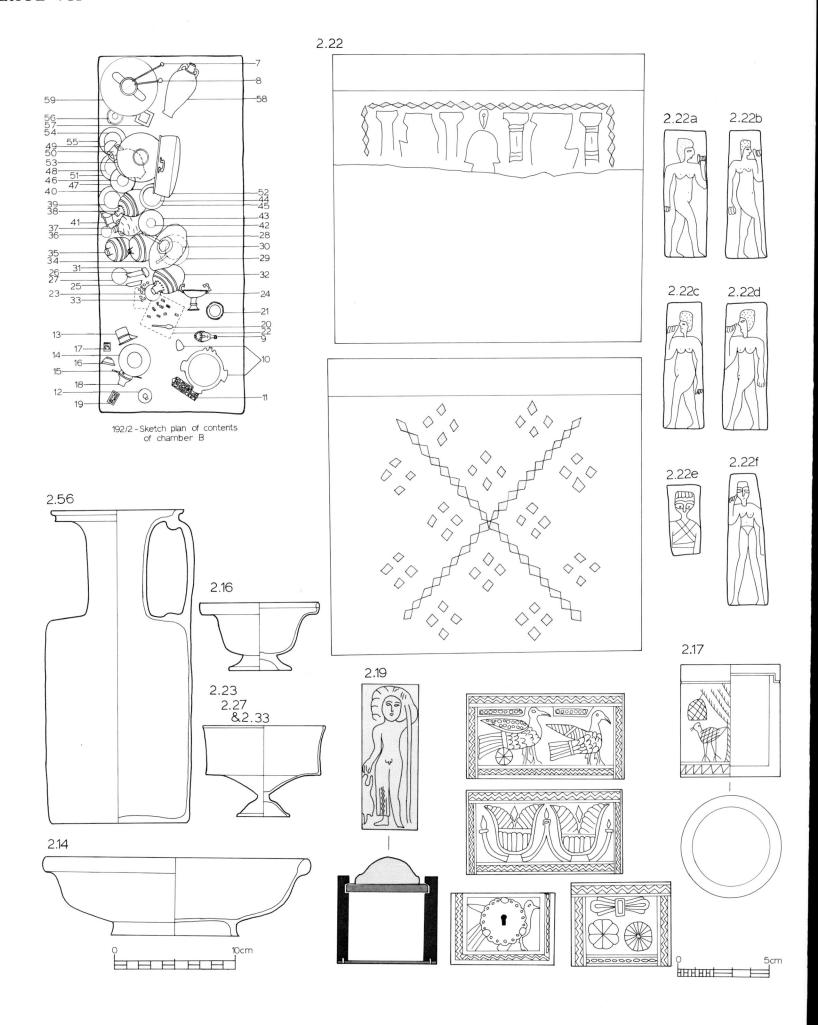

192/2 – Sketch plan of contents
of chamber B

2.22

2.22a   2.22b

2.22c   2.22d

2.22e   2.22f

2.56

2.16

2.23
2.27
&2.33

2.19

2.17

2.14

0   10cm

0   5cm

PLATE VIII

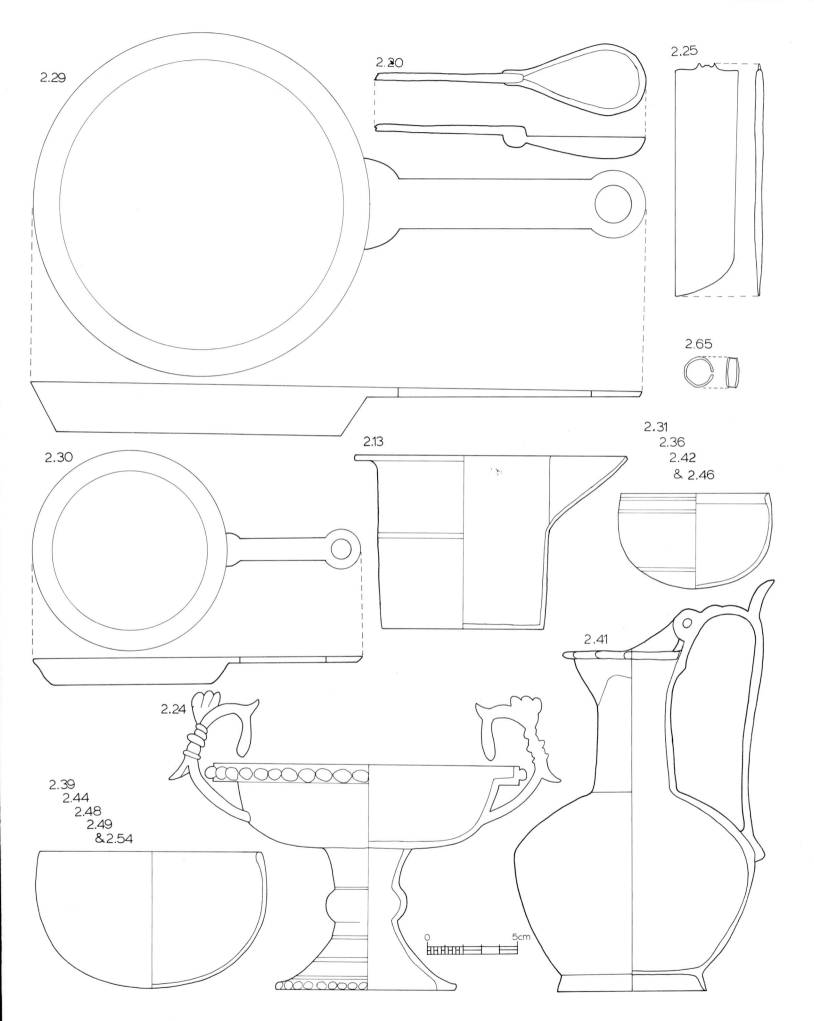

2.29

2.30

2.25

2.65

2.13

2.31
2.36
2.42
& 2.46

2.30

2.41

2.24

2.39
2.44
2.48
2.49
& 2.54

0   5cm

PLATE IX

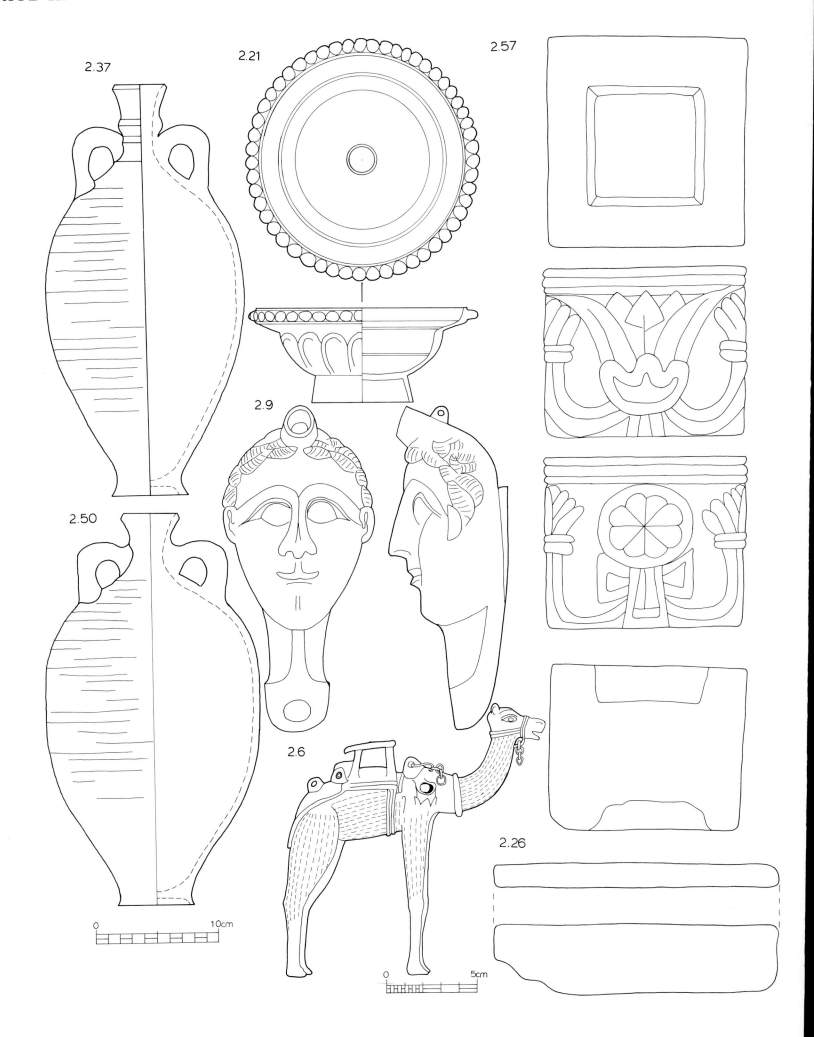

2.37

2.21

2.57

2.50

2.9

2.6

2.26

0   10cm

0   5cm

PLATE X

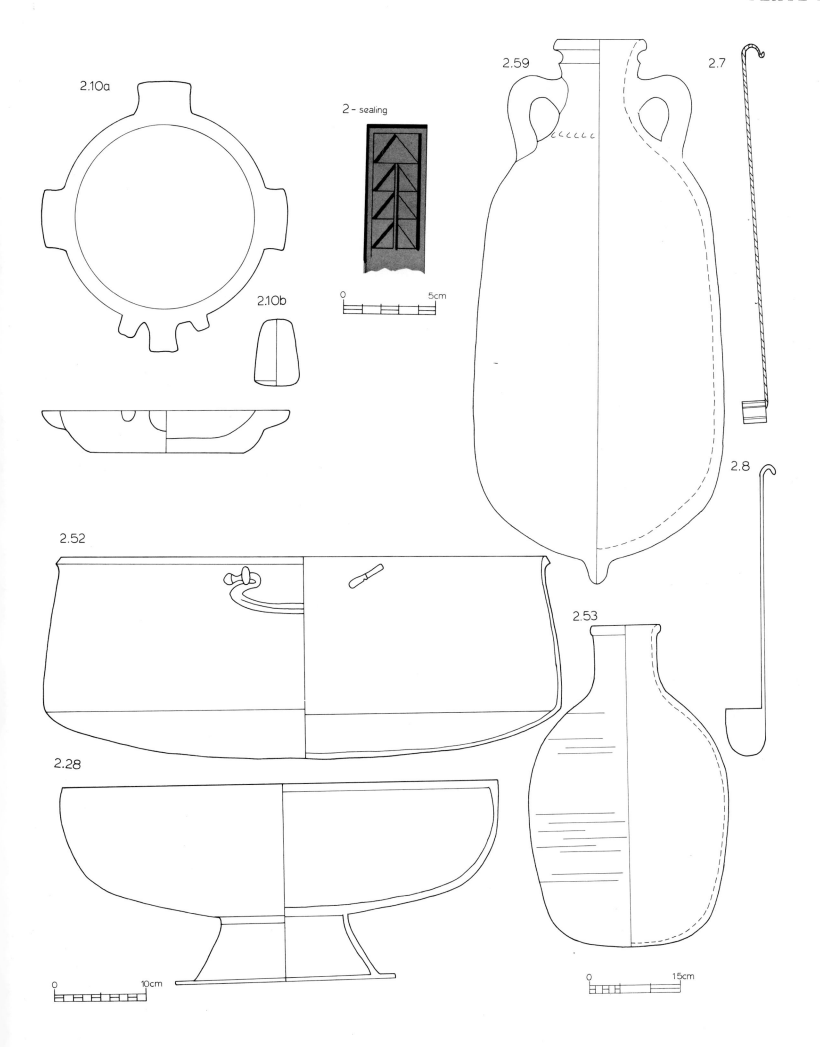

2.10a

2.10b

2 – sealing

0   5cm

2.59

2.7

2.8

2.52

2.53

2.28

0   10cm

0   15cm

PLATE XI

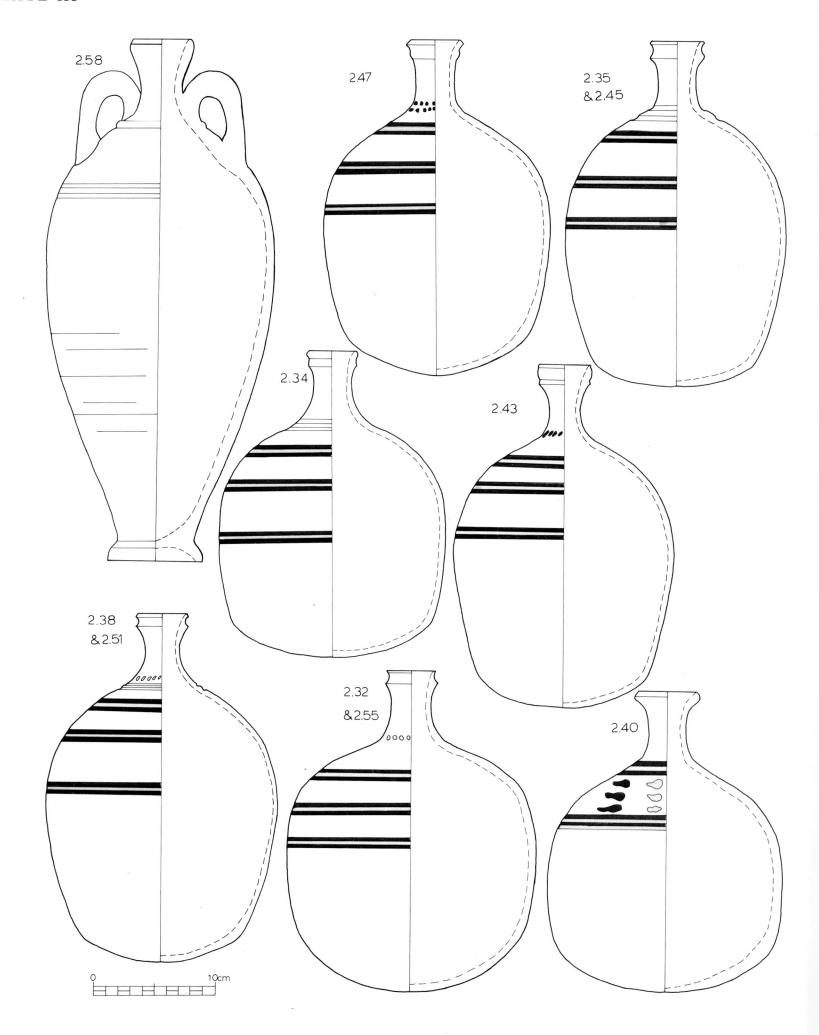

2.58

2.47

2.35
&2.45

2.34

2.43

2.38
&2.51

2.32
&2.55

2.40

0   10cm

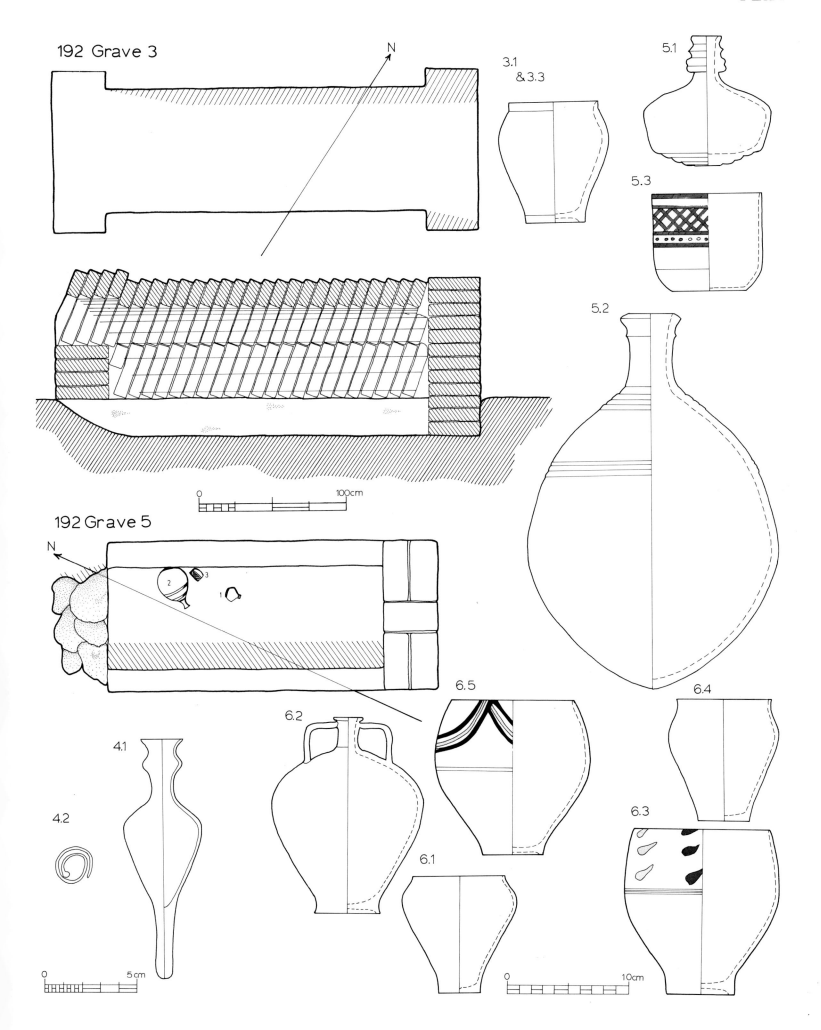

PLATE XII

PLATE XIII

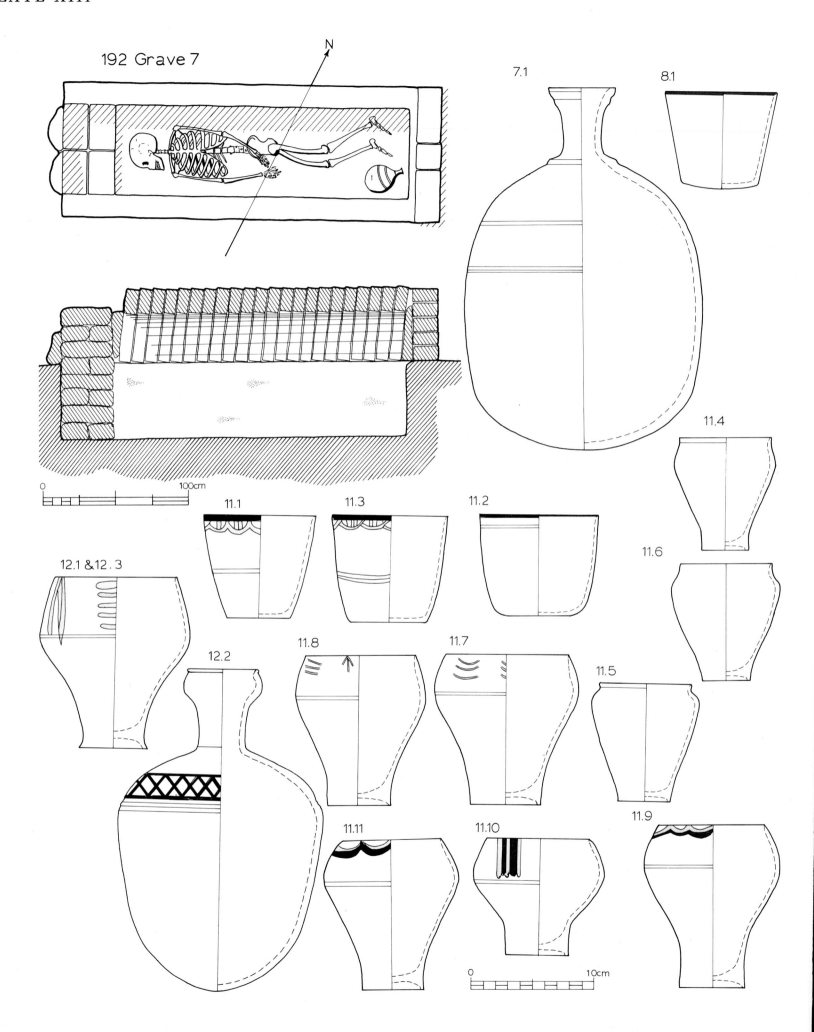

192 Grave 7

N

100cm

7.1

8.1

11.4

11.1

11.3

11.2

11.6

12.1 & 12.3

12.2

11.8

11.7

11.5

11.11

11.10

11.9

0   10cm

PLATE XIV

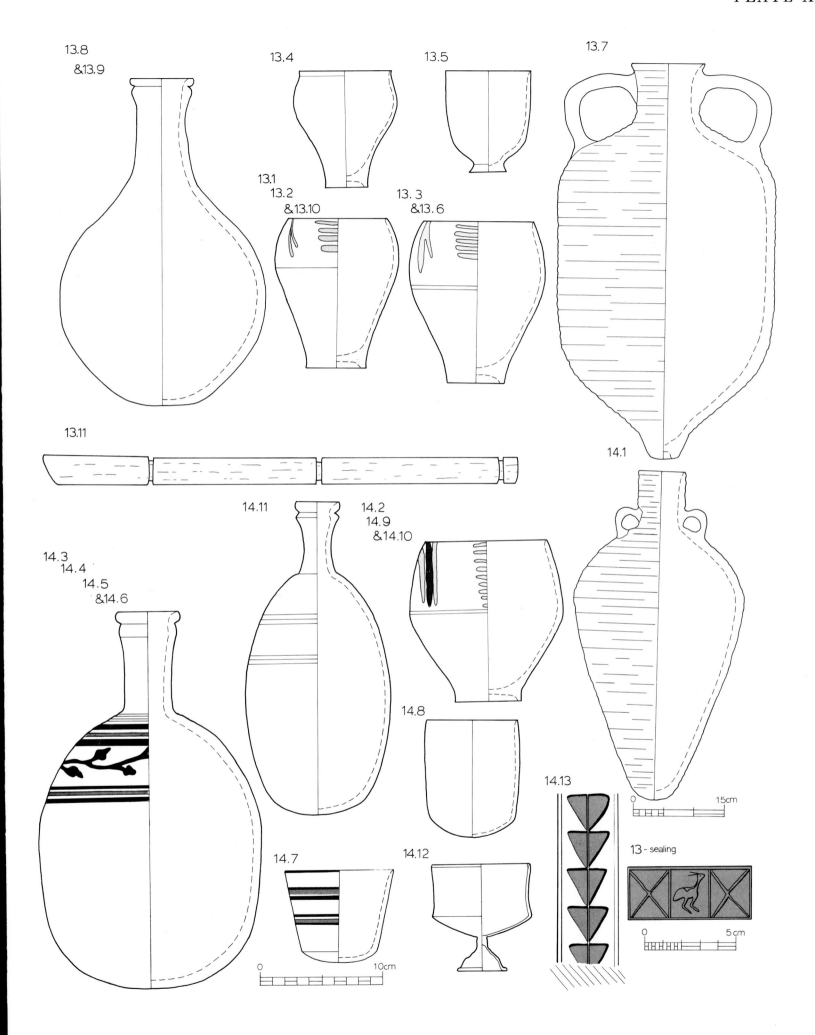

13.8
&13.9

13.4

13.5

13.7

13.1
13.2
&13.10

13. 3
&13.6

14.1

13.11

14.11

14.2
14.9
&14.10

14.3
14.4
14.5
&14.6

14.8

14.13

14.7

14.12

13 - sealing

0   15cm

0   10cm

0   5cm

PLATE XV

192 Grave 15

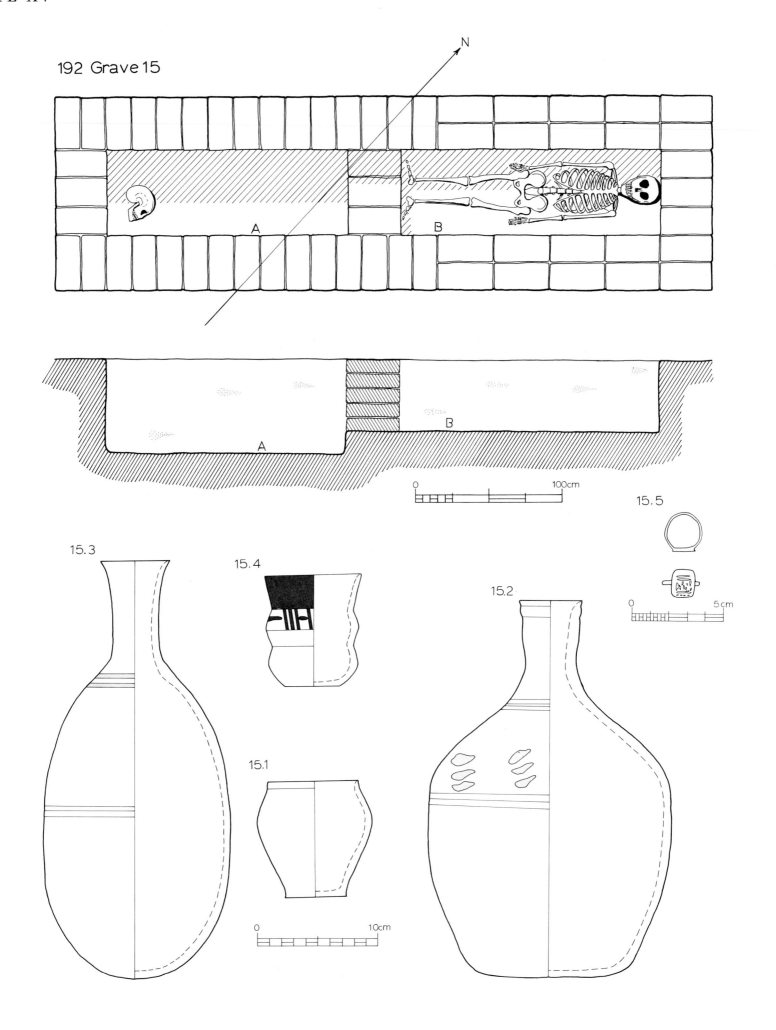

15.3

15.4

15.1

15.2

15.5

PLATE XVI

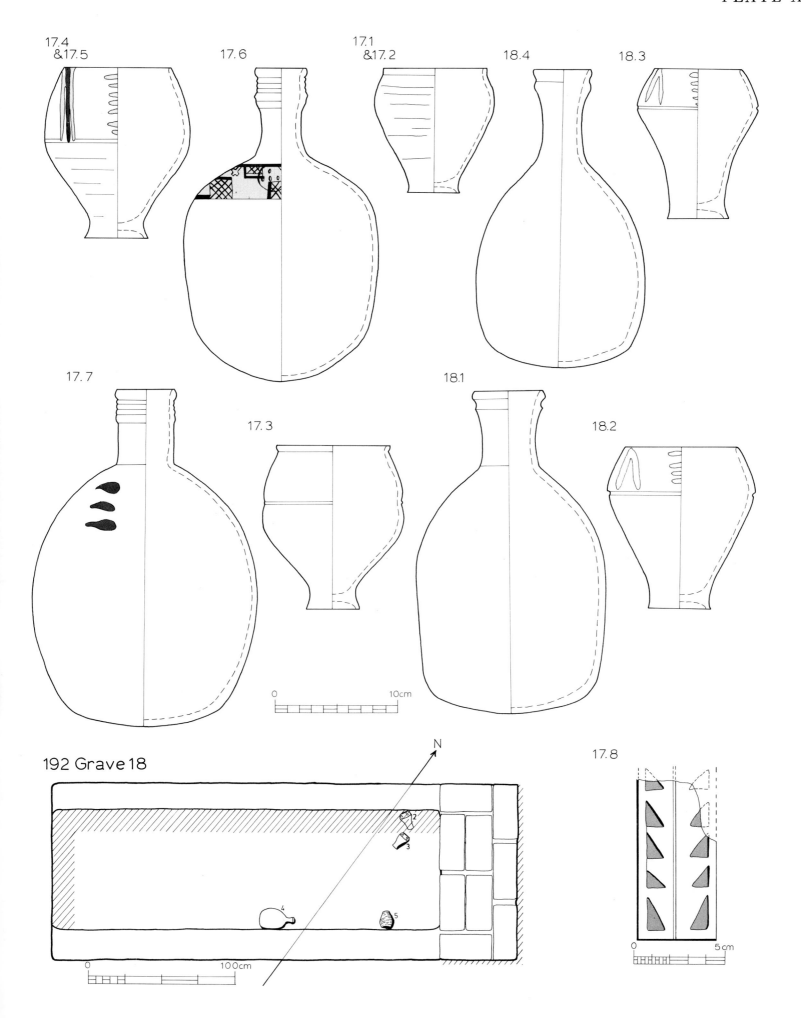

17.4
&17.5

17.6

17.1
&17.2

18.4

18.3

17.7

17.3

18.1

18.2

192 Grave 18

N

17.8

0   10cm

0   100cm

0   5cm

PLATE XVII

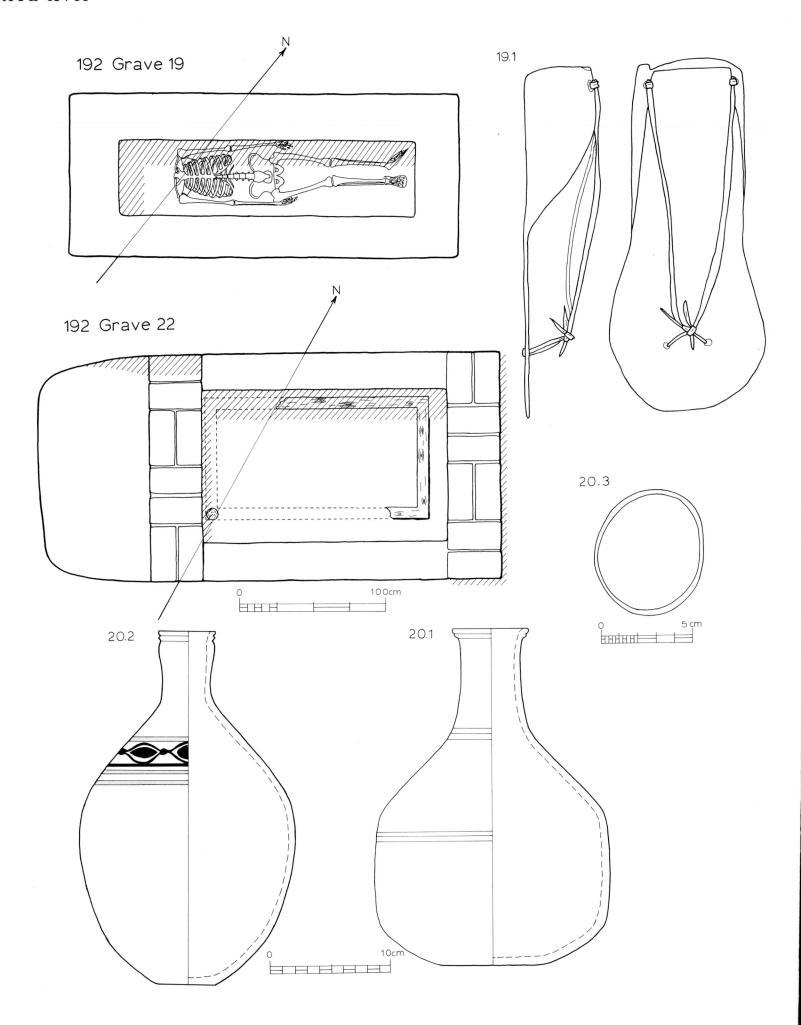

192 Grave 19

192 Grave 22

19.1

20.3

20.2

20.1

PLATE XVIII

192 Grave 21

21.2

21.4

21.3

21.11

21.7

21.5
& 21.9

21.6

21.8

21.10

21.1

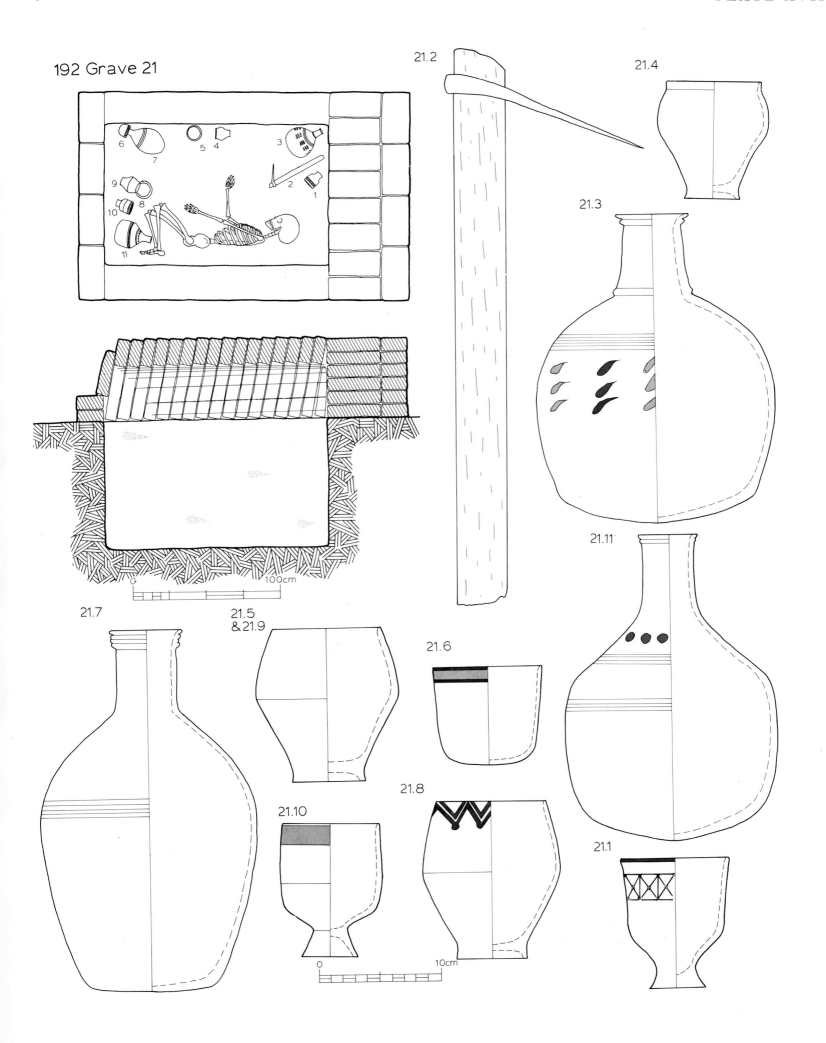

100cm

0   10cm

PLATE XIX

192 Grave 23

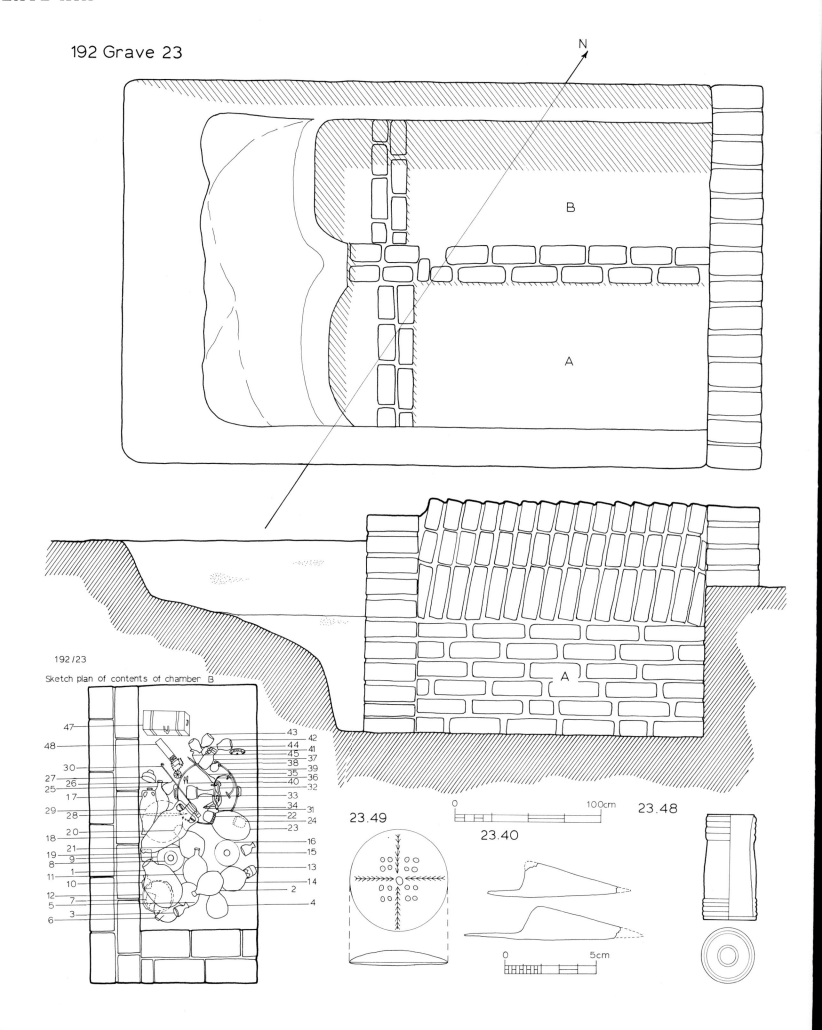

N

B

A

192/23

Sketch plan of contents of chamber B

A

23.49

23.40

23.48

0   100cm

0   5cm

PLATE XX

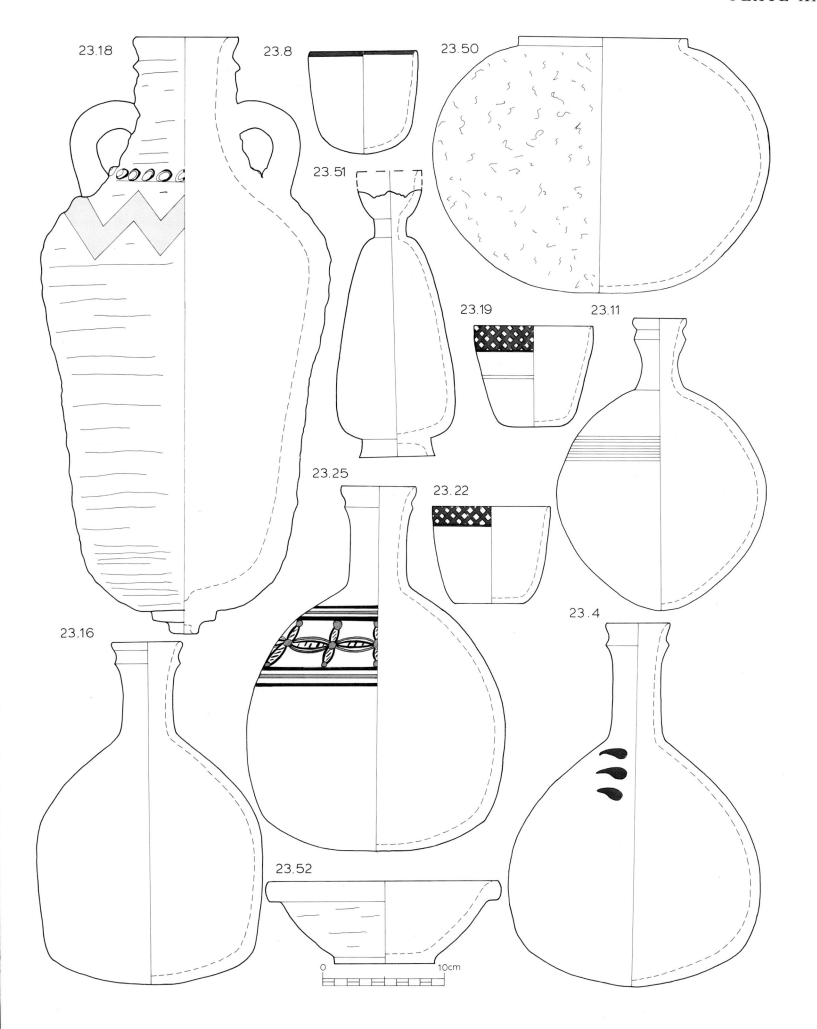

23.18

23.8

23.50

23.51

23.19

23.11

23.25

23.22

23.4

23.16

23.52

0   10cm

PLATE XXI

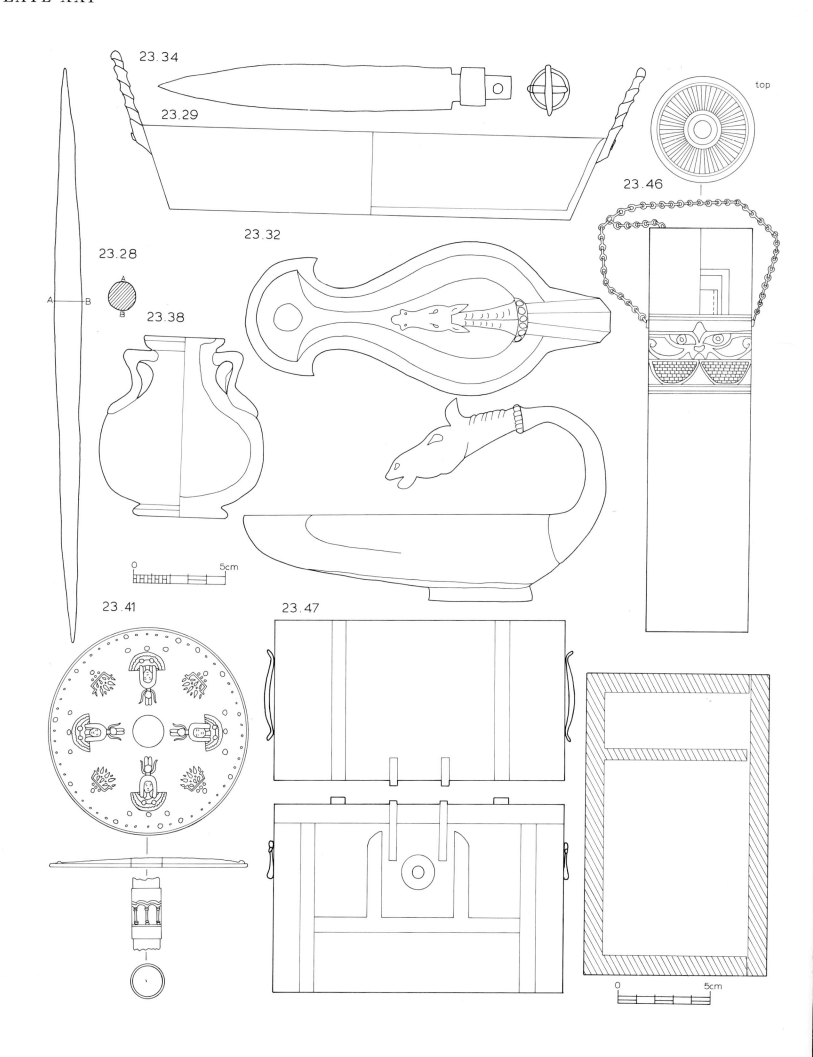

23.34

23.29

23.32

23.46

top

23.28

A
B

23.38

A B

5cm
0

23.41

23.47

0
5cm

PLATE XXII

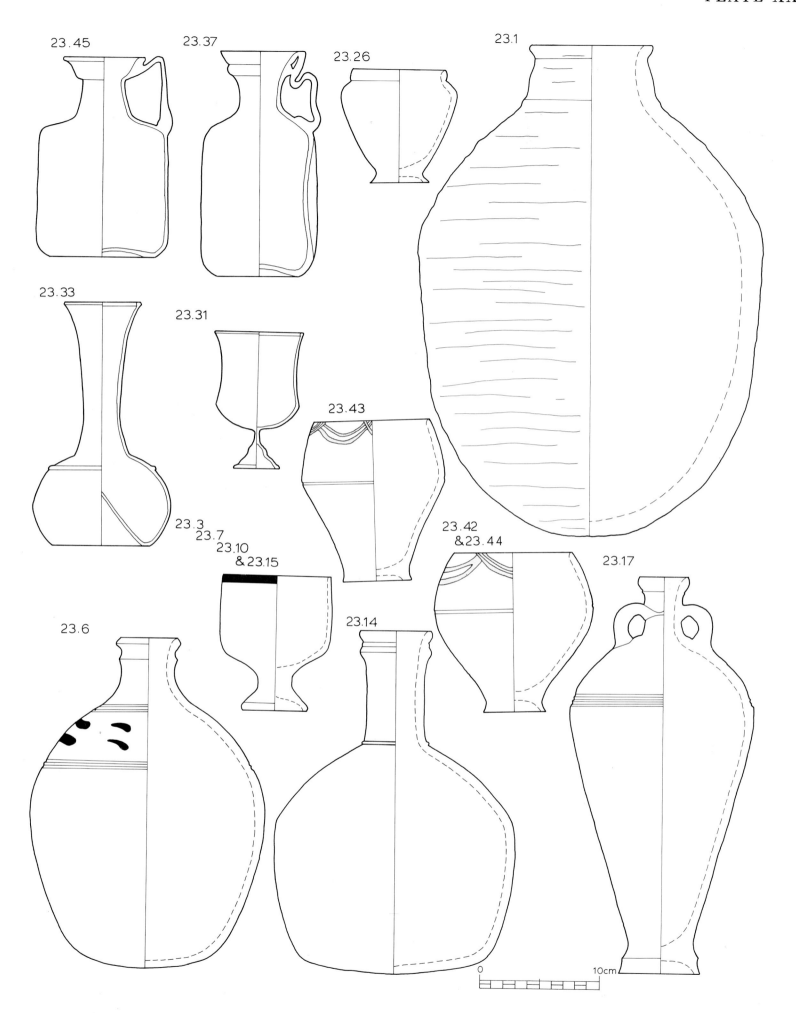

23.45 23.37 23.26 23.1 23.33 23.31 23.43 23.3 23.7 23.10 &23.15 23.42 &23.44 23.17 23.6 23.14

0 10cm

PLATE XXIII

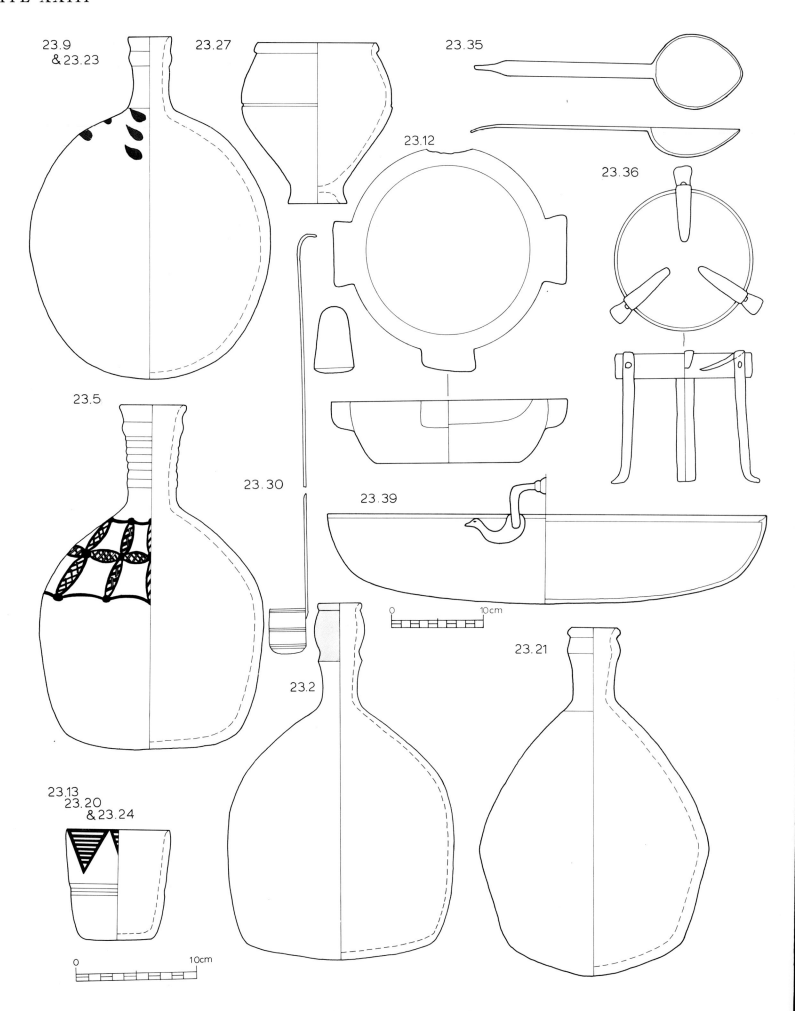

23.9
& 23.23

23.27

23.35

23.12

23.36

23.5

23.30

23.39

0   10cm

23.2

23.21

23.13
23.20
& 23.24

0   10cm

PLATE XXIV

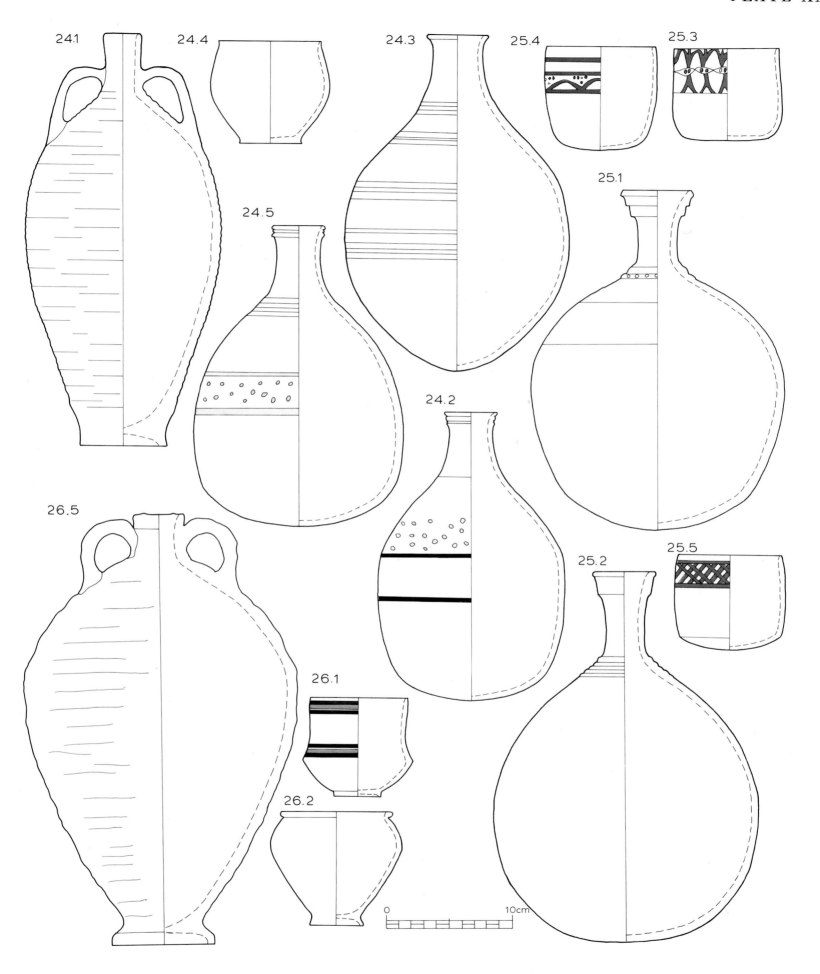

24.1 24.4 24.3 25.4 25.3 25.1 24.5 24.2 26.5 26.1 26.2 25.2 25.5

0 10cm

PLATE XXV

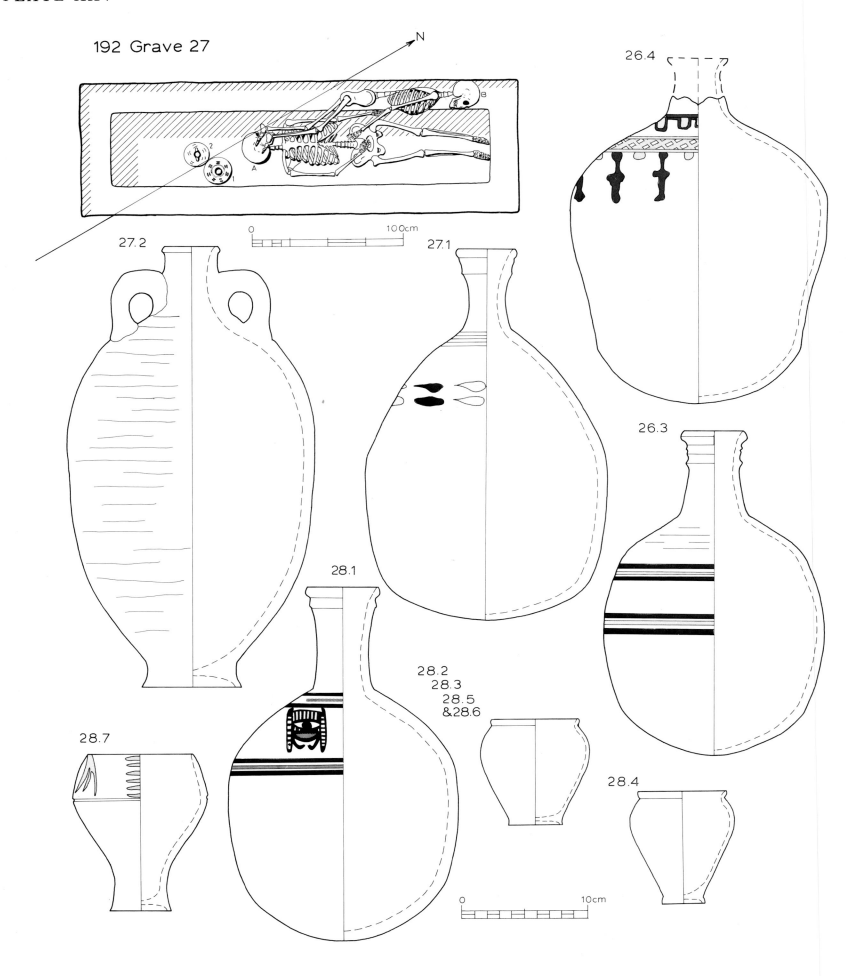

192 Grave 27

26.4

27.2

27.1

0   100cm

28.1

26.3

28.2
28.3
28.5
&28.6

28.7

28.4

0   10cm

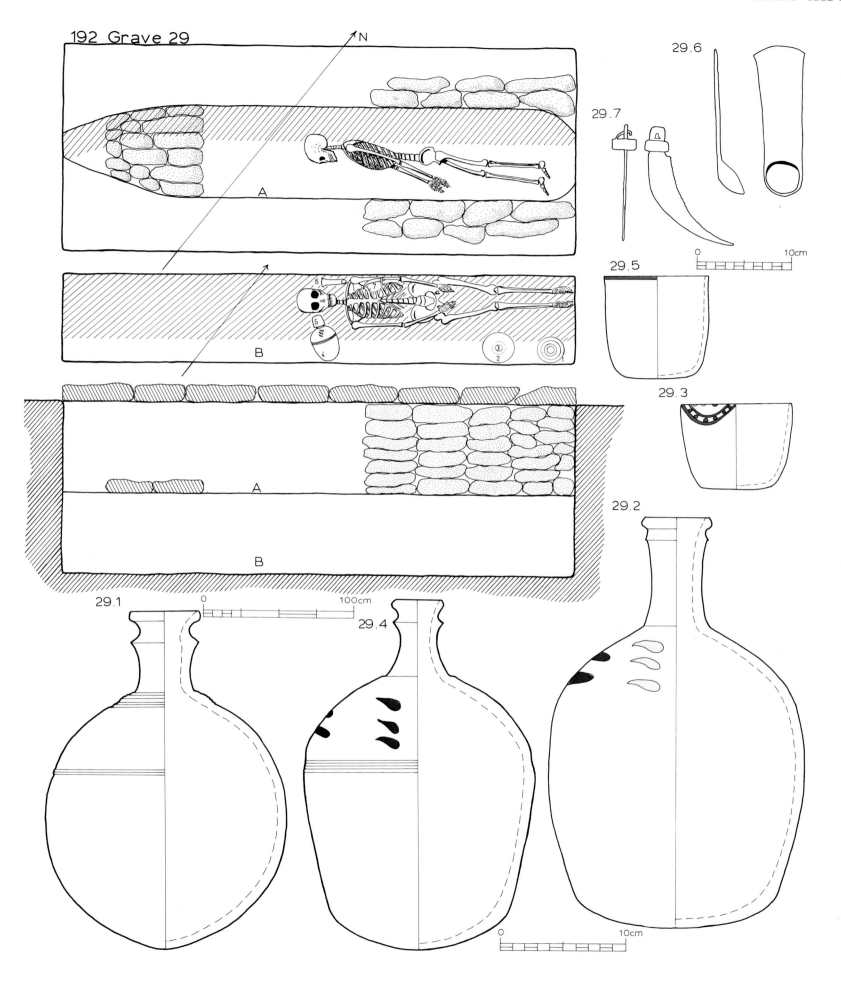

192 Grave 29

PLATE XXVI

29.6
29.7
29.5
29.3
29.2
29.1
29.4

0   10cm

0   100cm

0   10cm

PLATE XXVII

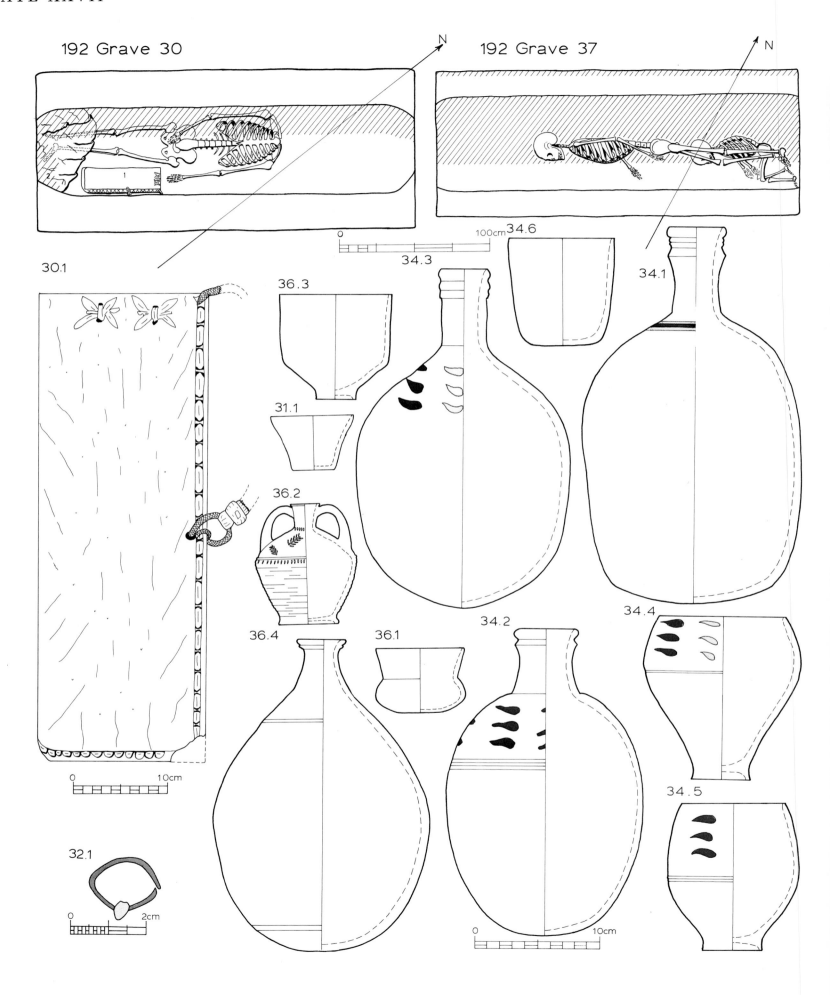

192 Grave 30

192 Grave 37

PLATE XXVIII

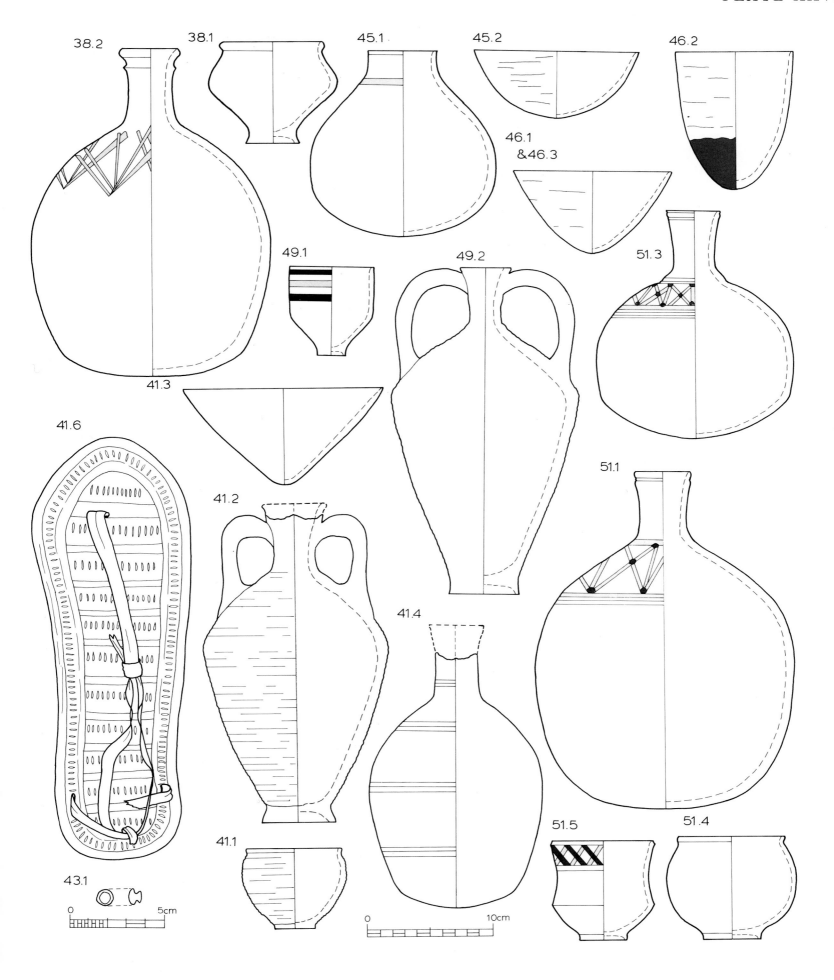

38.2

38.1

45.1

45.2

46.2

46.1
&46.3

49.1

49.2

51.3

41.3

41.6

51.1

41.2

41.4

43.1

0   5cm

41.1

0   10cm

51.5

51.4

PLATE XXIX

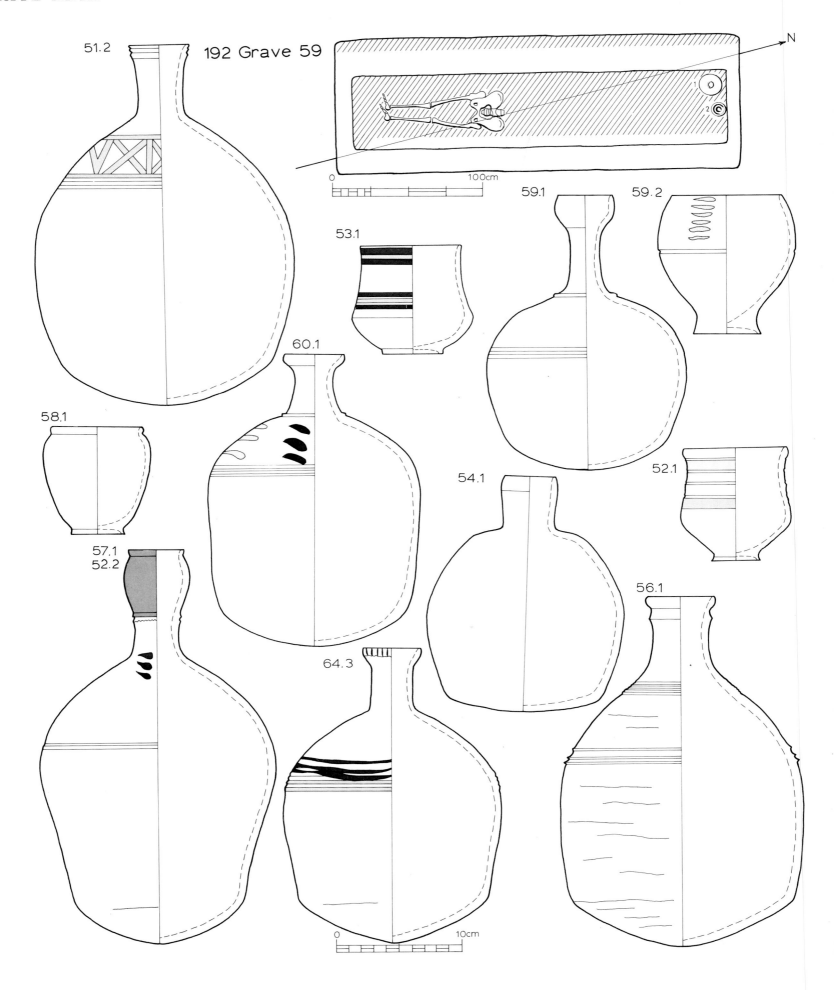

51.2

192 Grave 59

N

0   100cm

53.1

59.1   59.2

60.1

58.1

54.1   52.1

57.1
52.2

56.1

64.3

0   10cm

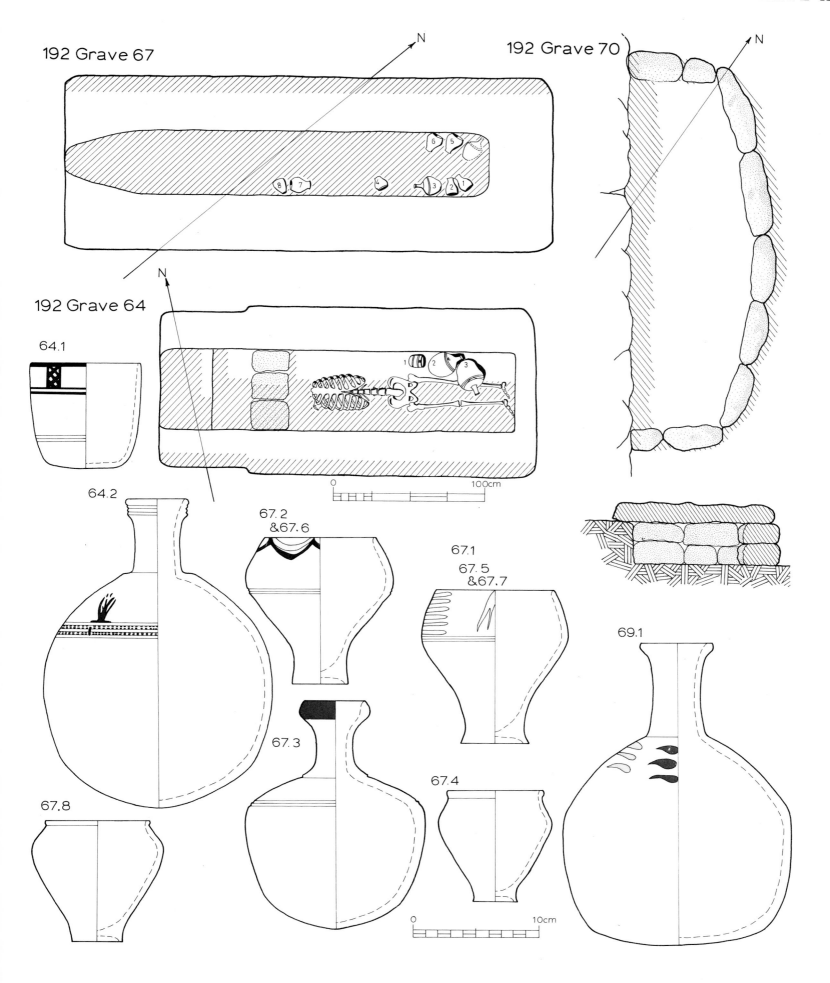

PLATE XXX

192 Grave 67

192 Grave 70

192 Grave 64

64.1

64.2

67.2
&67.6

67.1
67.5
&67.7

67.3

67.4

67.8

69.1

0   100cm

0   10cm

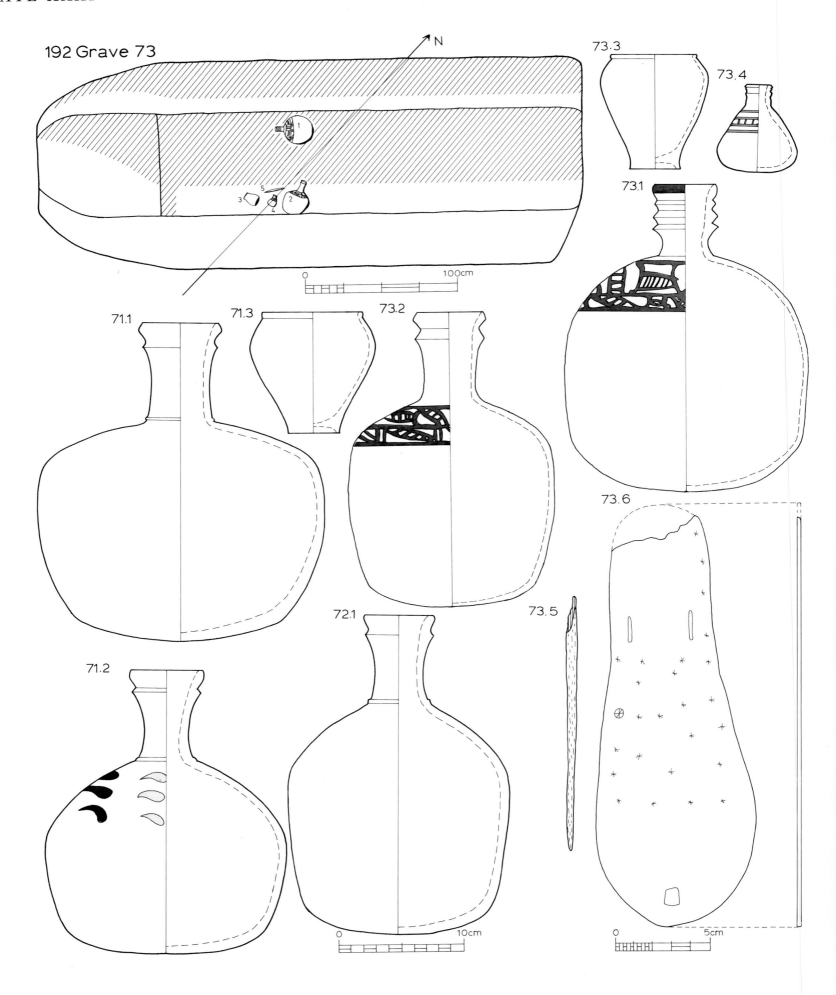

PLATE XXXI

192 Grave 73

N

73.3

73.4

73.1

73.6

71.1

71.3

73.2

72.1

73.5

71.2

0   100cm

0   10cm

0   5cm

PLATE XXXII

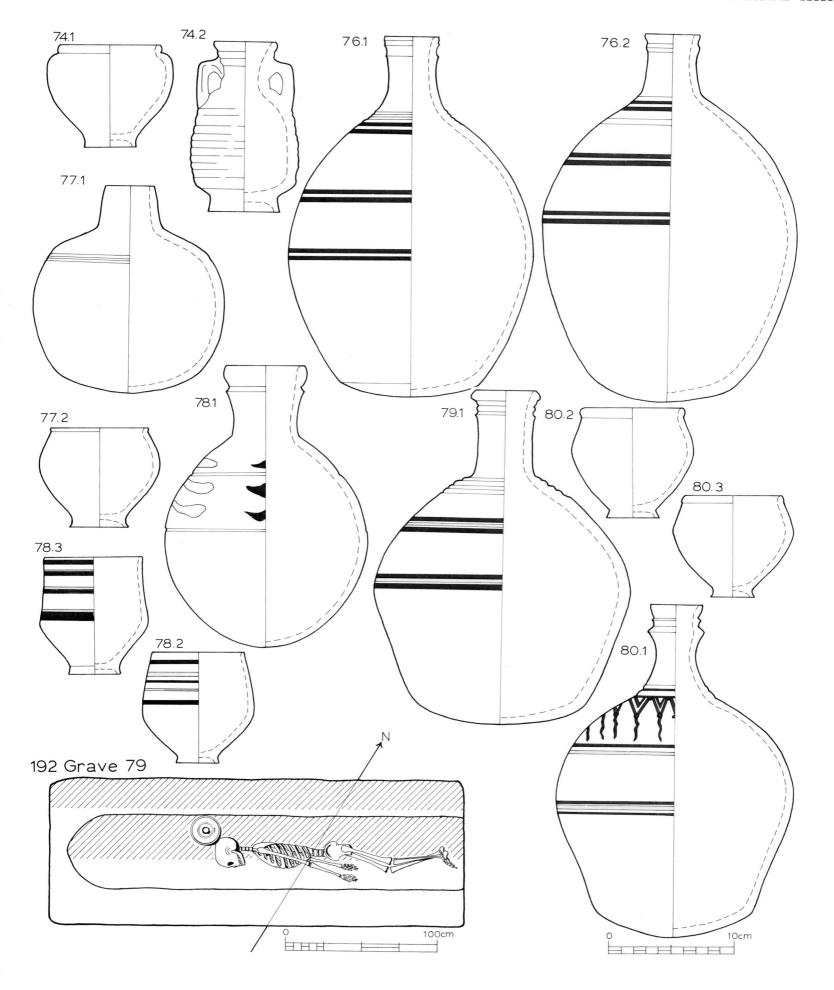

74.1

74.2

76.1

76.2

77.1

77.2

78.1

79.1

80.2

80.3

78.3

78.2

80.1

192 Grave 79

N

0   100cm

0   10cm

PLATE XXXIII

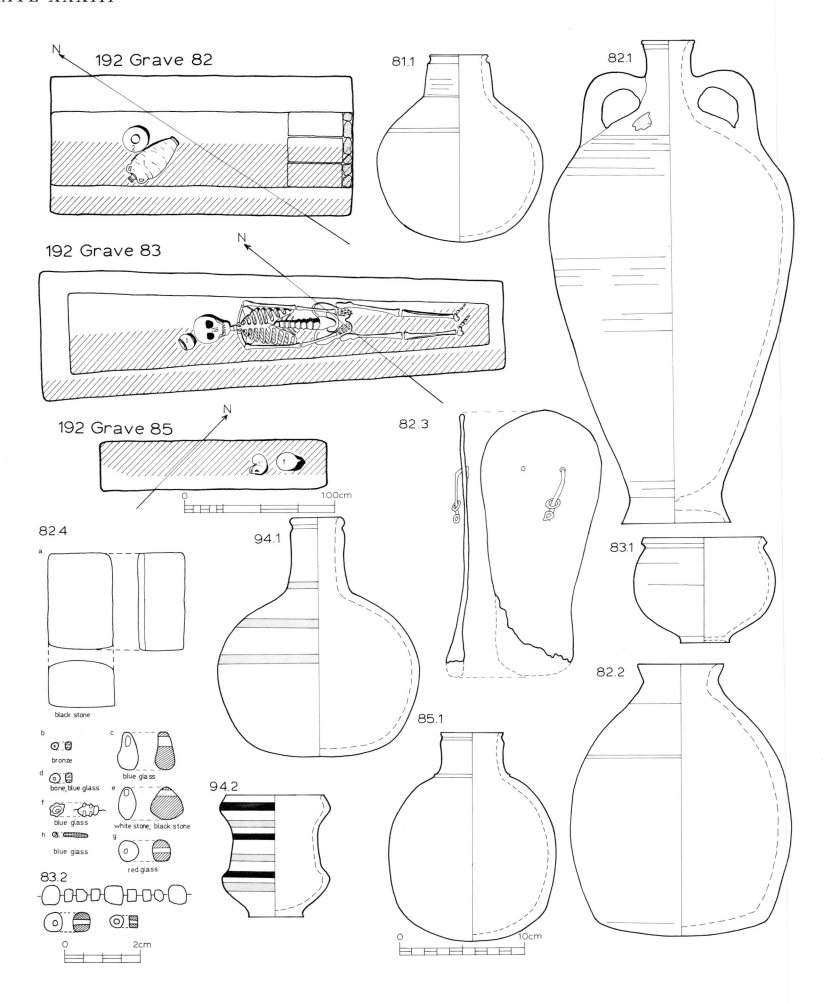

N

192 Grave 82

81.1

82.1

N

192 Grave 83

192 Grave 85

82.3

0   100cm

82.4

a

94.1

83.1

black stone

82.2

b

c

bronze

d

blue glass

bone, blue glass

e

f

85.1

blue glass

white stone, black stone

94.2

g

h

blue glass

red glass

83.2

0   10cm

0   2cm

PLATE XXXIV

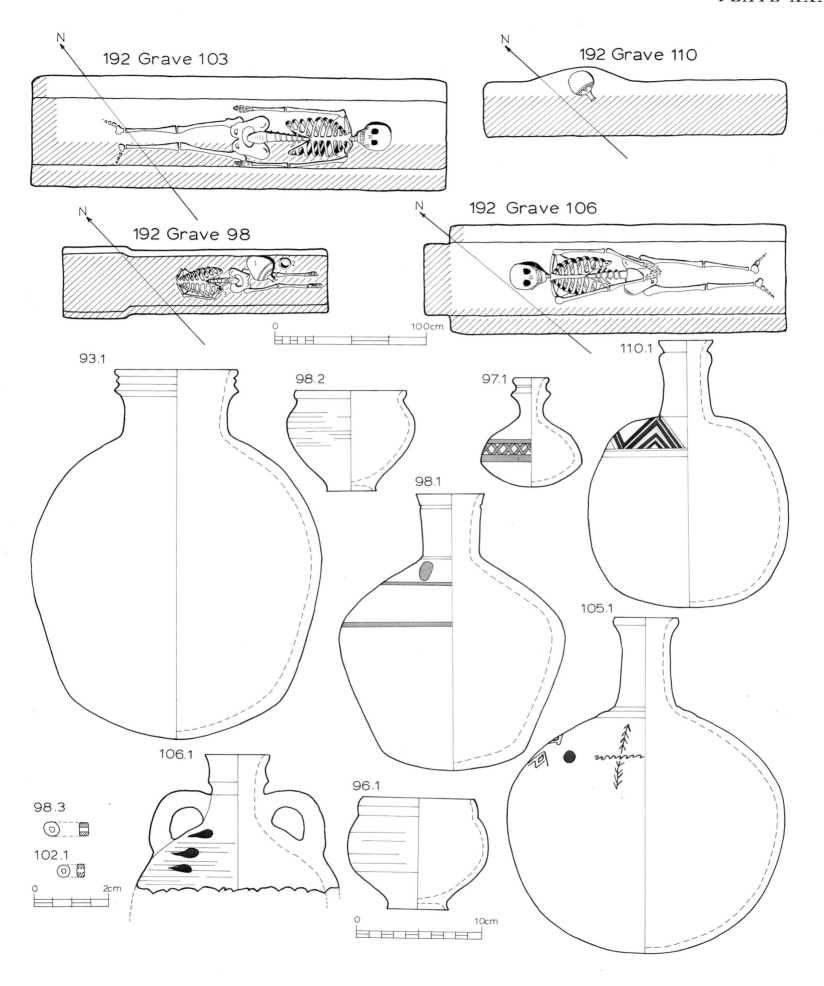

192 Grave 103

N

192 Grave 110

N

192 Grave 98

N

192 Grave 106

N

0   100cm

93.1

98.2

97.1

110.1

98.1

105.1

106.1

98.3

102.1

96.1

0   2cm

0   10cm

PLATE XXXV

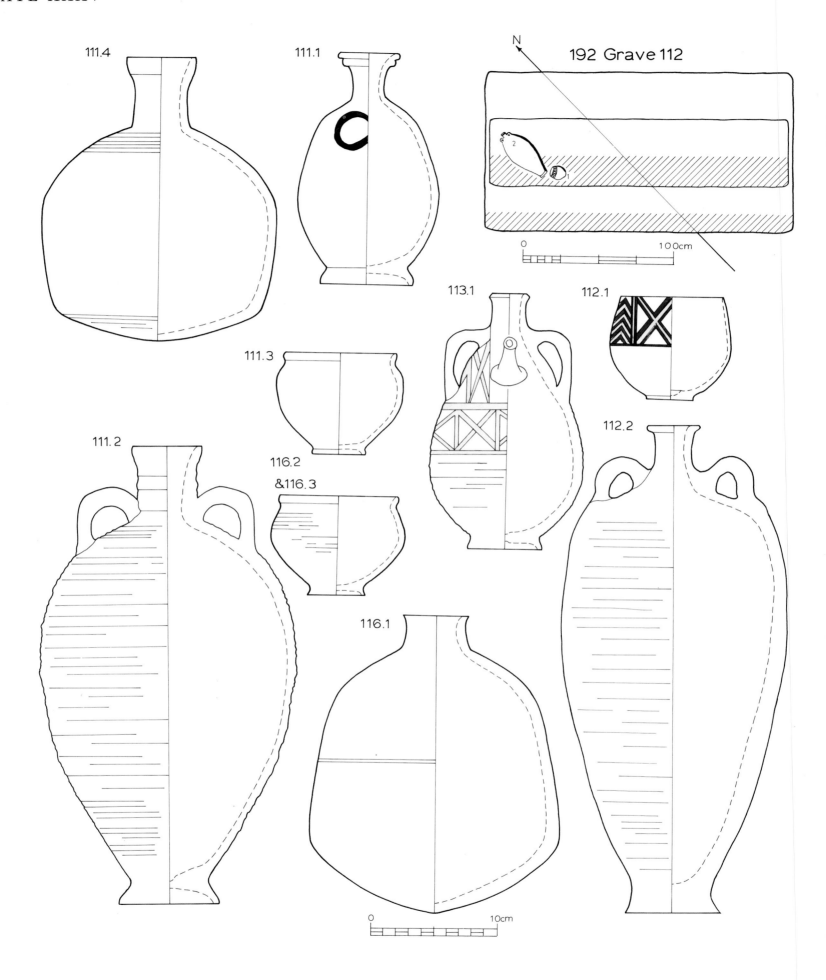

111.4

111.1

192 Grave 112

0   100cm

113.1   112.1

111.3

116.2
&116.3

111.2

112.2

116.1

0   10cm

PLATE XXXVI

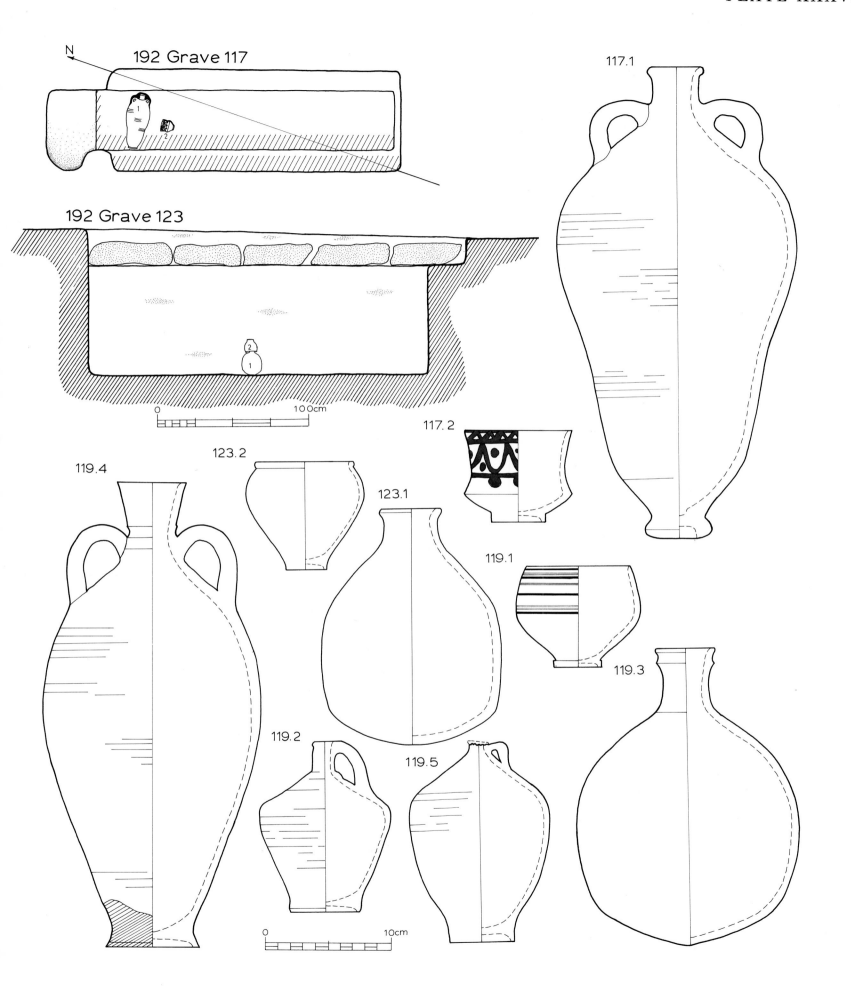

192 Grave 117

192 Grave 123

0   100cm

117.1

117.2

119.4

123.2

123.1

119.1

119.3

119.2

119.5

0   10cm

PLATE XXXVII

192 Grave 121

133.2

129.1

120·1

121.1
&121.2

133.1
&133.3

126.2

126.1

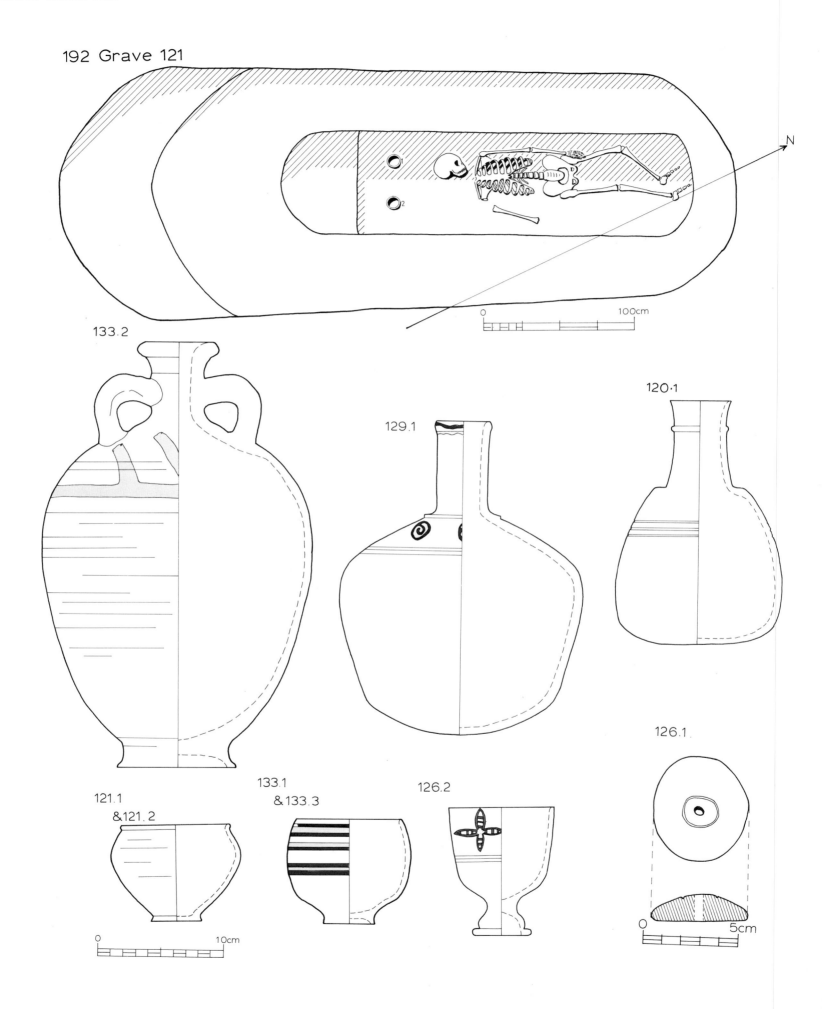

0   100cm

0   10cm

0   5cm

N

PLATE XXXVIII

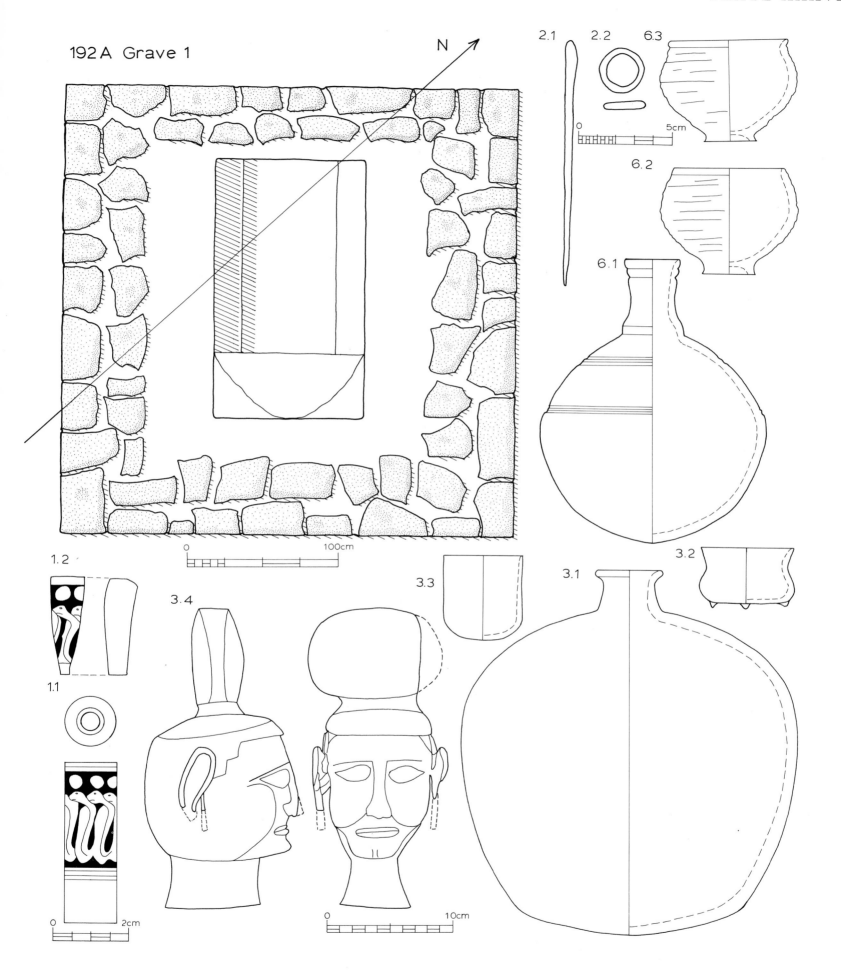

192 A Grave 1

N

2.1 2.2 6.3

0   5cm

6.2

6.1

3.3 3.1 3.2

1.2

1.1

3.4

0   100cm

0   2cm

0   10cm

PLATE XXXIX

192 A Grave 4

4.6

4.7

4.2

4.1

4.5

4.4

4.3

0   100cm

0   2cm

0   10cm

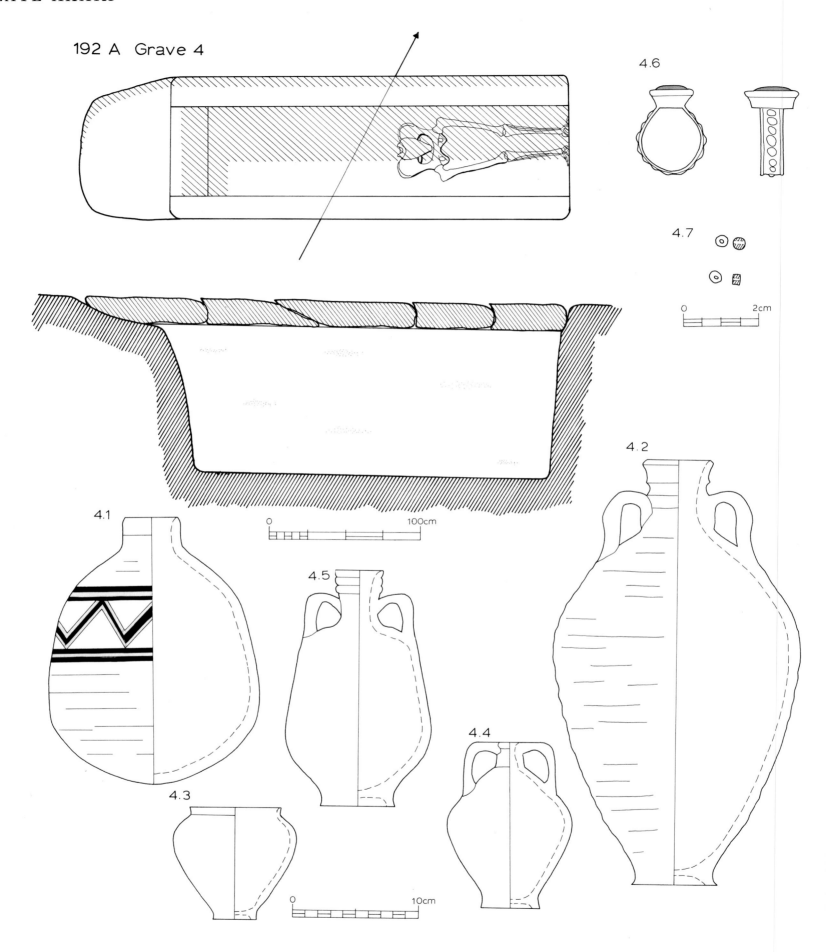

PLATE XL

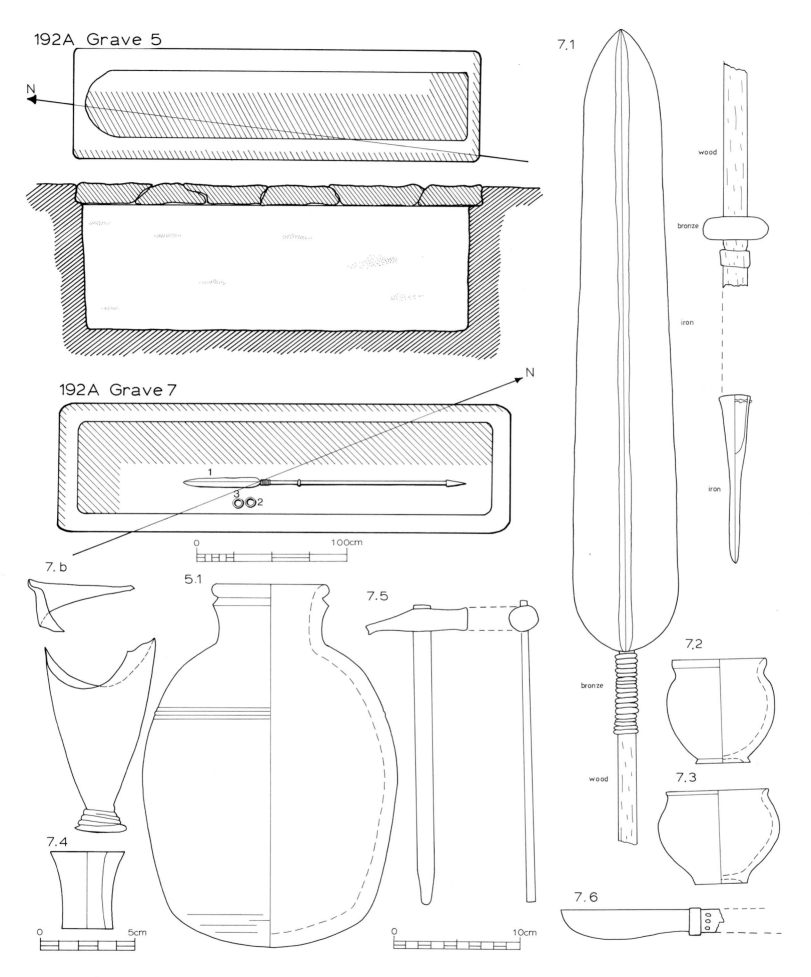

192A Grave 5

N

192A Grave 7

1

3 2

N

7.b

0   100cm

5.1

7.5

7.4

0   5cm

0   10cm

7.1

wood

bronze

iron

iron

bronze

wood

7.2

7.3

7.6

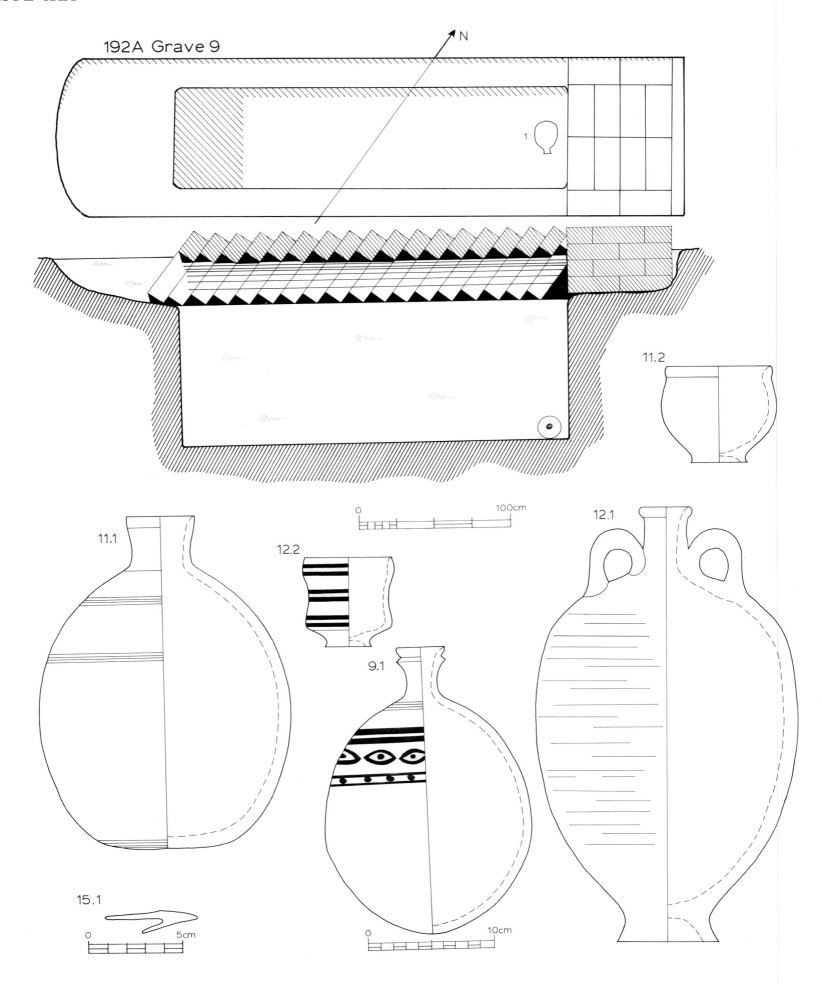

PLATE XLI

192A Grave 9

N

11.2

11.1

12.2

12.1

9.1

0   100cm

15.1

0   5cm

0   10cm

PLATE XLII

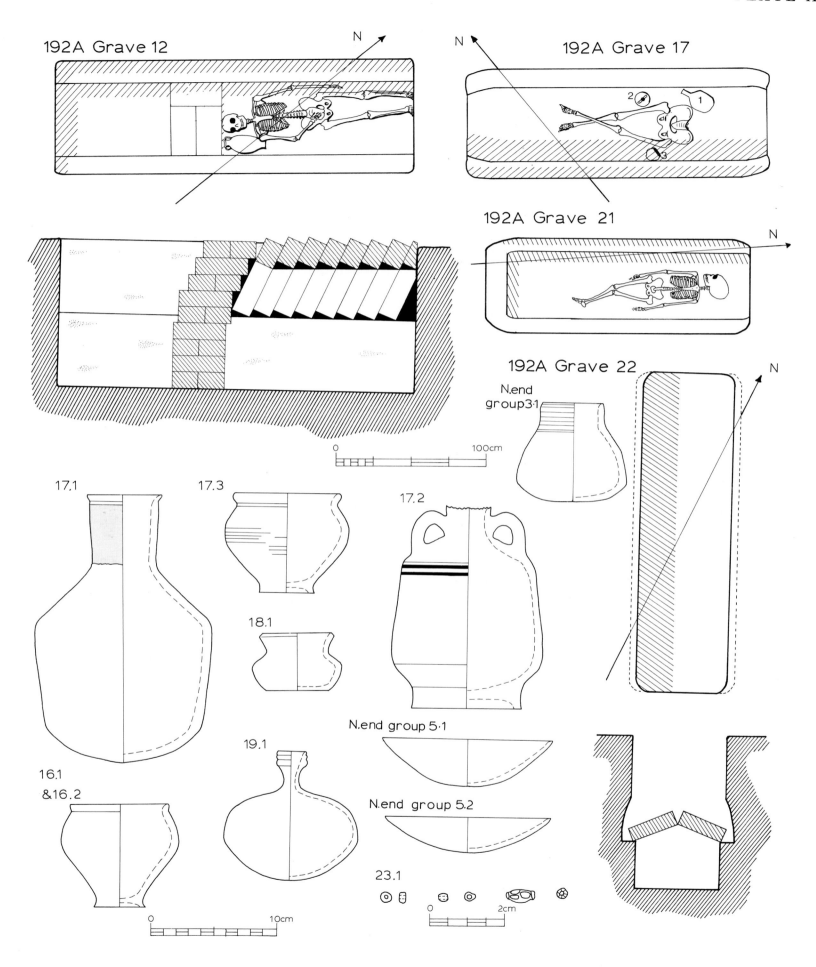

192A Grave 12

192A Grave 17

192A Grave 21

192A Grave 22

N.end
group3·1

17.1

17.3

17.2

18.1

N.end group 5·1

16.1
&16.2

19.1

N.end group 5.2

23.1

0   100cm

0   10cm

0   2cm

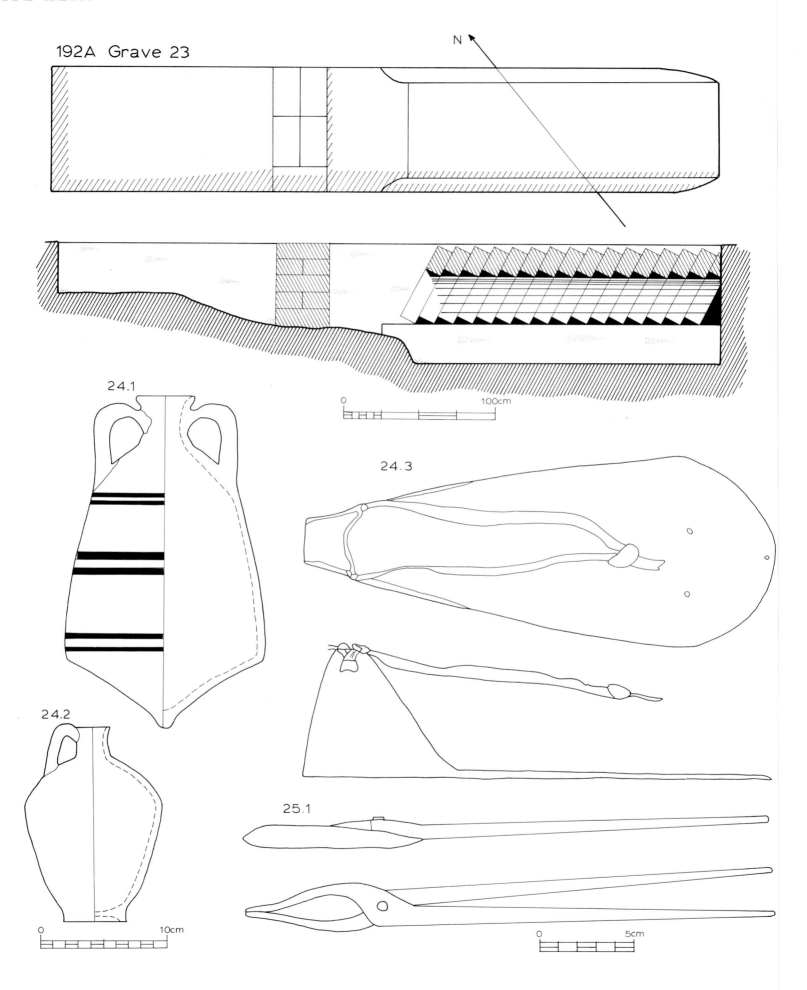

PLATE XLIII

192A Grave 23

N

24.1

24.3

24.2

25.1

0   100cm

0   10cm

0   5cm

PLATE XLIV

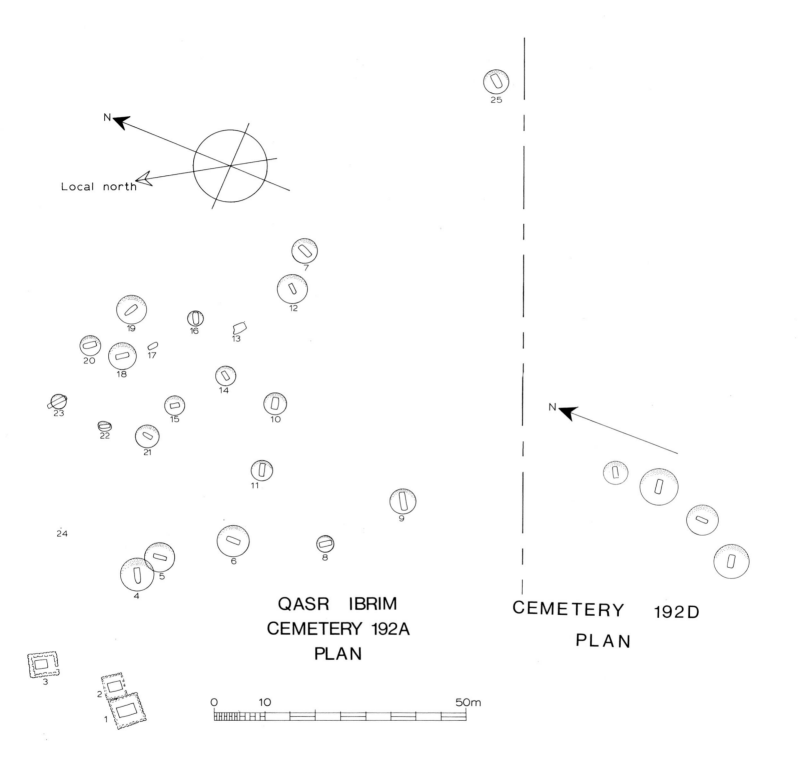

QASR IBRIM
CEMETERY 192A
PLAN

CEMETERY 192D
PLAN

Local north

N

0   10   50m

PLATE XLV

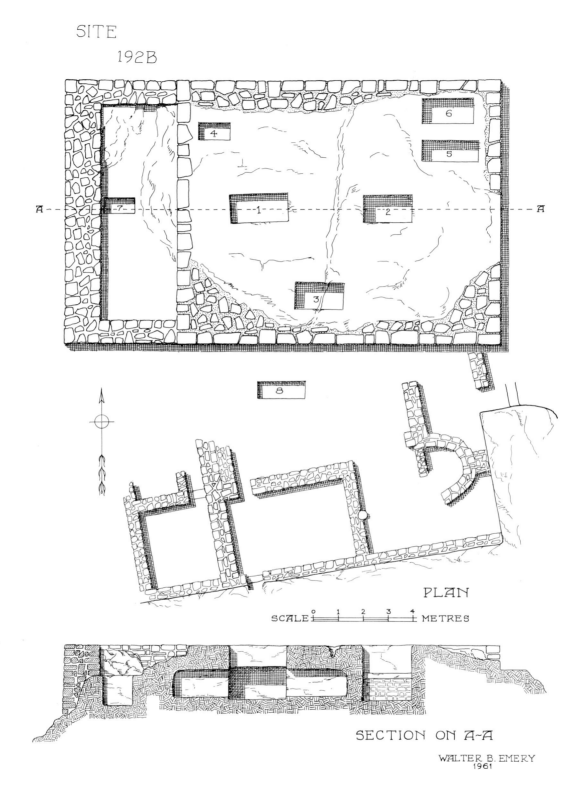

SITE
192B

6

4

5

A ---- 7 ---- 1 ---- 2 ---- A

3

8

PLAN

SCALE 0 1 2 3 4 METRES

SECTION ON A-A

WALTER B. EMERY
1961

PLATE XLVI

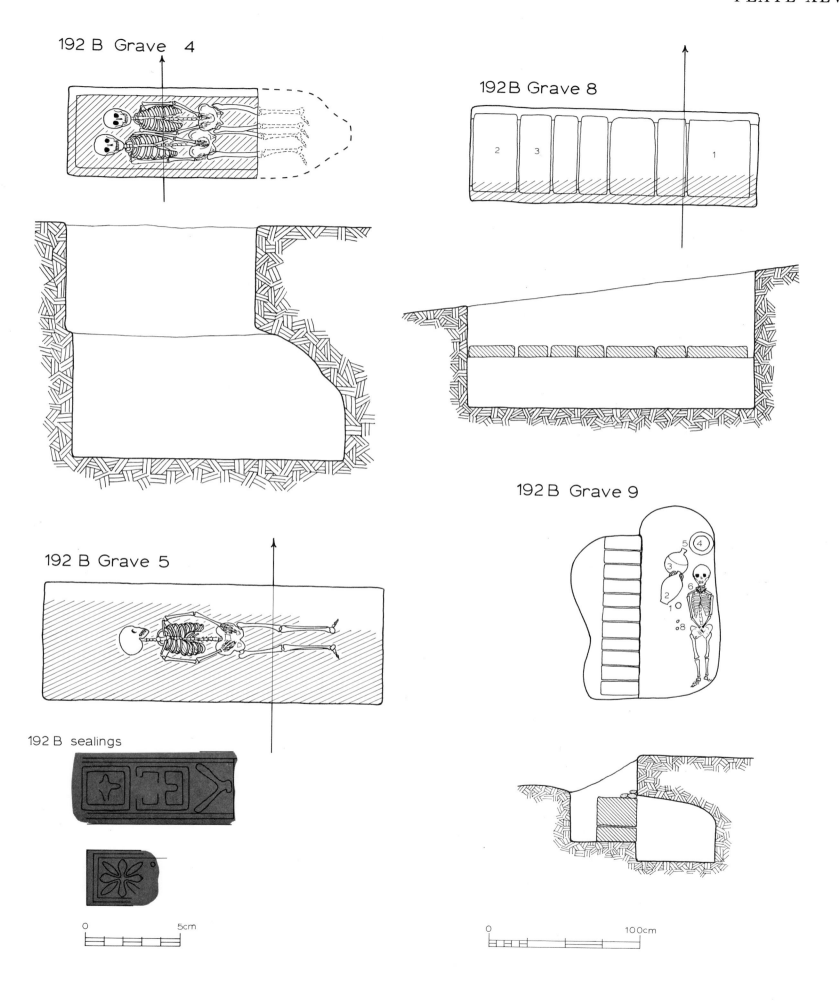

192 B Grave 4

192 B Grave 8

192 B Grave 5

192 B sealings

192 B Grave 9

0   5cm

0   100cm

PLATE XLVII

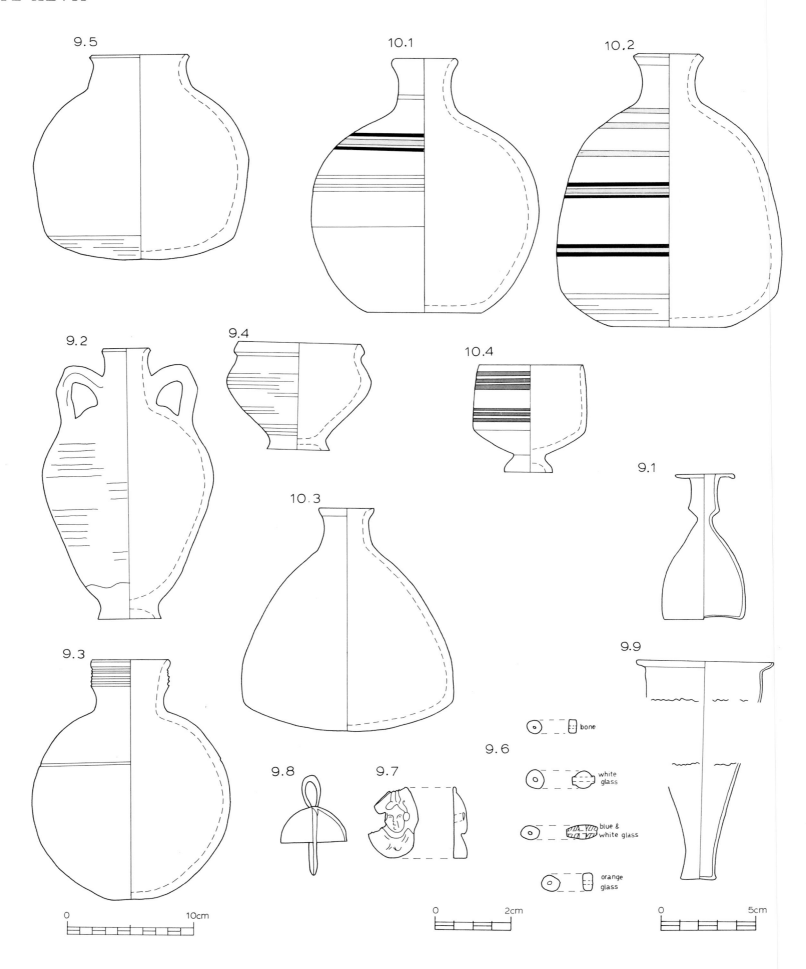

9.5

10.1

10.2

9.2

9.4

10.4

9.1

10.3

9.9

9.3

9.6

9.8

9.7

bone

white
glass

blue &
white glass

orange
glass

0   10cm

0   2cm

0   5cm

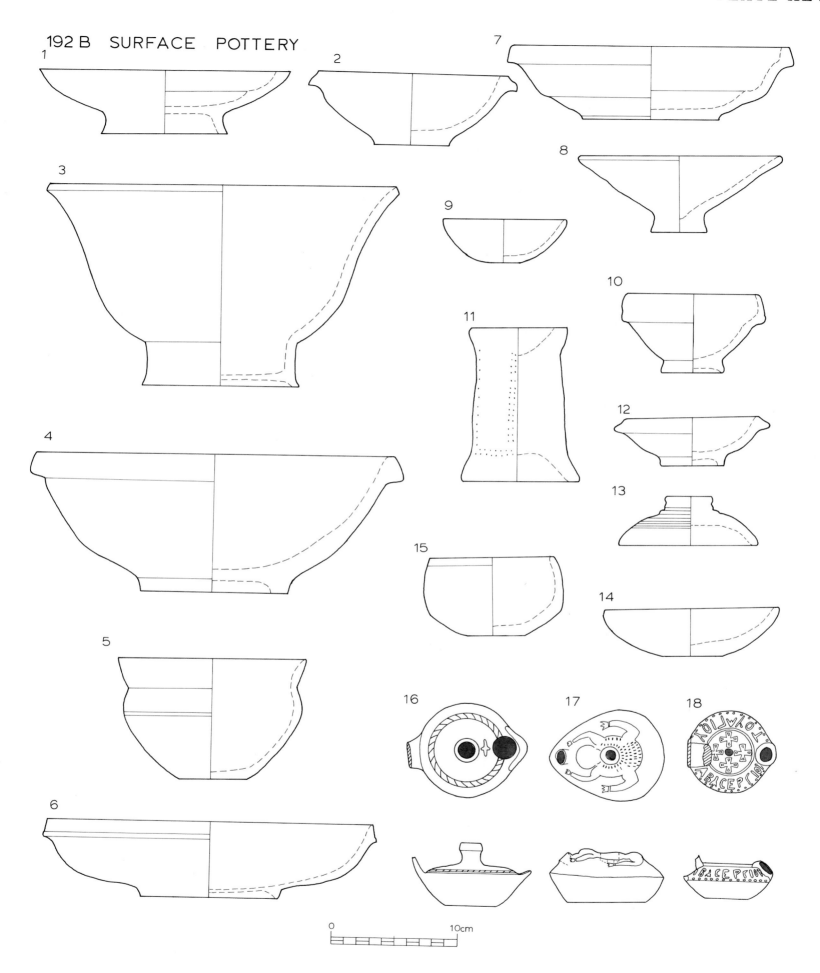

PLATE XLVIII

192 B SURFACE POTTERY

0   10cm

PLATE XLIX

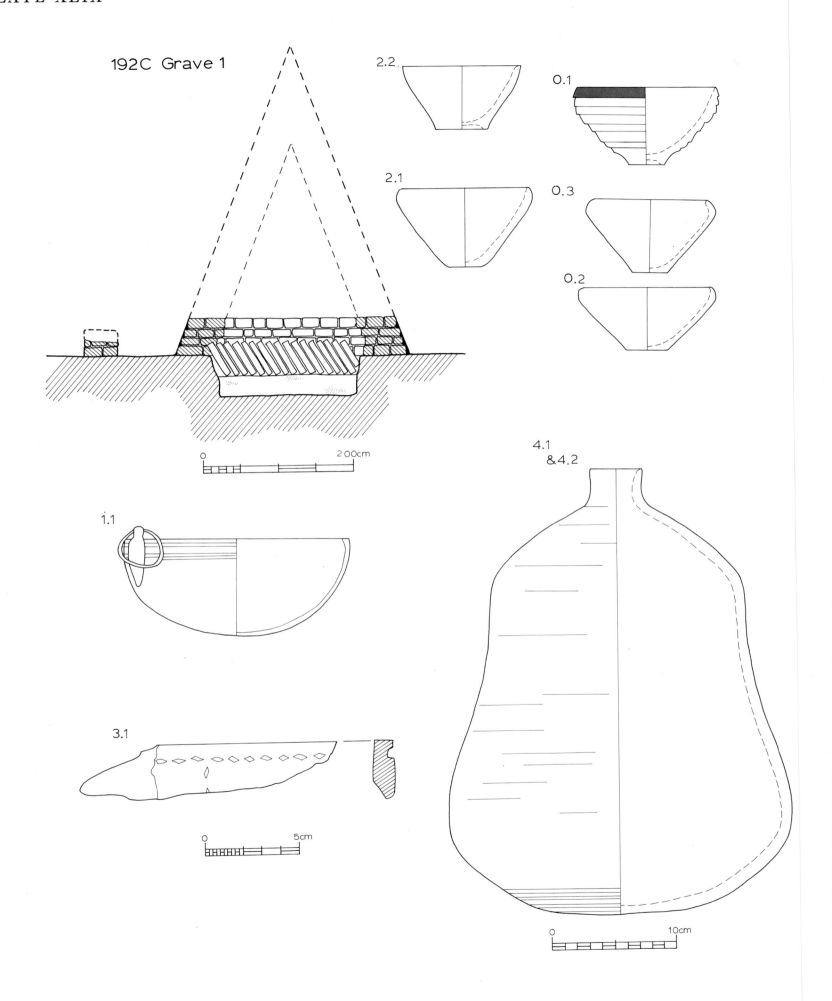

192C Grave 1

2.2

2.1

1.1

3.1

0.1

0.3

0.2

4.1
&4.2

0   2:00cm

0   5cm

0   10cm

PLATE L

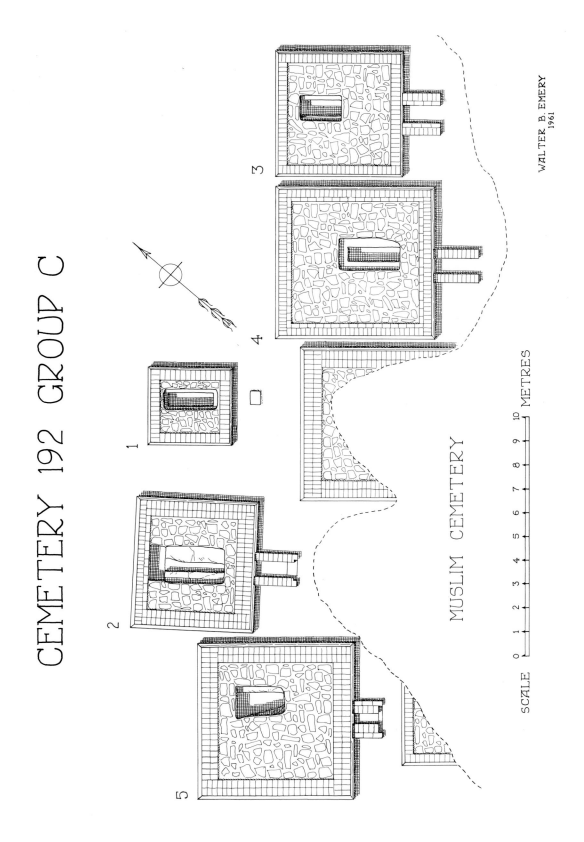

CEMETERY 192 GROUP C

MUSLIM CEMETERY

WALTER B. EMERY
1961

SCALE 0 1 2 3 4 5 6 7 8 9 10 METRES

PLATE LI

192D Grave 1

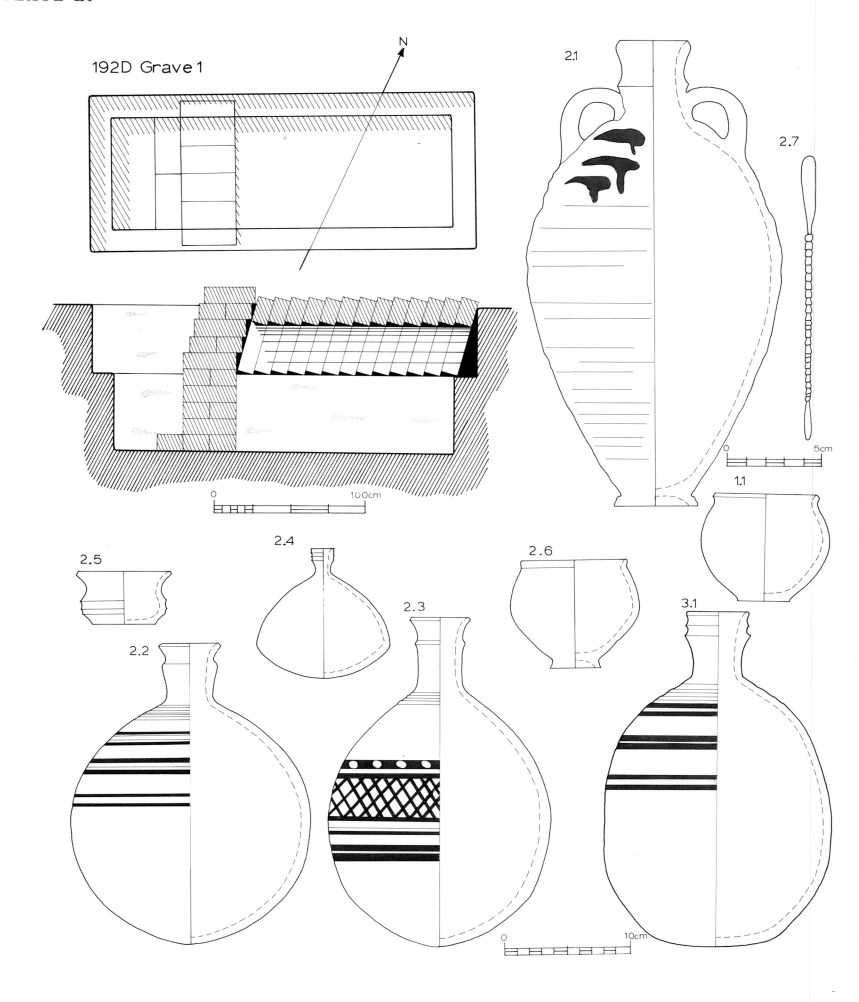

PLATE LII

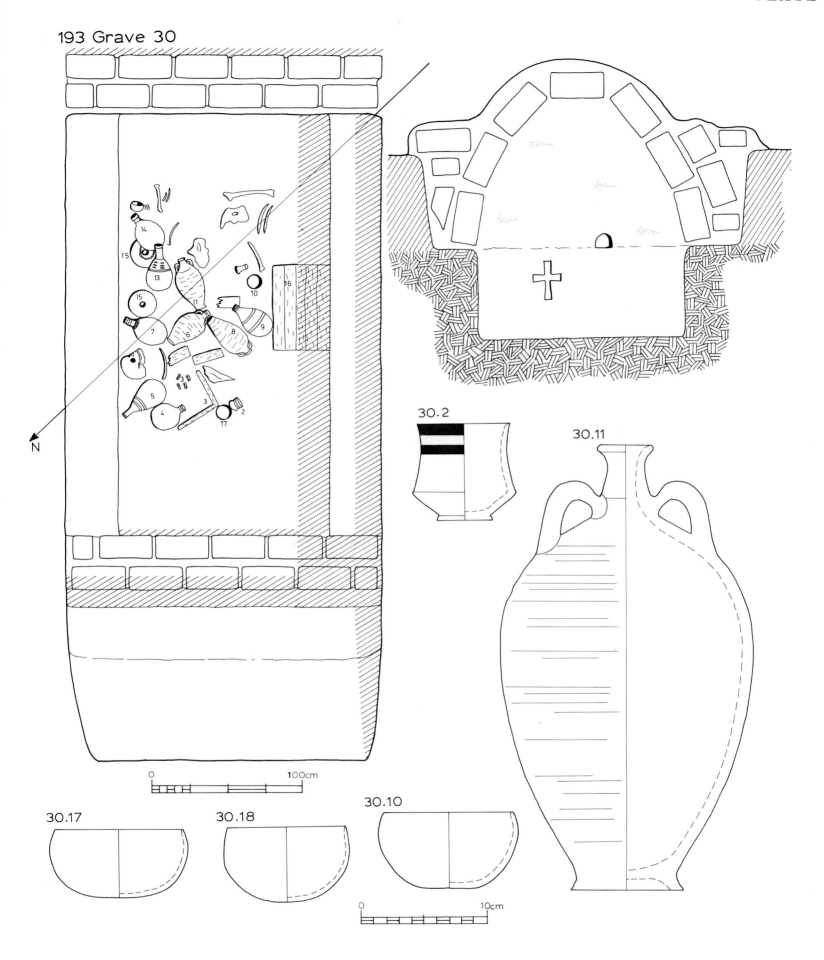

193 Grave 30

N

100cm

30.2

30.11

30.10

30.17

30.18

0   10cm

PLATE LIII

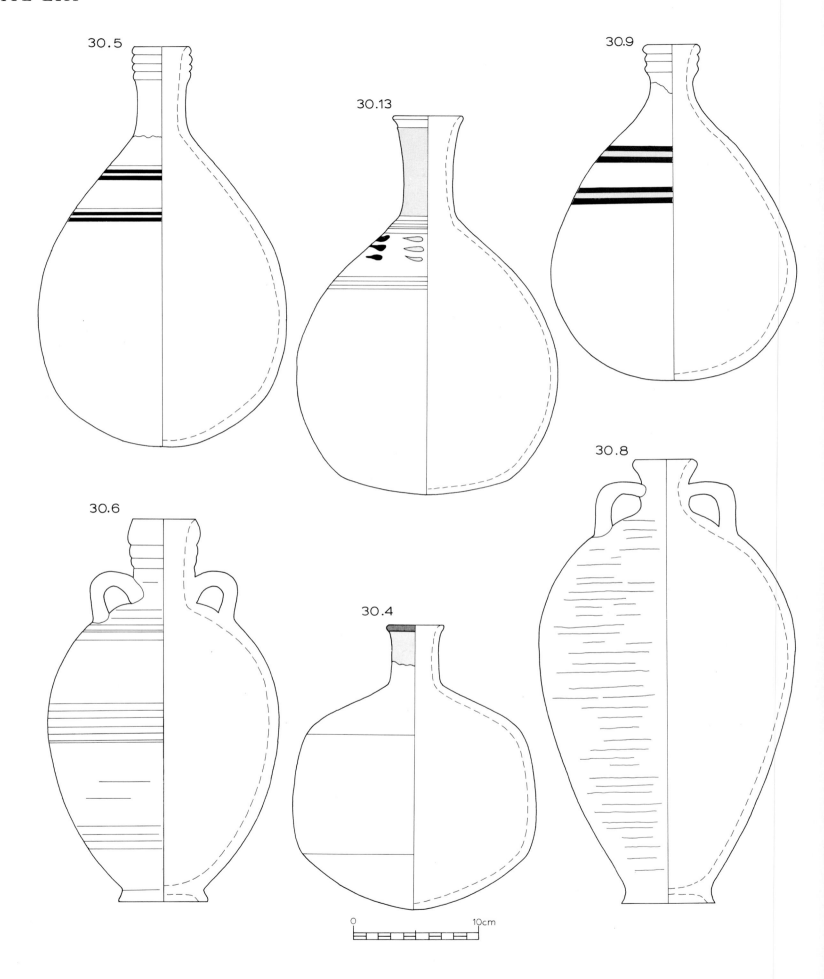

30.5

30.9

30.13

30.8

30.6

30.4

0   10cm

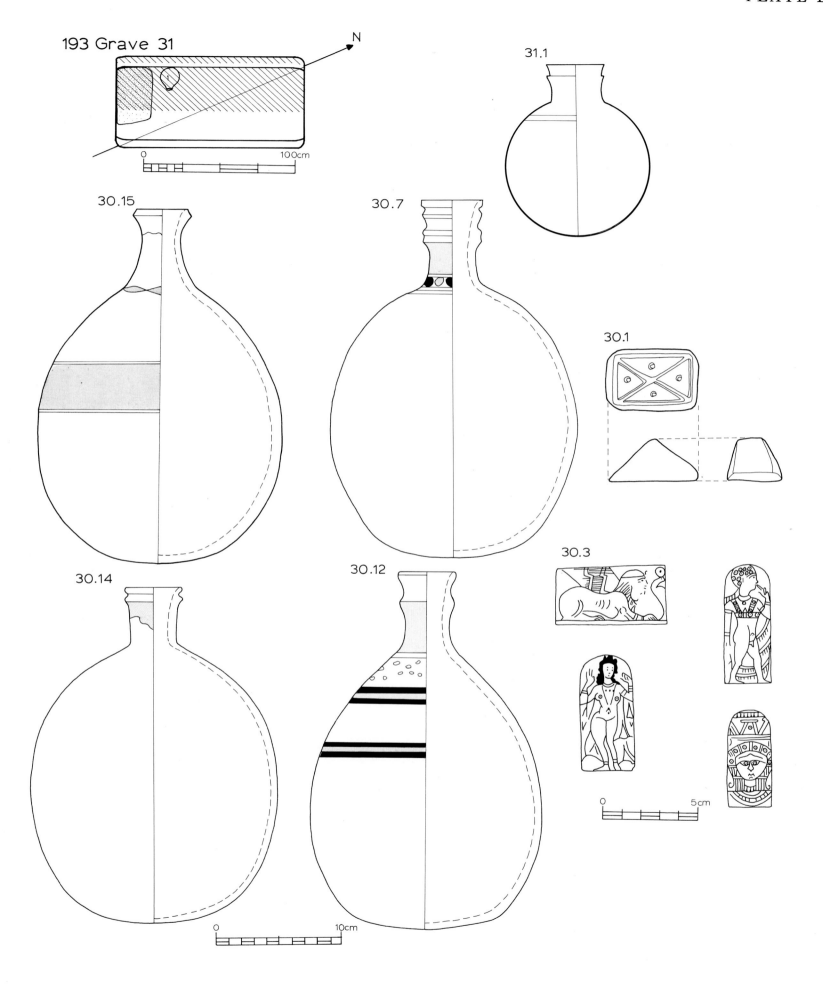

PLATE LIV

193 Grave 31

N

0   100cm

31.1

30.15

30.7

30.1

30.14

30.12

30.3

0   5cm

0   10cm

PLATE LV

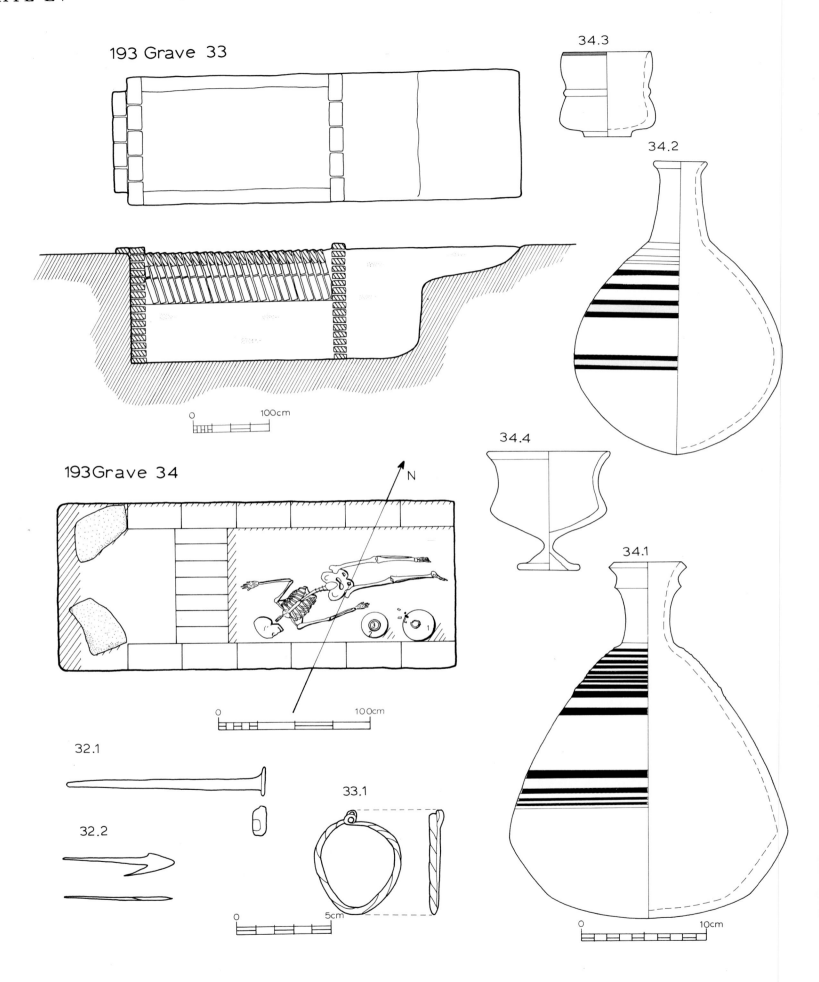

193 Grave 33

34.3

34.2

0   100cm

193 Grave 34

N

34.4

34.1

0   100cm

32.1

32.2

33.1

0   5cm

0   10cm

PLATE LVI

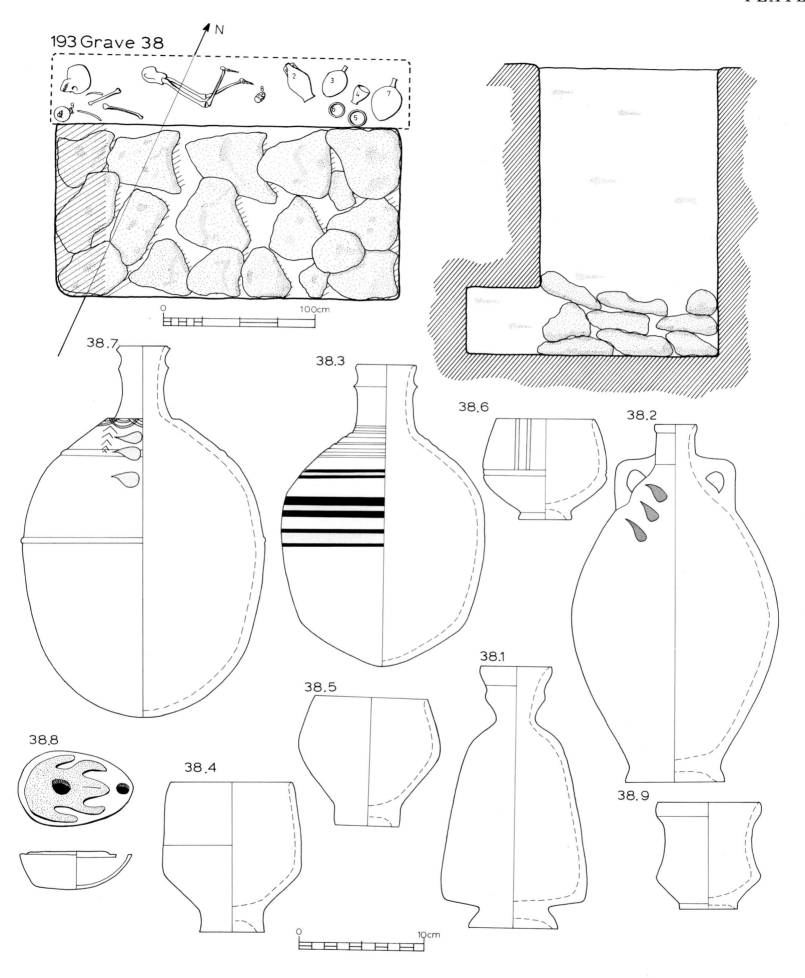

193 Grave 38

N

0   100cm

38.7

38.3

38.6

38.2

38.1

38.5

38.8

38.4

38.9

0   10cm

PLATE LVII

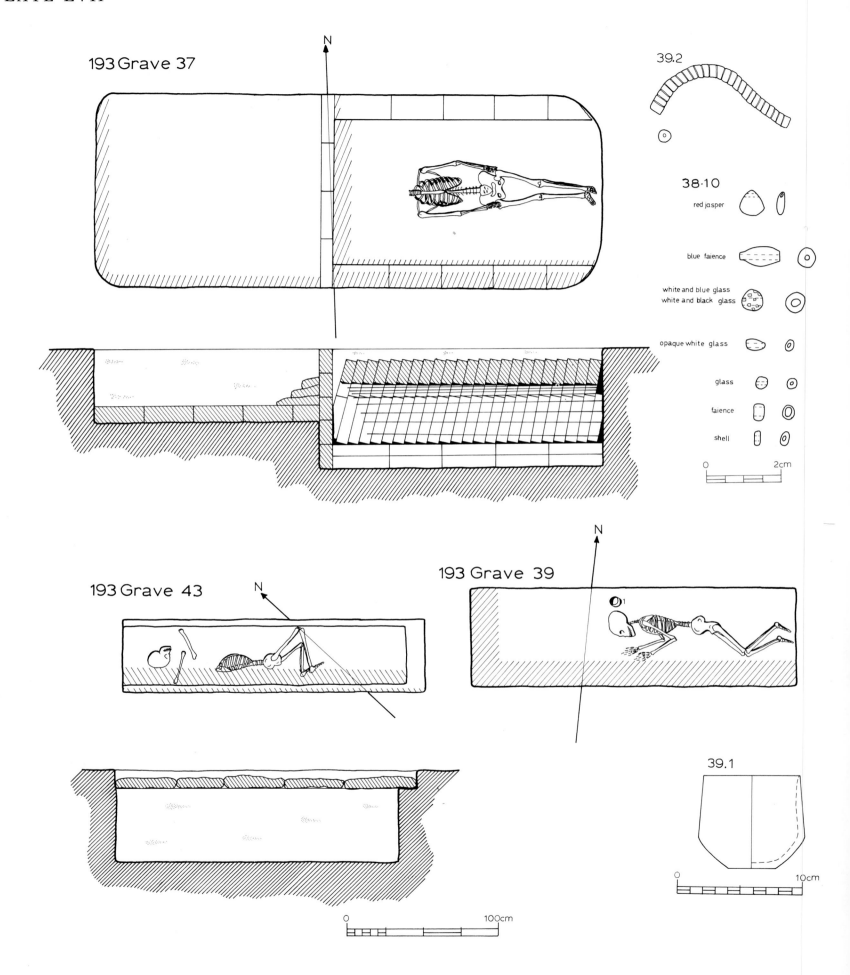

193 Grave 37

N

39.2

38·10

red jasper

blue faience

white and blue glass
white and black glass

opaque white glass

glass

faience

shell

0   2cm

193 Grave 43

N

193 Grave 39

N

39.1

0   10cm

0   100cm

PLATE LVIII

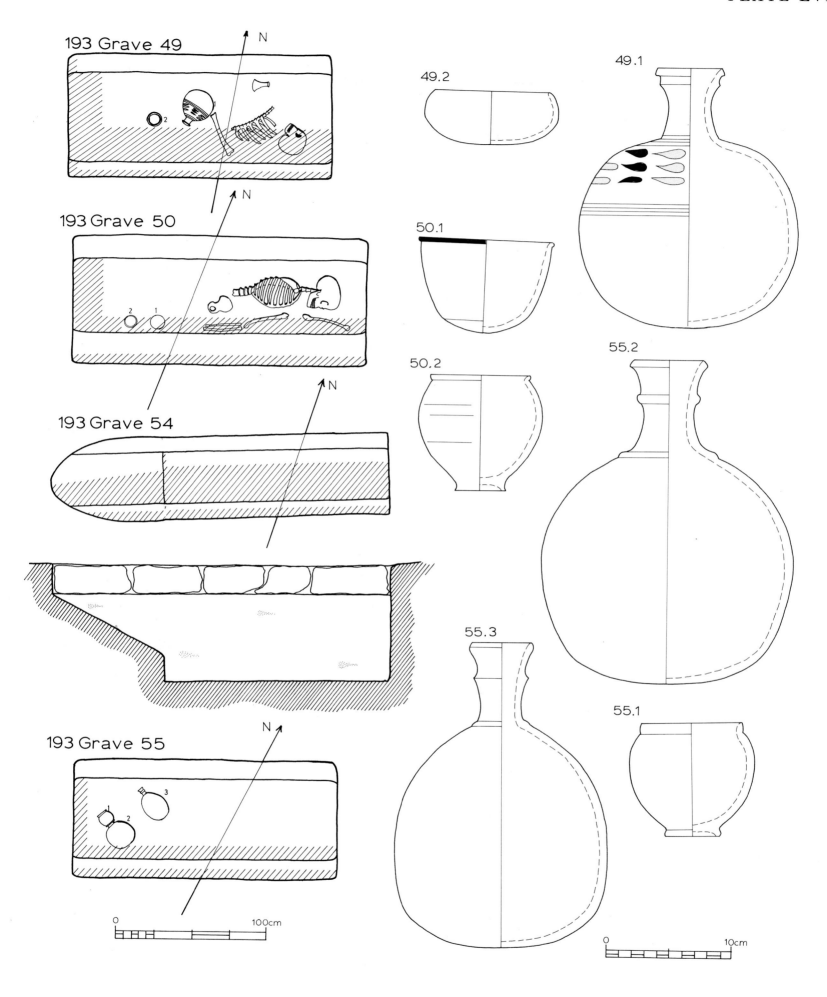

193 Grave 49

193 Grave 50

193 Grave 54

193 Grave 55

49.2

49.1

50.1

50.2

55.2

55.3

55.1

0   100cm

0   10cm

PLATE LIX

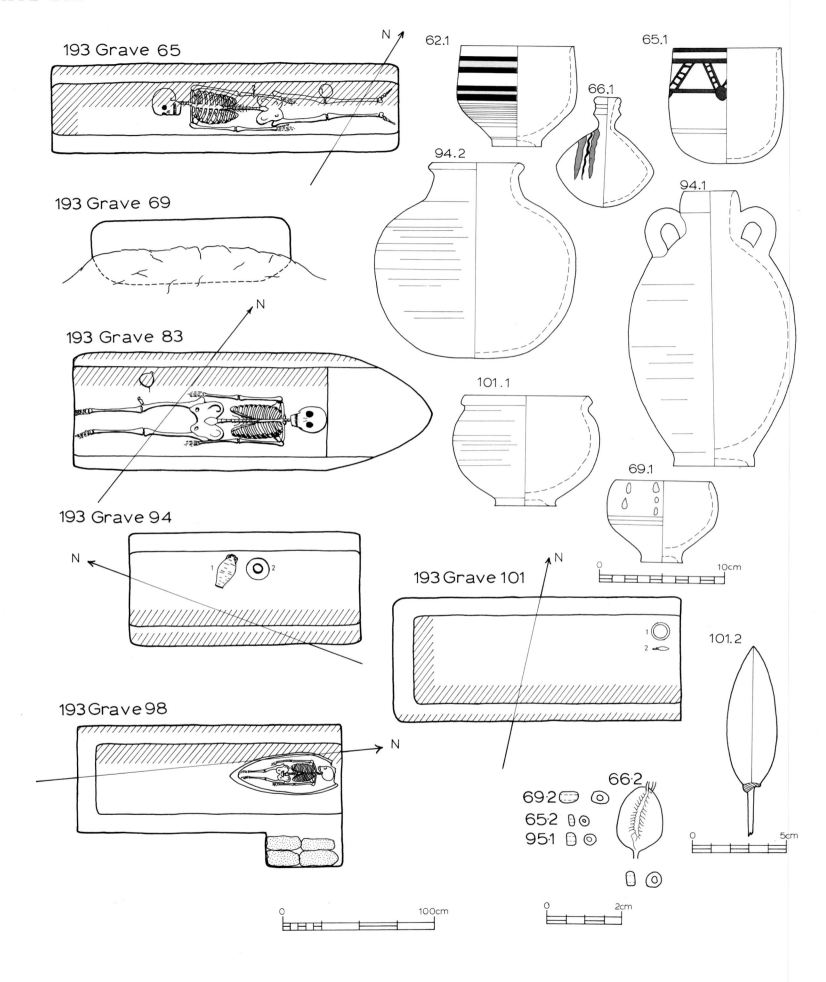

193 Grave 65

193 Grave 69

193 Grave 83

193 Grave 94

193 Grave 98

193 Grave 101

62.1

65.1

66.1

94.2

94.1

101.1

69.1

66.2

69.2

65.2

95.1

101.2

10cm

100cm

2cm

5cm

PLATE LX

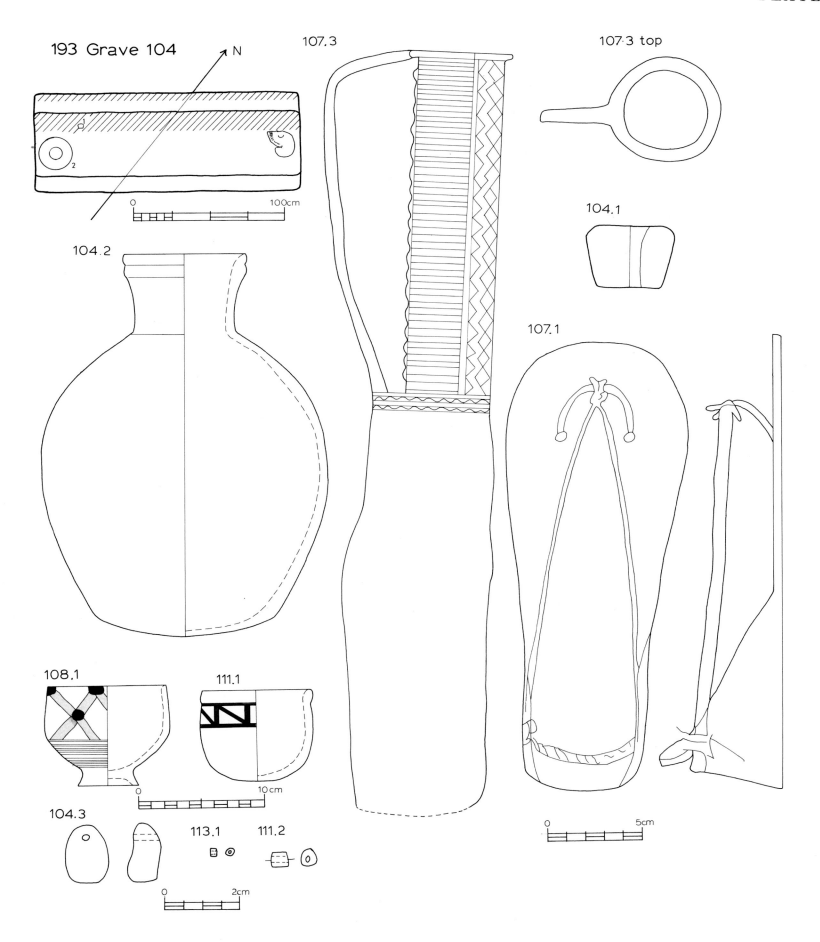

193 Grave 104

N

0   100cm

107.3

107.3 top

104.1

104.2

107.1

108.1

111.1

0   10 cm

104.3

113.1   111.2

0   2cm

0   5cm

PLATE LXI

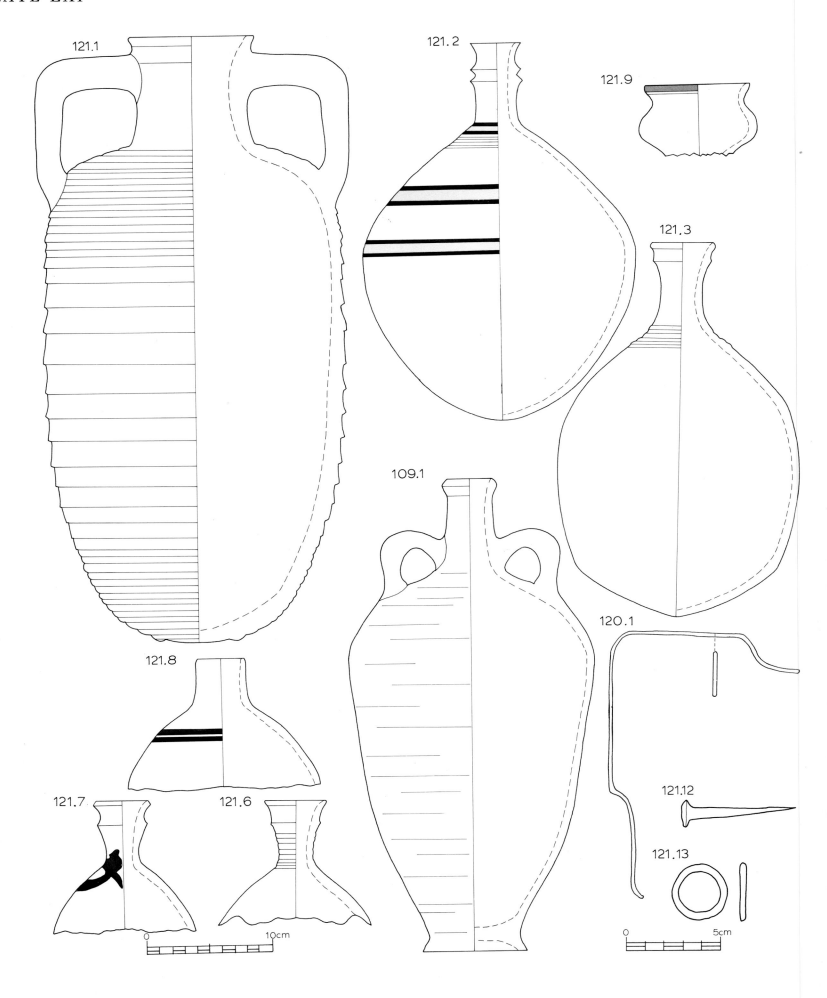

121.1

121.2

121.9

121.3

109.1

120.1

121.8

121.12

121.7

121.6

121.13

0   10cm

0   5cm

PLATE LXII

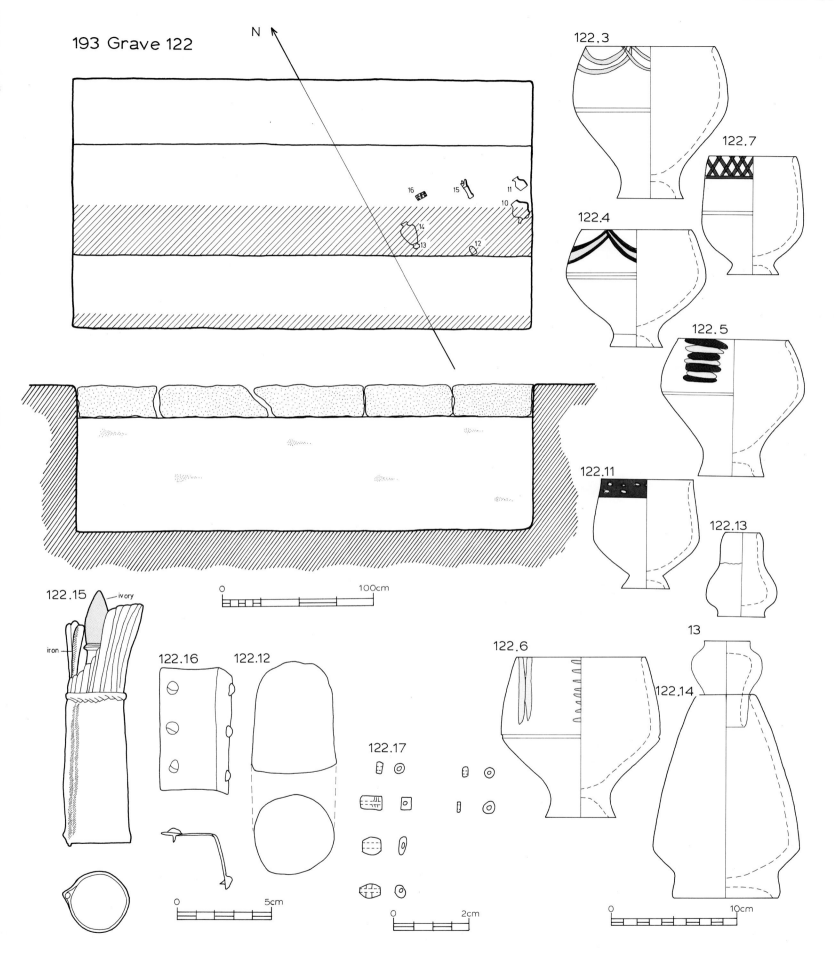

193 Grave 122

122.3

122.7

122.4

122.5

122.11

122.13

122.15

ivory

iron

122.16

122.12

122.17

122.6

13

122.14

0   100cm

0   5cm

0   2cm

0   10cm

PLATE LXIII

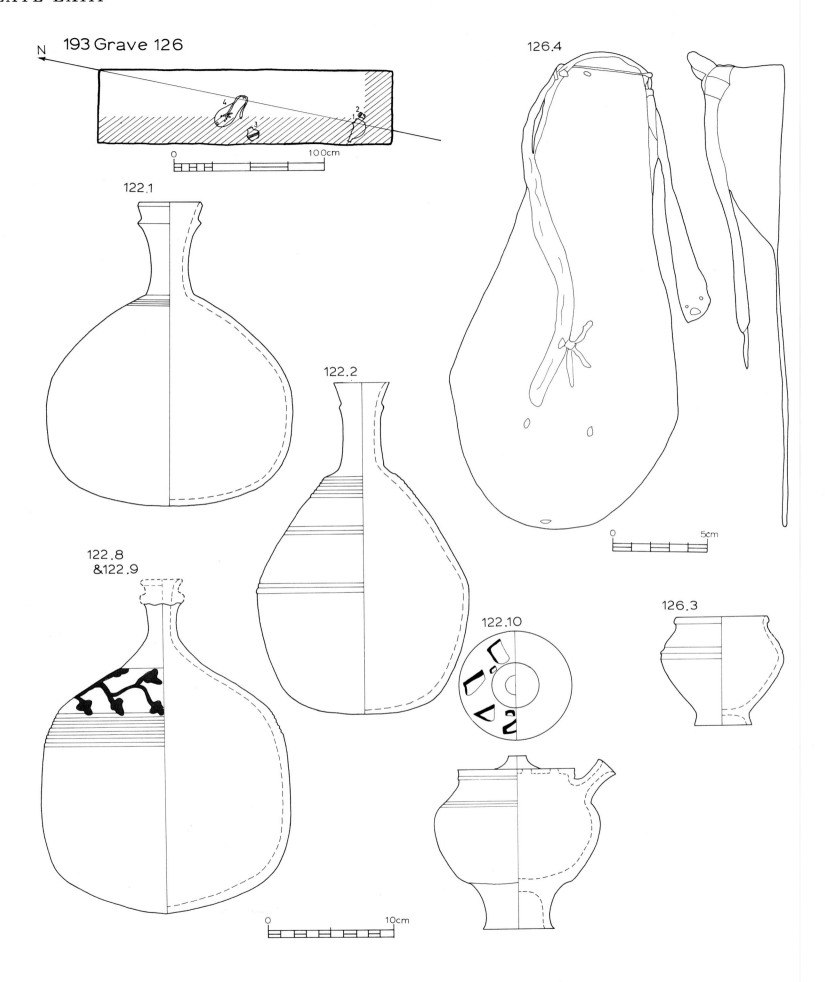

193 Grave 126

N

100cm

126.4

122.1

122.2

122.8
&122.9

122.10

126.3

5cm

10cm

PLATE LXIV

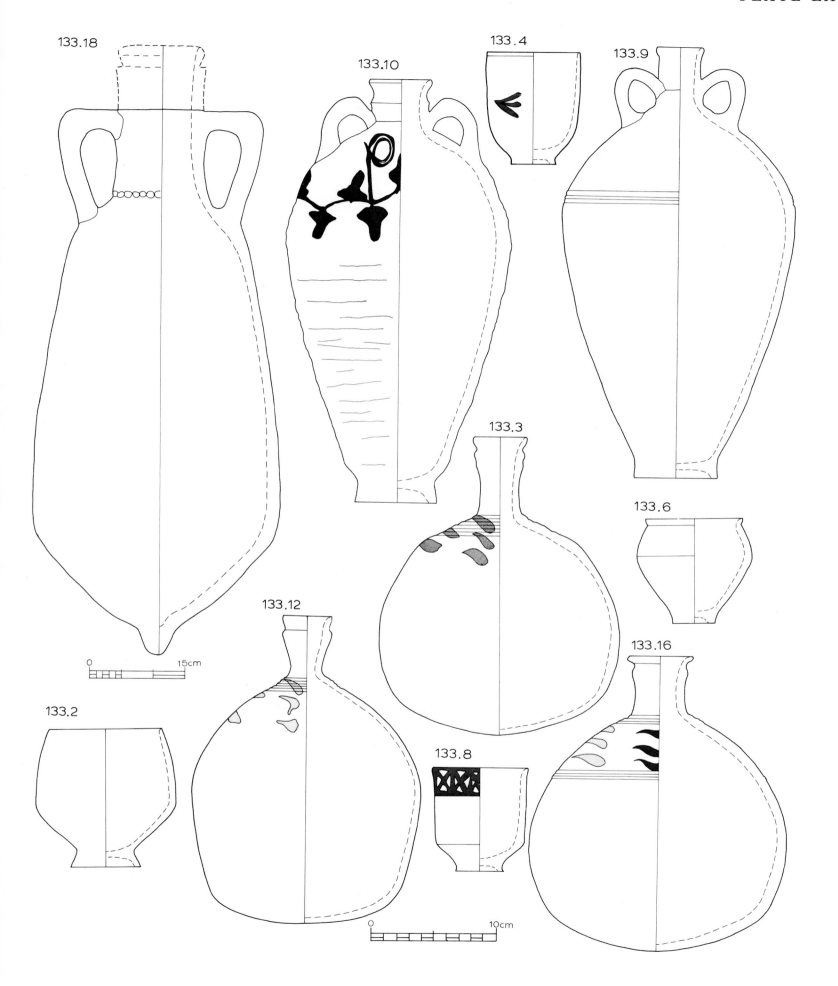

133.18

133.10

133.4

133.9

133.3

133.6

133.12

133.16

133.2

133.8

0   15cm

0   10cm

PLATE LXV

133.14   133.5 &133.7   133.11   133.13

134.3   133.15   134.1

134.2

134.5   134.4   134.6

133.17   133.1

134.7

0   10cm

0   5cm

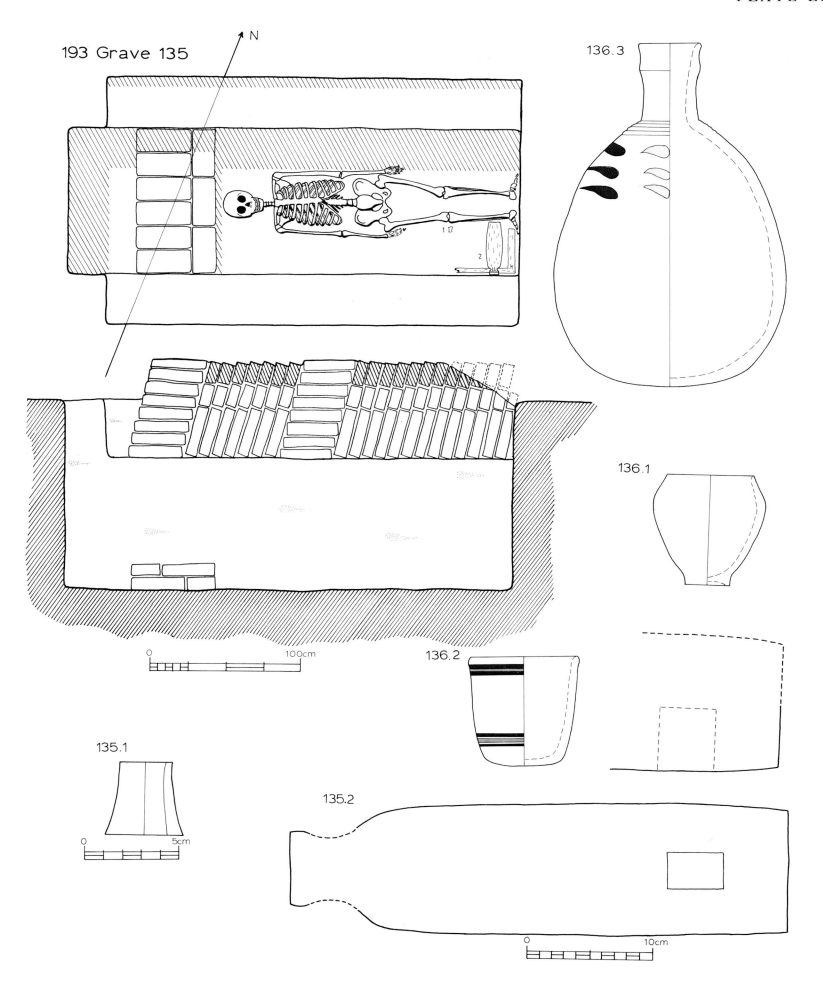

PLATE LXVI

193 Grave 135

N

136.3

136.1

136.2

135.1

135.2

0   100cm

0   5cm

0   10cm

PLATE LXVII

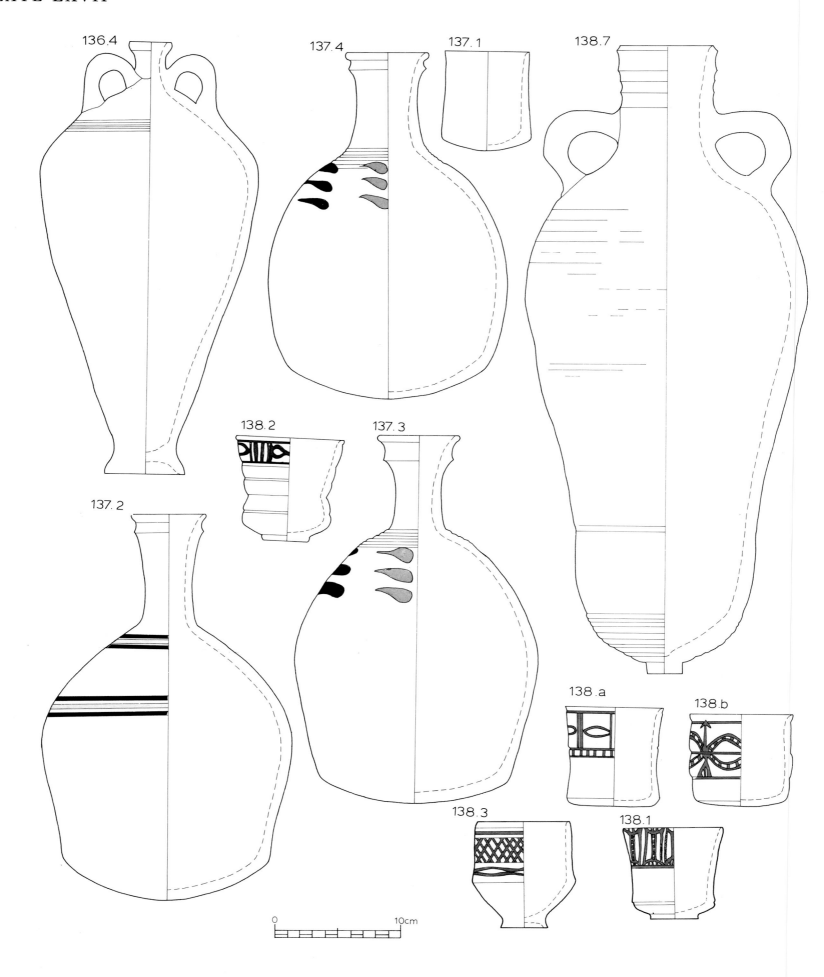

136.4

137.4

137.1

138.7

138.2

137.3

137.2

138.a

138.b

138.3

138.1

0   10cm

PLATE LXVIII

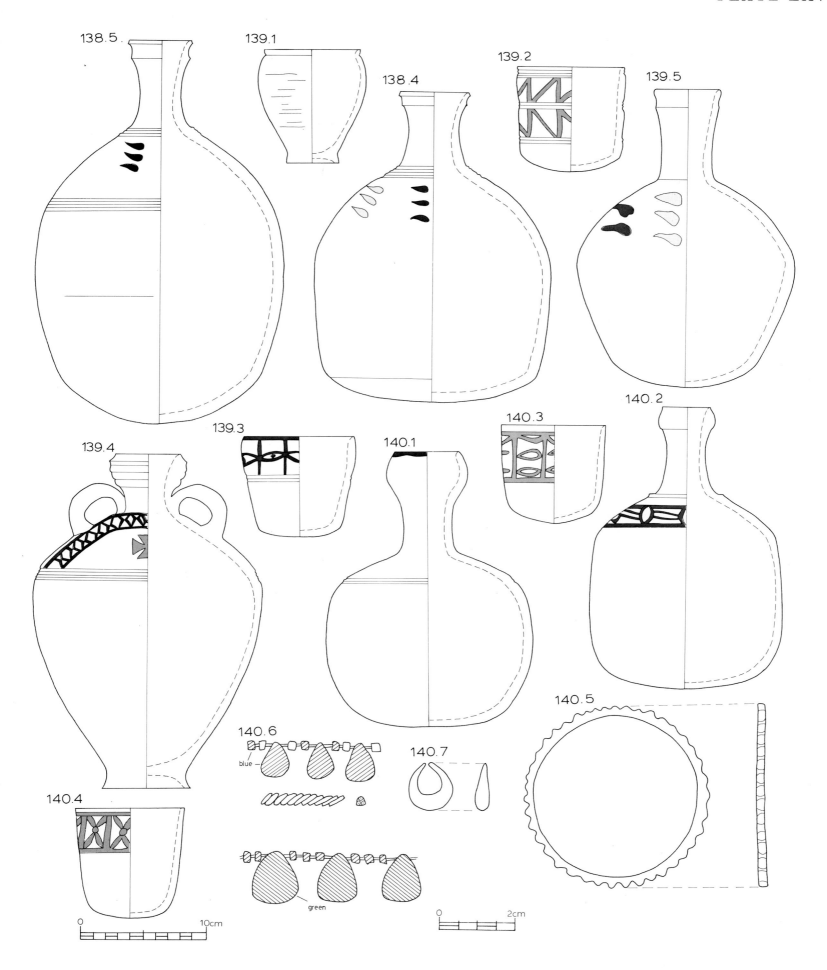

138.5

139.1

138.4

139.2

139.5

139.3

139.4

140.1

140.3

140.2

140.6

140.7

140.5

blue

green

140.4

0   10cm

0   2cm

PLATE LXIX

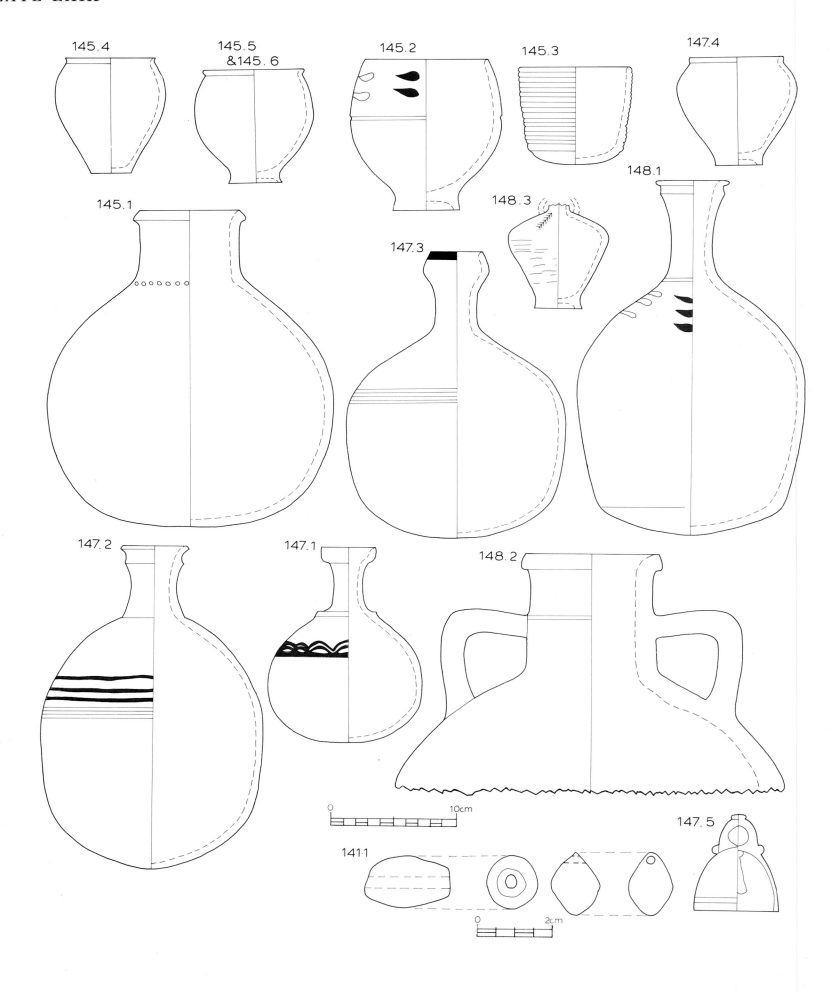

145.4

145.5
&145.6

145.2

145.3

147.4

145.1

148.3

148.1

147.3

147.2

147.1

148.2

0   10cm

141·1

147.5

0   2cm

PLATE LXX

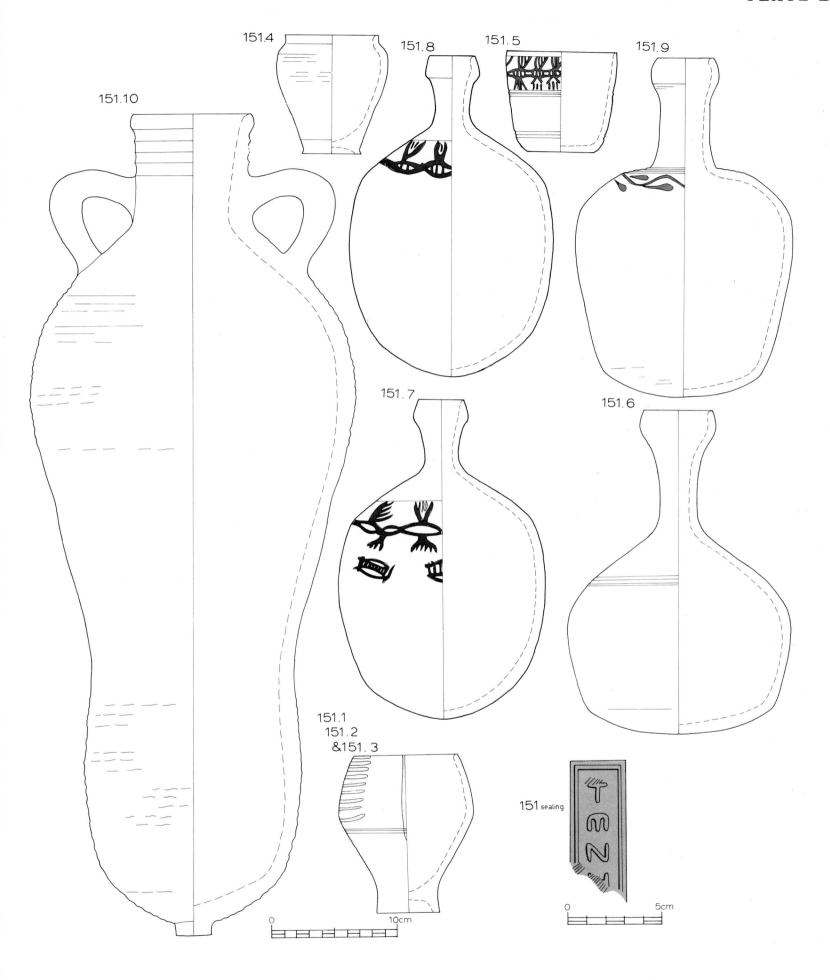

151.10

151.4

151.8

151.5

151.9

151.7

151.6

151.1
151.2
&151.3

151 sealing

0   10cm

0   5cm

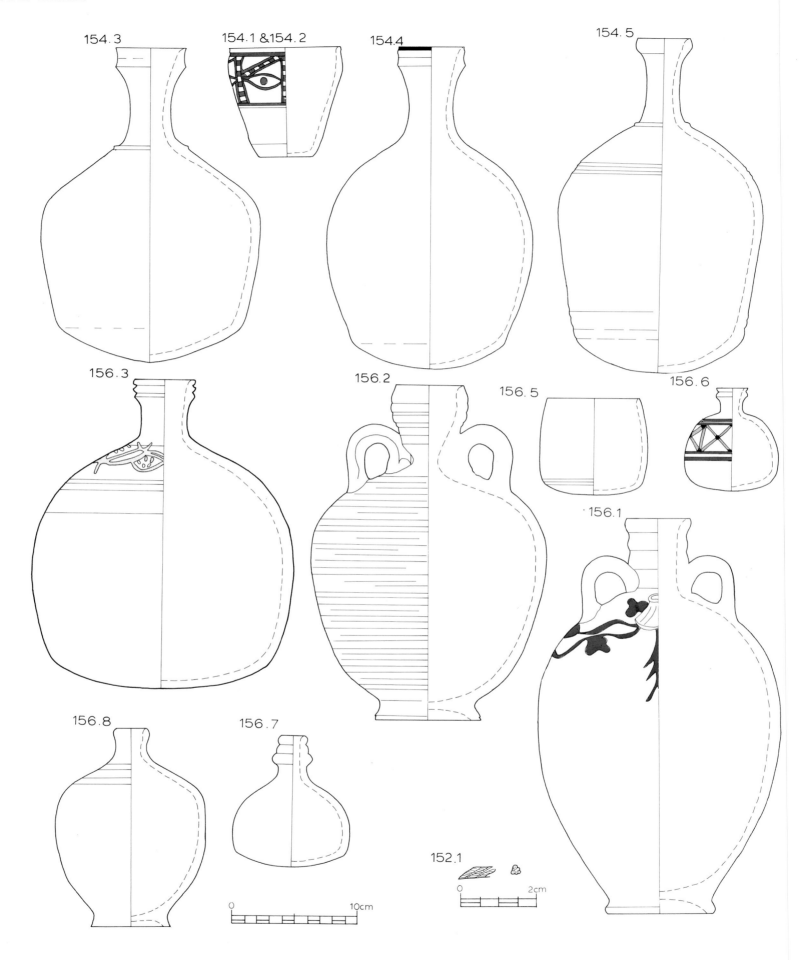

PLATE LXXI

154.3   154.1 & 154.2   154.4   154.5

156.3   156.2   156.5   156.6

156.1

156.8   156.7

152.1

0   10cm

0   2cm

PLATE LXXII

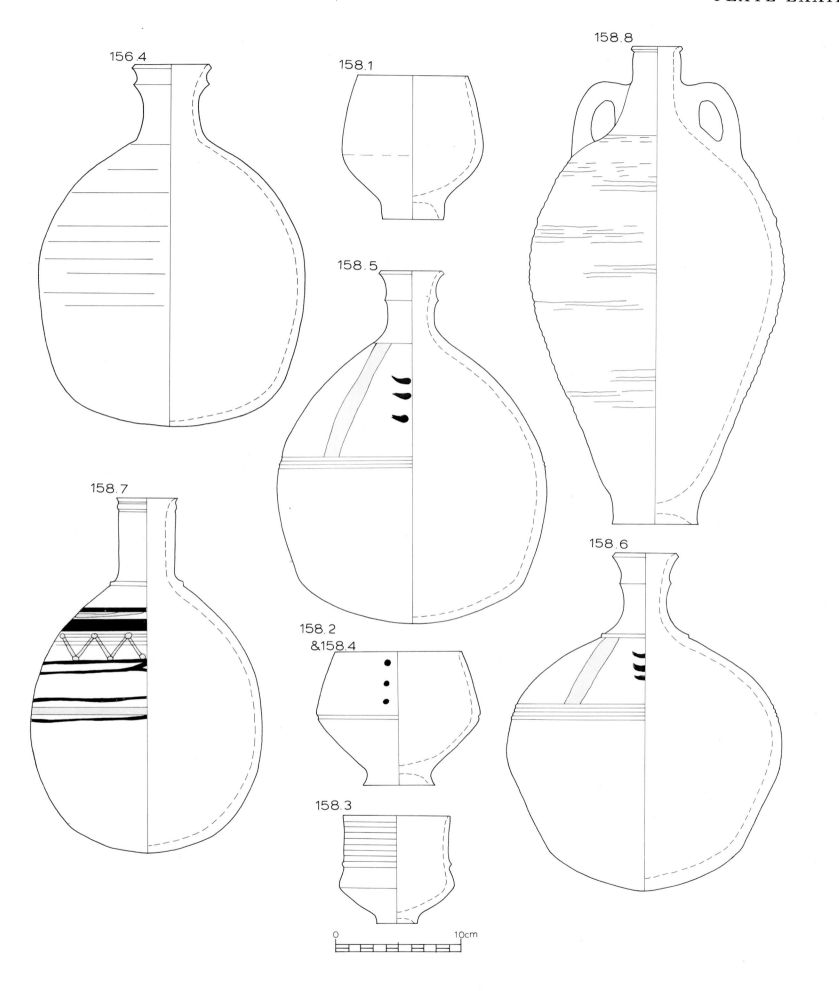

156.4

158.1

158.8

158.5

158.7

158.2
&158.4

158.6

158.3

0   10cm

PLATE LXXIII

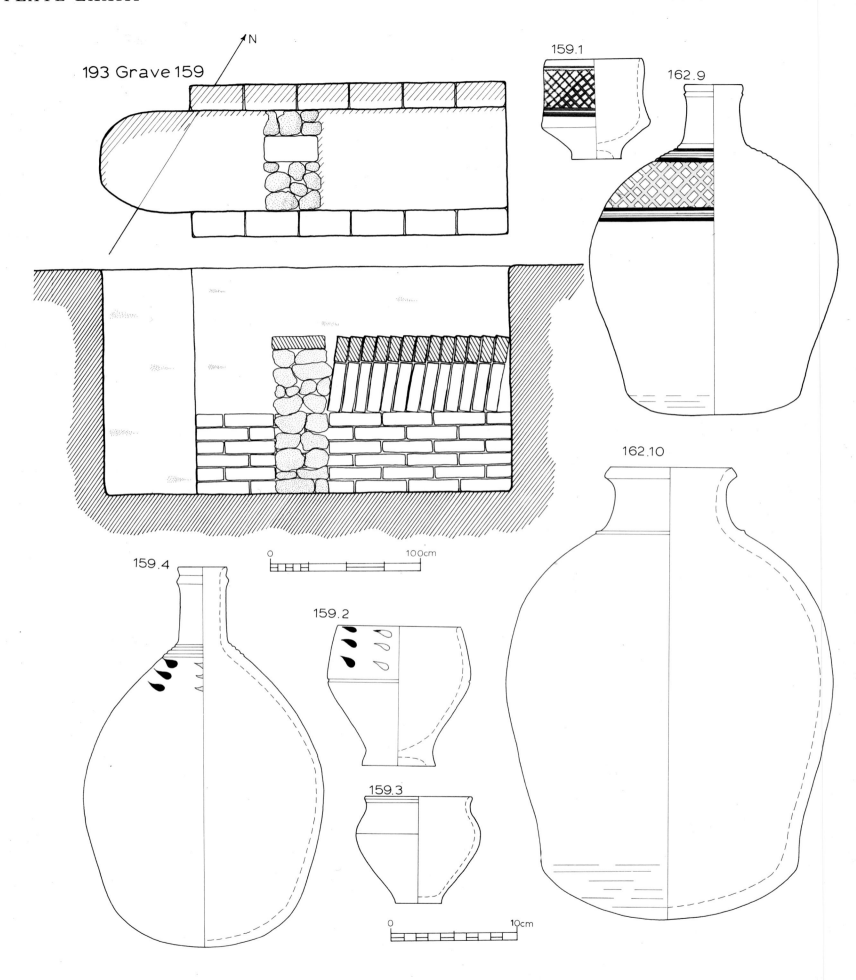

193 Grave 159

159.1

162.9

100cm

159.4

159.2

159.3

162.10

0   10cm

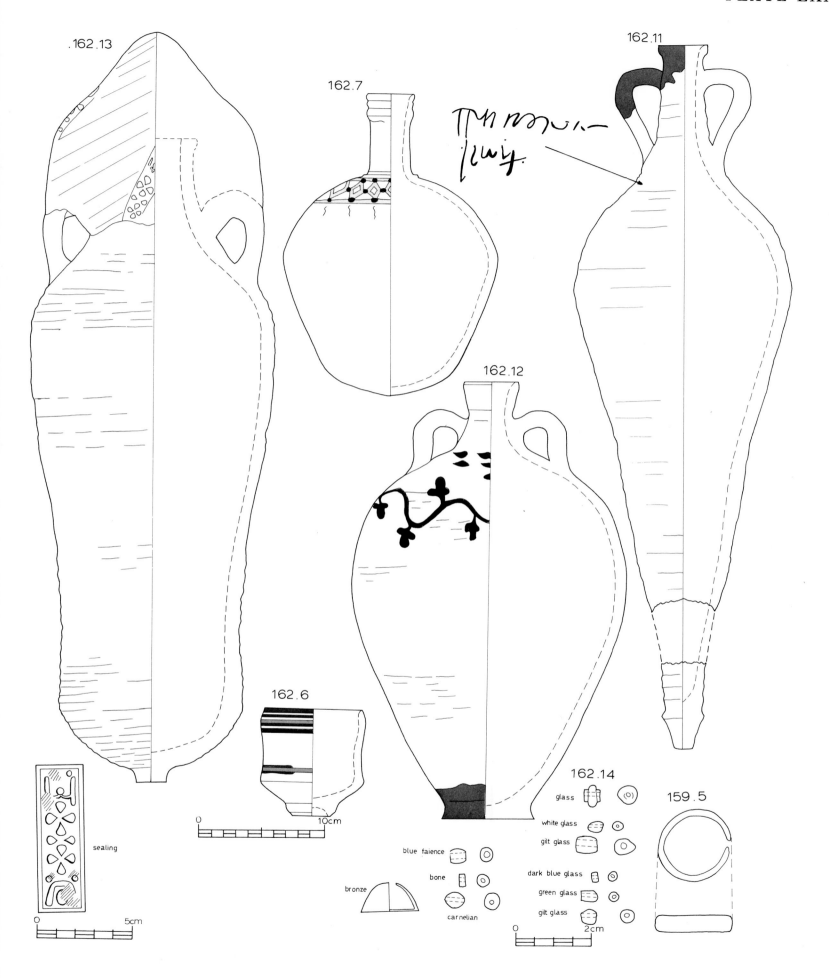

PLATE LXXIV

.162.13

162.7

162.11

162.12

162.6

162.14

159.5

sealing

glass

white glass

gilt glass

blue faience

bone

dark blue glass

green glass

gilt glass

bronze

carnelian

0   5cm

0   10cm

0   2cm

PLATE LXXV

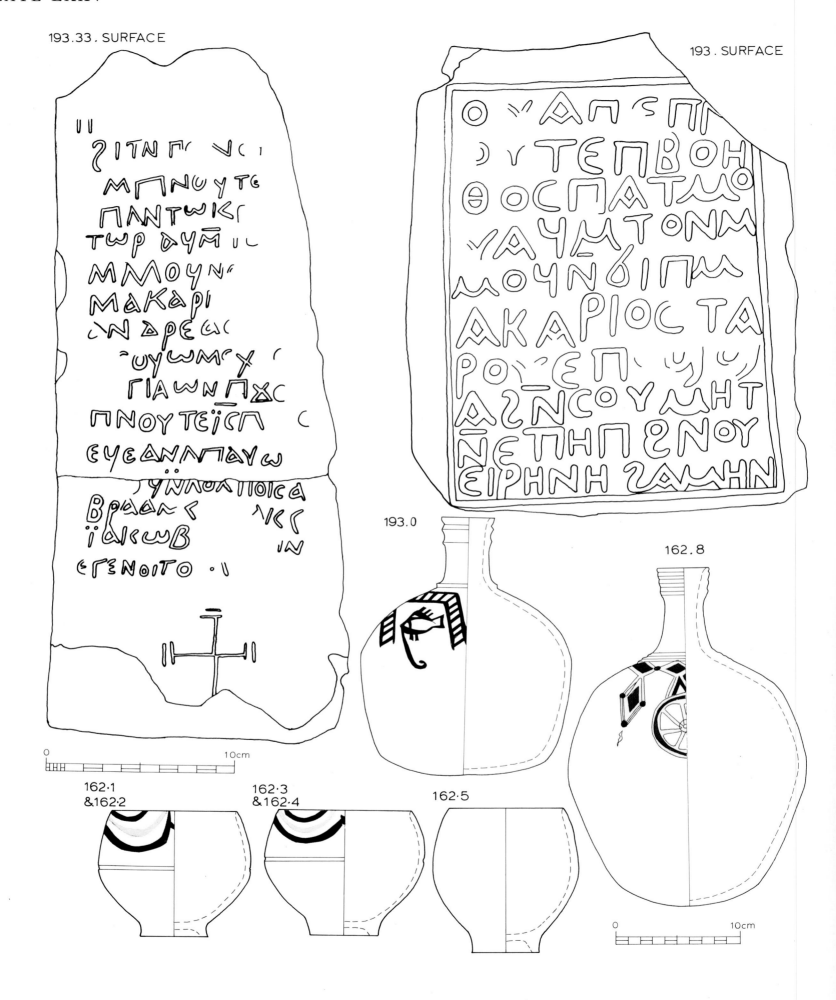

193.33 . SURFACE

193 . SURFACE

193.0

162.8

162·1
&162·2

162·3
&162·4

162·5

0   10cm

0   10cm

PLATE LXXVI

193. 33. SURFACE

193. SURFACE

192. SURFACE

10cm

0

PLATE LXXVII

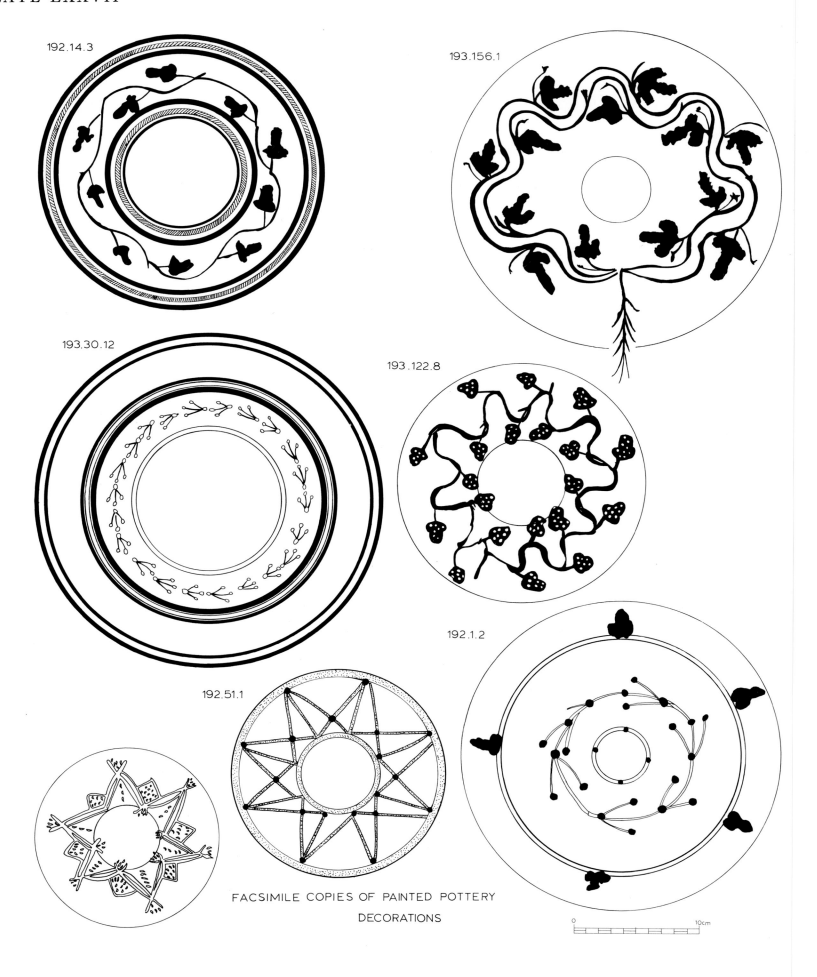

192.14.3

193.156.1

193.30.12

193.122.8

192.1.2

192.51.1

FACSIMILE COPIES OF PAINTED POTTERY
DECORATIONS

0   10cm

PLATE LXXVIII

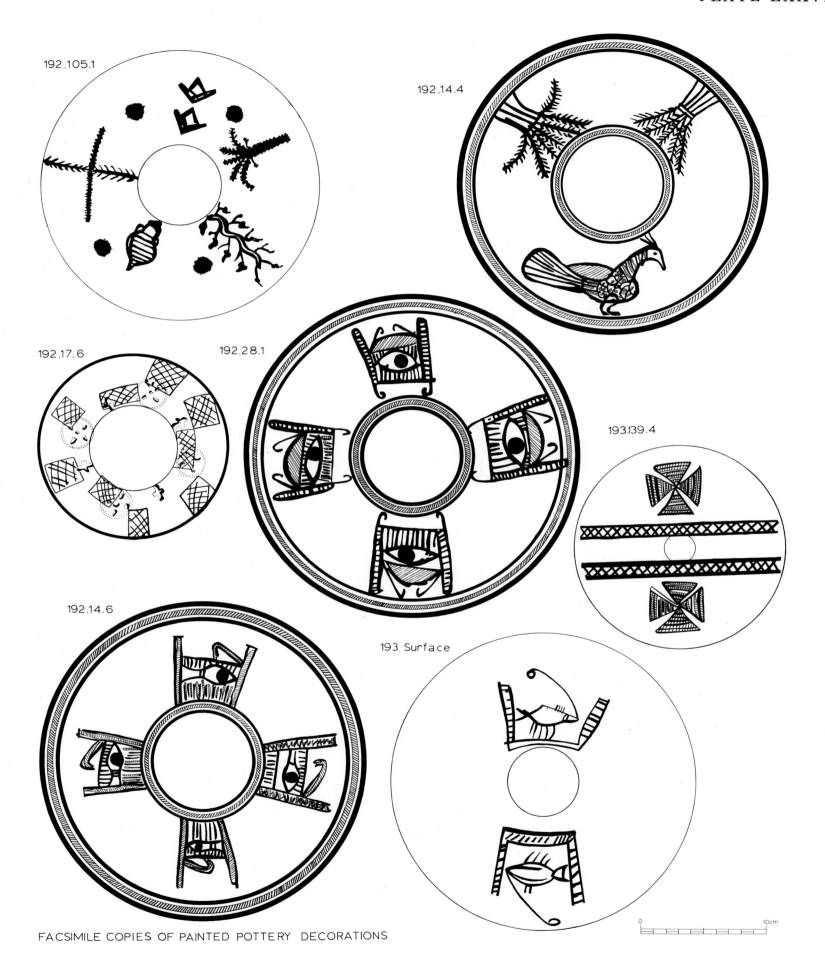

192.105.1

192.14.4

192.17.6

192.28.1

193.139.4

192.14.6

193 Surface

0   10cm

FACSIMILE COPIES OF PAINTED POTTERY DECORATIONS

PLATE LXXIX

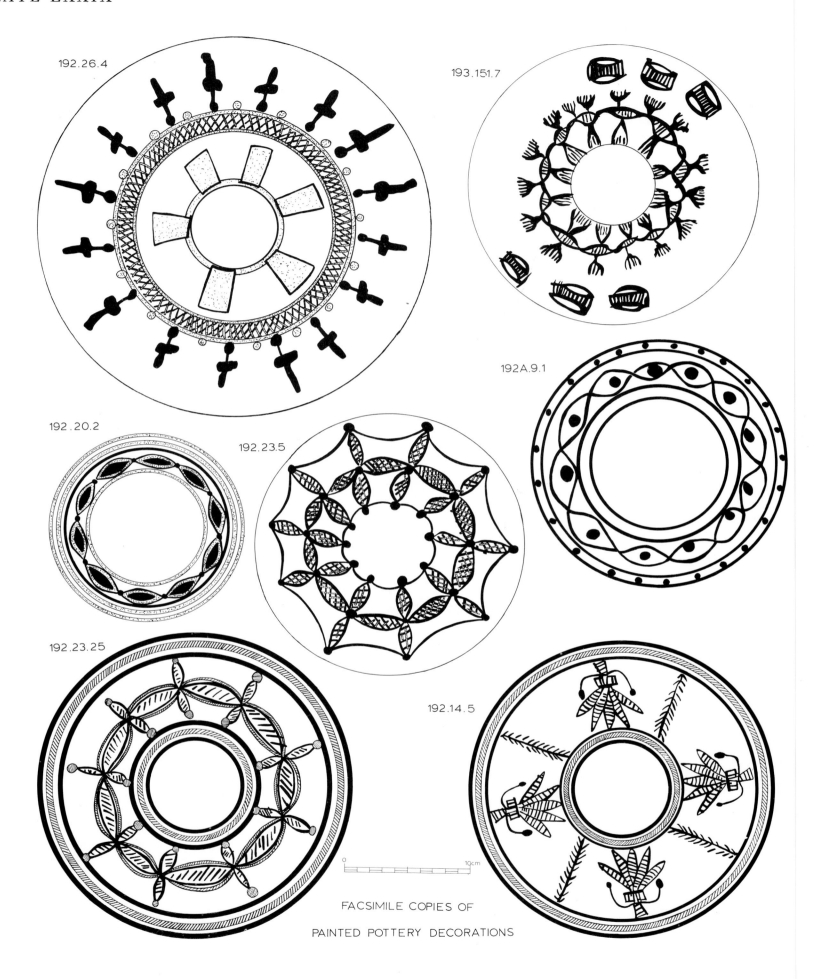

192.26.4

193.151.7

192A.9.1

192.20.2

192.23.5

192.23.25

192.14.5

0   10cm

FACSIMILE COPIES OF
PAINTED POTTERY DECORATIONS

PLATE LXXX

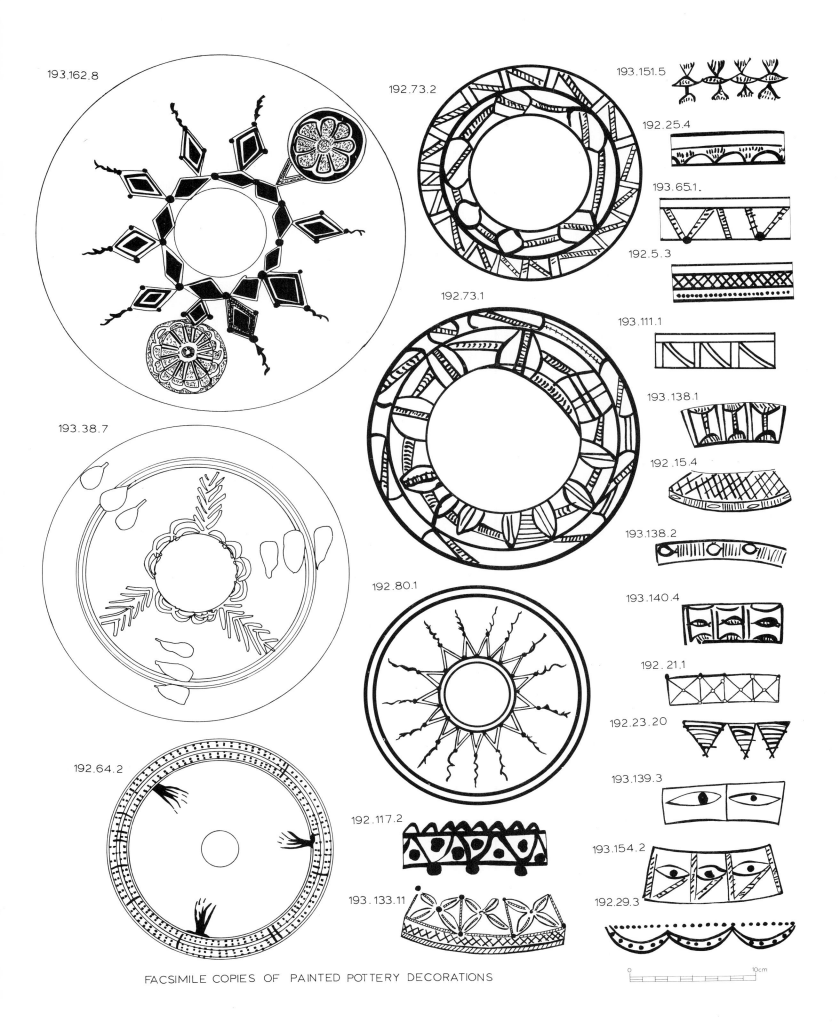

193.162.8

193.151.5

192.73.2

193.38.7

192.25.4

193.65.1.

192.5.3

192.73.1

193.111.1

193.138.1

192.15.4

193.138.2

192.80.1

193.140.4

192.21.1

192.23.20

192.64.2

193.139.3

192.117.2

193.154.2

193.133.11

192.29.3

FACSIMILE COPIES OF PAINTED POTTERY DECORATIONS

0   10cm

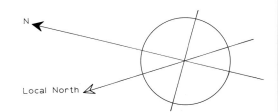

N

Local North

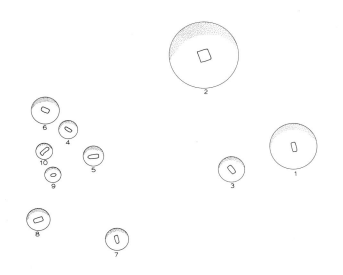

2

6

4

10

5

9

8

7

3

1

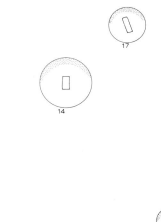

17

14

15

11

12

13

QASR   IBRIM
CEMETERY   192
PLAN

0   10   50m

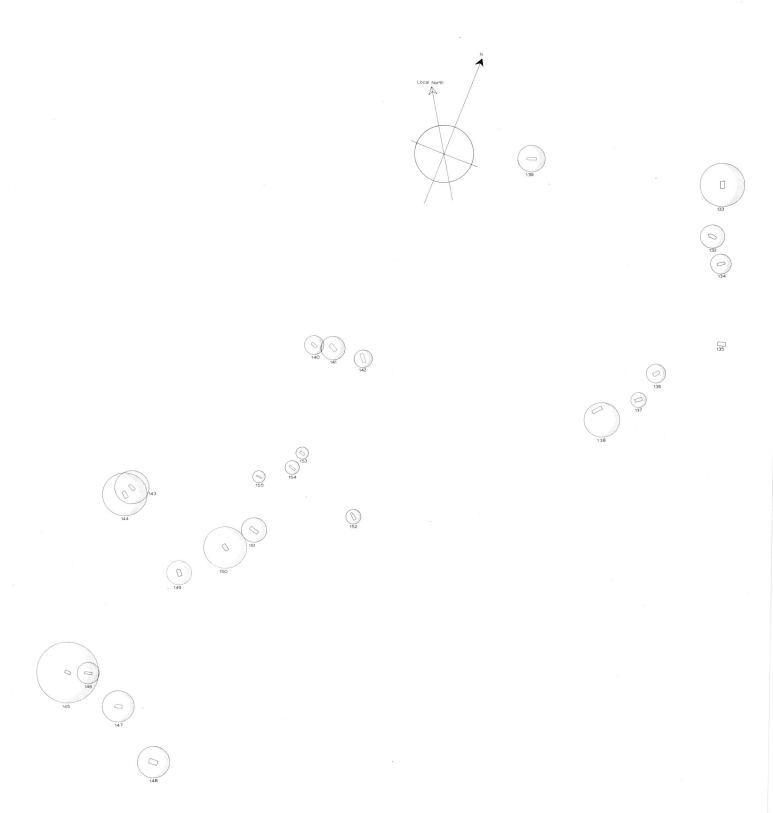

QASR IBRIM
CEMETERY 193
PLAN

0   10   50m

PLATE LXXXIII

PLATE LXXXIV

2. Site 192B after excavation

1. Cemetery 192. General view of tumuli from south

5. Tomb 192.2.6. Bronze camel lamp hanging *in situ* on the vaulting

4. Some of the objects *in situ* in Tomb 192.2

3. The vaults of the two chambers of Tomb 192.23

PLATE LXXXV

1. Some of the grave tumuli

4. Tumulus of Tomb 193.30 under excavation

2. Stone superstructures of Christian tombs

3. Mud brick *qubba* tomb structure

5. Chamber of Tomb 193.30. Note the incised cross to the left of the scale

CEMETERY 193

PLATE LXXXVI

1. 192.2.6: bronze camel lamp

4. 192.23.32: bronze horse-head lamp

2. 192.2.9: bronze face lamp

5. 192.29.7: iron sickle blade

7. 193.101.2: iron javelin point

6. 192A.7.1:
iron spear-blade
and butt

3. 192.2.9: bronze face lamp, side view

PLATE LXXXVII

1. Toilet objects from Tomb 192.2: nos. (from left to right) 19, 11, 15, 12

4. 192.2.56: glass flagon

2. 192.2.14: glass footed dish

3. 192.2.16: glass footed cup

5. 192.23.33: glass bottle

PLATE LXXXVIII

1. 193.105.1: woollen pile rug

2. 192A.0.1: sandstone offering table

4. 192A.0.3: fragment of sandstone offering table

3. 192A.0.2: sandstone offering table

5. 192C.1.2: sandstone offering table

PLATE LXXXIX

1. Tomb 192B.8: blocking stones *in situ*

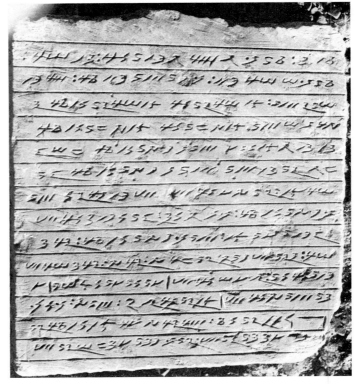

2. 192B.8.1: sandstone stela

3. 192B.8.2: sandstone stela

4. 192B.8.3: sandstone cavetto cornice with winged disc

PLATE XC

1. 192C.0.4: sandstone *ba* statue *in situ*

3. 192C.0.5: sandstone pyramid 'window'

4. 192C.0.6: wings of sandstone *ba* statue

2. 192C.0.4: sandstone *ba* statue

5. 192C.0.6: base of
sandstone *ba* statue

6. 192A.3.4: head of sandstone *ba* statue

PLATE XCI

1. 193.33.2

4. 193, surface

2. 193.33.3

3. 192, surface

5. 193, surface

6. 193, surface

SANDSTONE COPTIC FUNERARY STELAE

PLATE XCII

1. 192B, surface: ostracon

3. 192B, surface: ostracon

2. 192B, surface: ostracon

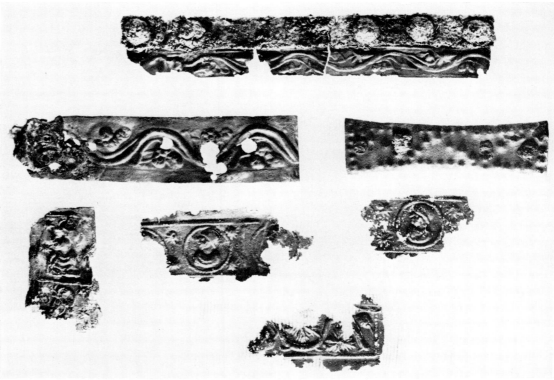

4. 192.23.47: bronze and iron casket fittings

PLATE XCIII

1. Small grains from Qaṣr Ibrîm (right side); modern grains of bulrush millet (*Pennisetum typhoides*) (left side)

2. Large grains from Qaṣr Ibrîm (right side); modern grains of sorghum (*Sorghum bicolor*) (left side)

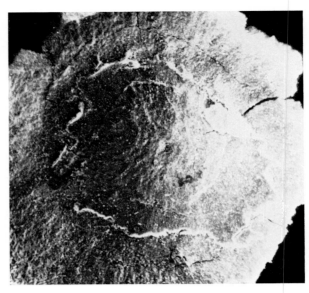

3. Inside surface of proximal end of pericarp of large grains, showing raised disc (× about 50; diameter = about 2.5 mm.)

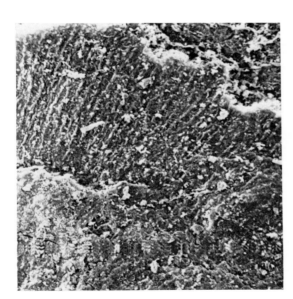

4. Part of edge of raised disc shown in 3 above (× about 250)

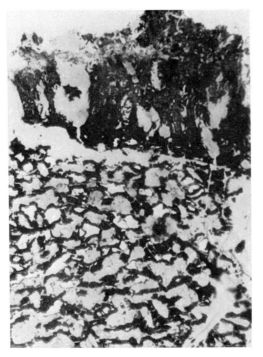

5. Section through outer layers of large grain from Qaṣr Ibrîm. The outer layers suggest pericarp and the inner endosperm

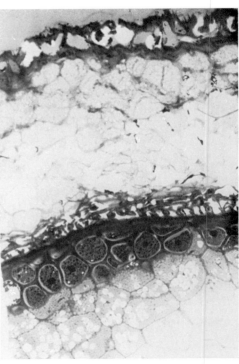

6. Section through outer layers of grain of modern *Sorghum bicolor*, race Durra. From the top down the layers are the collapsed outermost parts of the pericarp, the main tissue of the pericarp, and the innermost tube cells; then the aleurone layer of dark cells and the endosperm